STATE OF MARYLAND

Annual Report
Department of Education
A STATISTICAL REVIEW for the Year Ending June 30, 1987

showing condition of the Public Schools of Maryland by the State Board of Education

512747

STATE OF MARYLAND

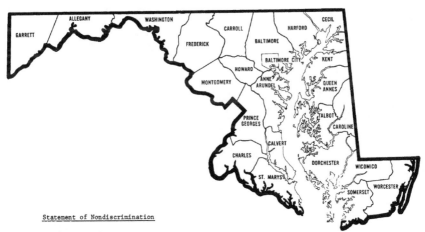

TABLE OF CONTENTS

TABLE OF CONTENTS

TABLE OF CONTENTS

TABLE OF CONTENTS

TABLE OF CONTENTS

TABLE OF CONTENTS

TABLE OF CONTENTS

TABLE OF CONTENTS

FOREWORD

The statistics in this report have been compiled to give administrators and interested members of the public a statistical overview of Maryland's schools and vocational rehabilitation programs in 1986-87.

There are numbers here that will help you understand the scope of services provided by the State Department of Education and local school systems. There are numbers also to give you insight into the diversity of students and the quality of services available to them.

But this report, valuable as it is to understanding our schools, can only give you raw data. We urge you to remember that behind these statistics are people: young children just beginning their schooling; middle school and high school students on the brink of making important decisions about their adult lives; and adults pursuing a second chance for an education or receiving rehabilitation services because they wish to become more knowledgeable, more productive, and more self-sufficient.

The numbers tell us much about our educational programs and the people in them. But true understanding, of course, will come only from direct involvement in the schools. And involvement and understanding by parents and other members of the community are essential to maintaining the strength of our schools.

Why not become involved in a school in your community? You can be sure it will be a valuable learning experience.

Sincerely,

JOSEPH L. SHILLING
State Superintendent of Schools

GENERAL INSTRUCTIONAL PROGRAM IMPROVEMENT

Program Assessment

The 1986-87 test results for public school students continued to improve in the four areas (reading, writing, mathematics, citizenship) of the Maryland Functional Testing Program required for graduation. Approximately 50,000 ninth grade students each year take the four tests. Ninth grade reading scores have leveled at 92.2 percent, mathematics and citizenship pass rates showed an increase, and a slight decrease was noted in writing. The 1.4 percent decrease in writing pass rate was attributed to a change in the date of testing, from the end of the school year to January. The change decreased the amount of available instructional time for test preparation. The drop in test scores is expected to be a one-year phenomenon.

On the California Achievement Test given to third, fifth, and eighth grade students in the fall, 1986, all three groups continued to perform above the 1976 national norm sample in the areas of reading comprehension, language, and mathematics, as evidenced by the following grade equivalent comparisons:

Grade	Reading		Language		Mathematics	
	Md.	Nat.	Md.	Nat.	Md.	Nat.
3	3.7	3 3	3 8	3.4	3.5	3.1
5	6.1	5 5	7 3	5.6	6.0	5.3
8	10.0	8:4	10:2	8.3	9.8	8.5

College bound Maryland student performance on the Scholastic Aptitude Test (SAT) continues to be above national averages as evidenced by the following SAT scale scores for the graduating class of 1987:

	Verbal	Mathematics	Written English
National	430	476	43.0
Maryland	437	477	43.6

Competency-Based Education

Maryland's massive statewide effort to implement a competency-based education program, Project Basic, was launched in 1977-78. Designed to ensure that students are competent in five areas of human activity before graduating from high schools, Project Basic is phased in as follows:

Basic Skills	
Reading	1982
Mathematics	1987
Writing	1989
Arts/Physical Education	1983
World of Work	1985
Survival	1985
Citizenship	1988

Instruction in Maryland schools continued to build in strength as local systems redesigned and adjusted programs to better prepare students with skills identified in the Declared Competencies Index. The result has been an increased level of performance on competency tests in mathematics, citizenship, writing, and reading. Simultaneously, local school systems have worked extensively to develop and improve appropriate assistance instruction to students, preparing them to retake competency tests which they previously failed.

Improvements in the Maryland Functional Testing Program which were suggested by Education Testing Service, Princeton, New Jersey, have now been implemented in virtually all areas of the Maryland Writing Test. The Maryland Testing Program has continued to gain national recognition for the courage of Maryland to address the accountability issue with more than rhetoric by linking performance on the tests with graduation requirements. Efforts to ensure that special education students are not disenfranchised by the tests have resulted in the development of special administration procedures that link the administration of the test to a student's individualized education program, which reflects input provided by parents and educators through the local Admission, Review, and Dismissal (ARD) Committees. Plans are underway to provide similar assistance to the non-English and limited English proficient populations, although an underlying assumption of these efforts upholds the importance of proficiency in the English language as a requirement for receipt of a regular Maryland high school diploma.

Strong efforts by local school districts continue to provide appropriate assistance and remediation to students who fail the functional tests at the ninth grade level, resulting in approximately a 50 percent pass rate on each successive trial for students in grades 10-12 who retake the tests.

All of these efforts resulted in the following pass rates for first time test takers, typically at the ninth grade level, for 1986-87:

Reading	92.2%
Mathematics	65.5%
Writing	67.1%
Citizenship	73.3%

Learning Technologies

The Division of Instruction is in the process of assessing its role given the advent of learning technologies within the public schools. To that end a task force is designing a concept paper on the role of the division in assisting schools in using new technology to enhance learning.

The task force has a direct link to another major activity entitled the Maryland Education Project, an effort among the local school systems served by Potomac Edison and the Maryland State Department of Education with the long term goal of providing a computer classroom in each of the schools served by Potomac Edison. A pilot project is underway at Boonsboro High

School in Washington County, and classrooms are being developed throughout the western part of the state during the 1987-88 school year. Additionally, staff development opportunities are being made available for classroom teachers related to hardware, software, and instructional practices utilizing the computer. Furthermore, three higher education institutions are also being equipped with computer classrooms for use in their teacher training programs in an effort to ensure that prospective teachers are trained in learning technologies utilization before entering the profession. This project will be a major initiative during the 1987-88 school year and thereafter.

The Maryland State Department of Education is providing both technical assistance and funding for the release of teachers and the hiring of substitutes so that teachers may receive indepth training in the job setting.

General Curriculum Development

A. Fine Arts

1. Focus and Frameworks

Focus areas for program development in the fine arts included development and field testing of curriculum frameworks, delivery of inservice education programs, technical assistance to local school systems, and preliminary development of a program in art safety. Curricular frameworks in dance and theatre education and a composite framework for fine arts education were completed. The framework for music education was prepared for pub-lication, and activities to support local school system implementation of the visual arts framework were continued. Inservice workshops were conducted to support implementation of programs in art and music education. Regional workshops conducted in Wicomico and Baltimore Counties provided school systems opportunities to focus on fine arts program improvement.

2. Art Safety

The State Superintendent appointed a task force to examine hazards posed by artistic media, materials and processes, and to develop an art manual to support implementation of local school system safety procedures.

B. Athletics

The Maryland Public Secondary Schools Athletic Association (MPSSAA) administered and regulated a statewide athletic program for students in Maryland public high schools. Over 73,000 students partici- pated in 22 interscholastic sports in the 151 member high schools. Seventeen state tournaments were conducted at the con- clusion of the fall, winter, and spring sports seasons. The MPSSAA trained and registered 6,000 game officials through a clinic and testing program. Finally, the MPSSAA sponsored an alcohol and drug prevention program geared to athletes. Twenty-two school teams were trained and now have active programs within their schools.

C. Environmental Education

A variety of grants in the science, social studies, and outdoor education areas ere awarded to assist local school systems develop and enhance environmental education programs. Inservice teacher training efforts focused on improving student understanding and participation in the restoration of the Chesapeake Bay watershed. An expanded Estuarine Field Studies Program in cooperation with the Chesapeake Bay Foundation, the Alice Ferguson Foundation, and Echo Hill Outdoor School enabled students to directly experience the beauty and the diversity of life found in the Chesapeake Bay area. Cooperative efforts among the Departments of Natural Resources, Environment, Agriculture, and Education enhanced each department's efforts to educate the youth of our state.

D. Health Education

1. Health Curricular Framework

Through efforts initiated by the Maryland State Department of Education, many local school systems are now working to implement comprehensive health educa- tion in K-12 curriculum. The Health Education Curricular Framework Task Force is in the second year of the development of

a comprehensive health education curricular framework. When completed, the document will include a recommended model for the design of grade K-12 health education curriculum. Issues addressed include drug abuse, teen pregnancy, youth suicide, AIDS, and child abuse. The frame-work is scheduled for completion in December 1988. At that time, it will be presented to the State Board of Education for adoption.

2. AIDS Prevention

The issue that has received the greatest amount of attention in the past year is AIDS. The Department began to address guidelines for school attendance for students who are HIV positive. The Interagency Committee on AIDS Education has been involved in the development and dissemination of instructional materials on AIDS prevention. The Committee has also produced a videotape on AIDS prevention and has provided technical assistance to several local school systems. In October 1987, a statewide inservice was held and attended by repre-sentatives from all 24 local school systems. The inservice was entitled "AIDS Prevention Education: Instructional Approaches." In October 1987, an emergency regulation was approved by the Administrative, Executive, and Legislative Review Committee that requires that all local school systems initiate AIDS education during the 1987-88 school year. In September 1987, MSDE received a cooperative agreement from the Center for Disease Control. The agreement is for a

6

five-year period and funding for FY 88 is $125,000. In FY 88 the funds will be used for programs in school systems with a high incidence of AIDS and to employ an AIDS Prevention Specialist to provide technical assistance to local school systems.

3. Child Abuse Prevention

State funds were again made available in fiscal year 1988 for development and implementation of child abuse and neglect prevention curriculum. State aid of $80,000 was designated to provide grants to local school systems. In FY 87, eight school systems were awarded grants of up to $10,000, and eight additional school systems will be awarded similar grants in FY 88. Each school system in the state received the grant application, and plans call for all 24 school systems to receive grants by the end of FY 89. Model curricula have been identified and are available from MSDE, and several school systems have received technical assistance from this Department.

4. Suicide Prevention

The Interagency Committee on Youth Suicide Prevention was established. This committee developed the Maryland Youth Suicide Prevention School Program designed to assist local education agencies (LEAs) in the development and implementation of a youth suicide prevention school program. Four regional meetings were held in spring 1987 to introduce the prevention program to the LEAs and to lend technical assistance to them in beginning their programs. Four regional meetings were held in winter 1988 to further meet the needs of the LEAs in starting local suicide prevention programs. Funds were made available through competitive grants to the LEAs for program funding.

5. Drug Free Schools

In April 1987, the Maryland State Department of Education and the Governor's Office of Justice Assistance completed a grant application for $2.66 million in funds through the Drug-Free Schools and Communities Act of 1986. The Department received approximately $1.86 million of which $1.6 million is to be distributed to local school systems. MSDE will use $86,000 to administer the program, employ a drug abuse prevention specialist, and provide technical assistance to local school systems. All local school systems have received applications. Each local school system is eligible to receive from a minimum of $15,000 up to a maximum of $297,000 according to the school-age population in the school system. School systems that receive funds must agree to implement K-12 drug abuse prevention education curriculum as well as intervention and support programs. The drug Abuse Prevention and Education Programs Advisory Council is reviewing grant applications and providing guidance to the Department. Members of the Council represent a variety of state agencies including the Governor's Office, the State Legislature, parent groups, and local government. The Department is providing technical assistance to many local school systems and is planning statewide conferences ad training to address drug abuse prevention issues. Federal funding for this program will continue through FY 89.

E. Mathematics

1. Mathematics Framework

The mathematics framework adopted by the Maryland State Board of Education is being implemented in all local school systems.

2. Mathematics Initiatives Grants

In its second year of operation, the Education for Economic Security Act (EESA) continued to support mathematics and science initiatives. Grants were made available to every local school system for improving grades K-12 mathematics/science programs through teacher training, conferences, and certification. Two science/statistics/communication conferences were held to encourage the cooperative efforts of science, mathematics, and language arts teachers. Special grants were made available to local school systems for designing an appropriate process of data collection in a science laboratory setting, the statistical display

of results of experiments, and the development of a writing scheme to portray the interpretation of these results. Drawing on an EESA exemplary grant from the previous year's funding, a three-year general mathematics curriculum guide was produced by a statewide committee and distributed to all local school systems.

3. Functional Mathematics

The Maryland Functional Mathematics Program was enhanced by continuing inservice days for mathematics, special education, and out-of-field teachers upon request of local school systems. In addition, a statewide inservice program was conducted.

4. Maryland Mathematics Week

In cooperation with the Maryland Council of Teachers of Mathematics, the Department sponsored a statewide middle school mathematics competition and provided every public and private school with activities and publications to enhance the celebration of Maryland Mathematics Week.

5. CCSSO Indicators

The Department assisted the Council of Chief State School Officers by participating in a mathematics indicators project. Curriculum materials, mathematics objectives, and indicators to measure expectations of achievement in mathematics were identified.

6. Retiree Outreach

With funding provided through a United States Department of Education discretionary grant, the Retiree Outreach Project was implemented as a means to attract persons with science, mathematics, and technology backgrounds to consider teaching as an alternative after retirement or as a change of career option. Various phases of the project have involved contacts with government, business, industry, higher education officials, and certification and personnel offices in the local school systems.

F. Middle Learning Years

The Maryland Task Force on the Middle Learning Years developed a mission/prespective statement to serve as the philosophical foundation for recommendations for the improvement of education for Maryland public school students aged 10-14. The Task Force will complete recommendations that will address organization and climate, staff preparation and development, curriculum and instruction, pupil services, and student activities for the middle learning years.

G. Study of High Schools

The first phase of a longitudinal study of the impact of the Maryland graduation requirements bylaw was completed resulting in a published and widely distributed study entitled "Pathways through High School." Recommendations contained in the study will be addressed in planning for the next fiscal year.

To aid in implementing the high school bylaws, a set of standards and processes have been developed to assist schools in assessing implementation and development of school improvement plans. The standards are based upon the recommendations for high school education in Maryland resulting from the study conducted by the Maryland Commission on Secondary Education.

Finally, to provide a resource for high school educators in Maryland, staff has developed a publication concerning graduation requirements. It includes regulations, explanations, and interpretations concerning frequently asked questions about the requirements. It will be published and distributed to local school systems.

H. Research on Effective Teaching Behaviors

The charge for Project BETTER (Building Effective Teaching Through Educational Research) was to research effective teaching behaviors, practices, and instructional strategies related to various content areas, levels, and/or specific student populations.

9

Phase II of this project includes summarizing research findings on content, level of schooling, and specific populations for physical education, language arts, social studies, mathematics, and thinking skills. For all Phase II research findings, a review process by recognized authorities is being used to validate the findings, to establish consistency in reporting style, and to achieve consensus on the worth of the findings for broad teacher audiences.

I. Physical Education

The 1986 physical education bylaw served as an impetus for curriculum development in several local school systems. An increasing emphasis on services to "special needs" youth, promotion of lifetime fitness concepts, and the use of varied student assessment techniques are valued educational trends reflected in the new guides.

Other major activities included:

o A workshop on "Maximizing Learning in Physical Education through Effective Instruction" that attracted over 250 teachers.

o A conference for 60 educators from 20 local education systems. Most of the participants became certified boating safety instructors. The two state agencies cooperatively developed instructional materials and provided technical assistance to school systems planning boating safety education activities.

o The Maryland Physical Education Demonstration School Project, a national recognition program, remained in effect for the sixth year. Fifteen promising finalists were selected for on-site evaluations; up to 10 will be chosen as exemplary grade K-12 models in February 1988. Three long-term winners served as Honor Roll Schools this years in addition to the nine continuing state demonstration centers, which displayed their exemplary programs to visitors each month and at the state physical education association convention.

o Approximately 20 school systems reported use of the Maryland Superfit Test at three or more grade levels to assess the physical fitness of students. The state test was initiated by the Maryland Commission on Physical Fitness and produced with assistance from the Department and other support groups in the state. Presently these groups are cooperatively developing an instructional handbook of activities to help students improve their fitness level and increase their understanding of important fitness concepts.

J. Science

1. Science Initiatives

Title II funds under the Education for Economic Security Act, PL. 98-377, enabled the awarding of grants to each local school system to train science teachers and plan exemplary programs. Seventeen local school systems in Maryland conducted one or more programs for the training and retaining of science teachers. The implementation phase of these programs was monitored through site visits and assistance provided by the Department. Title II exemplary funds were used to conduct a conference on "Science, Statistics, and Communication." Following the conference, grants were awarded to six local school systems to conduct similar workshops for science, mathematics, and English language arts teachers in the local school systems.

Carroll, Howard, and Washington counties conducted all or part of their "Science, Statistics, and Communication" programs. Anne Arundel, Baltimore, and St. Mary's counties will complete their projects in 1988. The implementation phase of these programs was monitored and assistance provided.

The work of the Maryland Human Genetics Advisory Committee was supported by a Title II grant. With the active involvement of the Department, this Committee produced and disseminated an 80-slide set with script on genetic screening. In the first phase of dissemination, slide sets were distributed to each local school system. Phase two of the dissemination process provided staff development programs using a trainer-of-trainers model. Planning for this phase was funded by a $10,000 grant from MARHGN (Mid-Atlantic Region Human Genetics Network).

K. Social Studies/Citizenship

The focus of the citizenship education efforts was staff development through statewide and local workshops for teachers, through a network of educators sharing ideas for instructional strategies, and through appropriate assistance provided to local school systems. Targeted audiences for special assistance included students in the 1988 graduating class who had not met the requirements for the Maryland Test of Citizenship Skills, special education students, and student speakers of other languages.

The Department provided various opportunities to assist local school systems in implementing the social studies bylaw and framework. Several statewide workshops provided Maryland educators with instructional strategies and materials. The development of Maryland and Your World, a curriculum publication for middle school student use, supports an under-standing of Maryland's international role.

The State Superintendent appointed a task force to examine social studies curricula and instructional programs at the

11

local school system level. The task force will make recommendations for future direction and emphasis in Maryland's social studies program.

L.   English Language Arts

A 1987 supplement to the state writing guide was published in August. The guide presents revisions to the writing test made as a result of task force recommendations. In addition, the guide explores stages in the writing process and presents related instructional activities.

A conference planned jointly by the Thinking Skills, English Language Arts, and Reading and Communication Skills specialists drew 600 participants for presentations on Improving Thinking and Learning through Language Connections.

In a teacher-research project, some teachers of basic writers are methodically examining events in their classrooms to understand and improve their teaching practice and their students' learning. The project will close with a conference for teachers of basic writers from around the state.

A project investigating writing and computers will culminate in a publication that will feature software evaluation, suggested units, and suggestions for classroom management of various computer configurations.

Last year, over 54,700 students in 414 schools participated in the Maryland Reading Certificate of Merit Program. This program requires the reading of at least ten books between November and April and thus promotes reading as a personal activity.

Bookmarks to foster students' self-monitoring of their comprehension were developed, and over 30,000 were distributed to schools and LEAs.

M.   Second and Foreign Language

Some 8,000 students, most of them Asian and Hispanic, last year represented over 150 linguistic and cultural heritages in 24 Maryland school systems. Funding from several federal programs provides assistance for locals and funding for coordination and assistance at the state level.

Current funds are being used to provide for statewide data collection regarding numbers of limited English proficient (LEP) students and services provided to these students. An MSDE task force on LEP students was formed and a policy statement on non-English and limited English proficient students was drafted. Additional activities include general technical assistance to locals, Bilingual Education Guidelines and completion of the writing section in the ESOL Bilingual Education Instructional Handbook.

12

Final revisions are being completed on the State Foreign Language Curriculum Framework. The framework should be published and disseminated by fall 1988.

N. Thinking Improvement Program

1. Curriculum

As a result of Department-sponsored pilot projects, model curricula have been developed for the following areas: teaching analogical reasoning (early learning years), integrating critical thinking skills (elementary), teaching thinking skills and learning strategies (elementary), including thinking skills throughout the curriculum (middle school), enhancing critical analysis in social studies (high school), and teaching thinking through writing (K-12).

2. Instruction and Staff Development

A Department-sponsored Training of Trainers Institute has resulted in the development of inservice courses for teachers. To date, 17 state approved workshops on teaching thinking are available to educators throughout the state.

A two-day conference launched Phase II of Project Ten (Teachers Effectiveness Network), which will focus on training teachers in methods for improving student thinking. The conference involved 60 teacher educators from Maryland institutions of higher education and staff

development personnel from local education agencies.

A major conference, "Improving Student Thinking Through Language Connections," focused on the importance of teaching thinking as a route to improved literacy and writing. A sell-out audience of 600 educators attended.

3. Assessment

A working group of state and local experts are completing the design of a model for assessing dimensions of thinking. The model, along with resource materials, will be made available to Maryland educators.

Early Childhood Education

A. Extended Elementary Education Program

Progress in early learning programs included development of a mission and philosophy for the early learning years, a prekindergarten curricular framework, and a home-school cooperation position paper. Further progress included accreditation and validation of nine Extended Elementary Education Programs (EEEP) by the National Association for the Education of Young Children (NAEYC) and completion of a comprehensive examination of the age of entry to public school issue.

During the 1986-87 school year, $2.25 million in State Aid monies enabled 56 elementary schools in 12 LEAs to

13

participate in EEEP. Approximately 2,331 four-year olds were served in this program. Technical assistance was provided to all participating school systems. Standards for Implementing Quality Prekindergarten Education was published and used by nine EEEP schools in field testing a joint national (NAEYC) accreditation and state (MSDE) validation process. All schools were successful in this endeavor.

Finally, an Early Learning Support Center was established in Baltimore City to serve as a training and observation site for persons interested in improving the quality of their early learning programs. The Support Center provided field experiences for new and experienced early learning staff to work in a collegial relationship with their peers. Here teachers strengthen and/or revitalize their knowledge and skills in particular areas related to early learning programs.

Three major early learning issues-- curriculum/philosophy, entry age, and home-school cooperation were identified for examination. The State Superintendent appointed early learning committees to develop a mission and philosophy for the early learning years and a prekindergarten curricular framework, to examine the issue of age of entry to public schools and make recommendations to the Department, and to review home-school cooperation efforts in Maryland. Written reports including a survey of research, conclusions, and recommendations to the Department were completed for all committees.

Three evaluations were made to identify the strengths and weaknesses of Maryland's Early Learning Programs. Dr. Irving Lazar from the Consortium for Longitudinal Studies and Dr. Cynthia Wallat, Florida State University, conducted an external evaluation of eight EEEP prekindergartens in five local school systems. A "Survey of Policies and Practices in the Early Learning Years" was administered to principals and teachers, prekindergarten-3, in 76 elementary schools in 21 LEAs. The survey covered organization, expectations, curriculum, delivery of instruction, assessment, and home-school cooperation. Results will be used to make decisions about future priorities and needs in the early learning years. Finally, a study entitled "Survey of School and Social Behavior" was made to look at EEEP's impact on students' later social development.

B.   Early Identification and Intervention Program

During the 1986-87 school year, the state's 745 elementary schools screened approximately 44,141 kindergarten students using the Maryland Observational Screening Checklist for Kindergarten (MOSCK). Of this number, 5,594 (12.7 percent) were referred for risk of potential learning problems. In grades 1-3, 15,486 students new to Maryland public schools were screened. Of this number, 2,821 (18 percent) were recommended for referral of potential learning problems.

14

The Department continued to provide LEAs processing and data analysis services in early identification. LEA 1986-87 MOSCK Administrative Reports were prepared and disseminated. In addition 1986-87 state level screening data were used to conduct an item analysis and a reliability analysis of the MOSCK screening instrument.

Teachers and administrators in several LEAs were given inservice training on early identification guidelines. Early identification procedures were monitored in 10 LEAs. The <u>Language and Concept Development Guide</u> prepared by Frederick County was published and disseminated to kindergarten and first grade teachers in the state. The follow-up study, "A Correlational and Classificational Analysis of the Predictive Validity of the Early Identification and Intervention Program Screening Process," was completed.

INSTRUCTIONAL IMPROVEMENT

School Library Media Services

In July 1986, the Board enacted a bylaw, COMAR 13A.05.04.01 Public Library Programs, which establishes school library media programs, plans for their integration into the local education agencies' instructional programs, the use of implementation documents, and an ongoing review process. <u>Standards for School Library Media Programs in Maryland</u> was approved for use in the review process. Onsite review dates have been scheduled for six LEAs and review teams identified.

Staff inservice and training programs focused on techniques for evaluation of overall programs. A state program provided models for evaluation of library media programs as they relate to the curriculum. Inservice activities focusing on the evaluation and selection of computer software and innovative technology, as it relates to the curriculum, were conducted for teachers, school library media specialists, and administrators. Sessions in various school systems were developed as follow up to help strengthen programs and functions of those programs.

Local education agencies participated in inservice sessions highlighting selection skills and the need for materials in citizenship, Black history, and writing. A Traveling Materials Collection of approximately 3,000 items circulated to the school systems to provide a hands-on preview of new items. Requests for information on computer programs successfully used with students continued to be answered through the Maryland Instructional Resources Network database. A Series of publications dealing with building library collections were published and disseminated to appropriate personnel.

The State Media Services Center began the initial phase of an automated bibliographic retrieval and circulation system to help in the delivery of information to over 1,500 requests for online searches during the year. The software package has been purchased, and modifications to adapt the software to State Media Services Center needs are being completed. A time-line for implementation of the system is being developed.

Public Libraries and State Library Network Services

The Governor's Task Force on Regional Library Resource Centers recommended a five-year plan to increase state funding for the three regional library resource centers located on the Eastern Shore, Southern Maryland, and Western Maryland. An increase in funds was provided in the 1988 budget to be used primarily for acquisition of books and other materials.

The State Library Network program began a pilot project in Essex Community College and Cecil County Public Library of dial-up access to the online bibliographic database, MILNET. The project is funded until June 1988 with federal library funds. The state bibliographic database became available in CD-ROM format as well as microfiche.

The State Board of Education enacted a revised bylaw on certification of public librarians, requiring academic or inservice training credits for certificate renewal.

The state aid formulas for public libraries were increased by the Maryland General Assembly from $6.50 to $6.75 per capita. An $8.00 per capita program is recommended by the Maryland Advisory Council on Libraries.

Public library staff responses to reference and information questions have improved by 22 percent as a result of extensive training programs conducted by the staff of the Public Library Branch of the Division of Library Development and Services.

Literacy programs in public libraries of Garrett, Allegany, Washington, and Cecil counties have begun as a result of federal library grants for literacy programs. This brings the number of public libraries with programs to combat illiteracy in their counties to 16.

A major cooperative effort to serve the hard-of-hearing is underway in public libraries on the Eastern Shore, with purchase of equipment and materials, and employment of a regional staff coordinator.

Instructional Technology

The Division of Instruction Television was renamed the Division of Instructional Technology during 1987. This was done to more accurately reflect the areas of responsibility that have been added to the Division. In addition to the traditional instructional television activities, the Division is now providing guidance and technical support to schools in instructional computing and other emerging technologies, such as interactive videodisc and CD-ROM.

16

A. Video Design and Production

During the 1987 calendar year, 804 minutes of broadcast and closed circuit programs were designed and produced by Maryland ITV, the production arm of Maryland Instructional Technology.

The major accomplishment was the completion of two series: "Writer's Realm," fifteen 15-minute telelessons that teach the process approach to writing to middle schoolers, and "Transitions: Building Bridges," five 30-minute programs which train teachers and administrators to assist the school's special education population in making the leap to the world of work. "Writer's Realm" is currently being broadcast nationwide through the Agency for Instructional Technology. Other noteworthy programs include:

o   "AIDS: What Every Student Should Know" (high School)

o   "The Freedom Station," an original drama to assist schools in their observance of Black History Month

o   "Steps in Time: Scenes from 1840 Baltimore," a drama produced in cooperation with Baltimore's City Life Museums and School for the Arts

o   "Opening the Doors" and "Excellence at Work," two documentaries for the Division of Vocational Technical Education

o   A Public Service Announcement with Sugar Ray Leonard to help promote the televised G.E.D. series

o   "Save Our Schools" Theme Week

o   "Ask the Students" and "Ask the Superintendents," two prime time hour programs produced in cooperation with Maryland Public TV.

Developmental work continued on the primary science series, "Wee Wonders," which is funded by a $1.3 million grant from the National Science Foundation. A project director and support staff were hired, scripts were begun, and the pilot programs was given a national evaluation to enhance the series design. Full funding is still being sought for the production phase and proposals have been submitted to the Corporation for Public Broadcasting and a variety of other foundations and corporations.

B. Video Utilization Services

The Field Support Section continued its strategy of visiting schools and teacher training institutions to promote ITV. Also, a one-hour teleconference on using ITV information and techniques was broadcast to schools last spring, with a special attempt made to reach building-level ITV Coordinators. And, in response to much LEA interest in the use of local cable systems for interactive teaching, the "Governor's Conference on the Use of Interactive Cable Television in Public

17

Schools" was held in Annapolis in December. Over 140 attended the conference.

C. Broadcast Television

During 1986-87, the daytime television broadcast schedule and nighttime taping service included 64 instructional series: 51 were leased and 13 were Maryland-produced. Instructional programming was provided in 15 curricular areas, with approximately 23 percent of broadcast time devoted to intermediate and 37 percent to junior/senior high school. The major portion of instruction across grade levels was provided in science and social studies (21 percent each).

D. Special Broadcast Services

1. Night Owl Taping

Special late-night broadcasts continue to provide additional oppor-tunities for taping selected series off the air. By setting the timers on their VCRs, teachers and parents can record instructional programming aired between 12:30 a.m. and 6:30 a.m. each Tuesday throughout the school year.

2. Special Programming Hour

This service is offered five hours each week. Programs, scheduled at 11:30 a.m. every weekday, include selected Maryland Public Television rebroadcasts of National Geographic Specials, NOVA, and Great Performances. Live teleconferences,

as well as documentaries and original, theme-based programs are also presented during this hour.

3. Coming Attractions

Twice a day, this five-minute video bulletin board announces Special Programming and Night Owl offerings.

4. Critique Week

Maryland teachers participate in the selection of instructional programs by screening possible selections for the next school year. Their recommendations assist the Division of Instructional Technology programmers in making final the annual ITV Schedule.

5. Publications

Print support materials accompany most of Maryland's instructional tele-vision productions. In addition, schedule catalogs provide information about the Division's offerings. Eight publications were developed in 1987.

E. Instructional Technology Systems

During the 1987-88 school year, the MARYLAND EDUCATION TECHNOLOGY NETWORK increased from the seven original sites in six counties to 31 sites located in 12 counties and Baltimore City. These sites provided 1,046 teachers and 17,364 students access to computer networks for use in

18

their instructional programs in almost every curriculum area.

"How to Start a Business," an inter-active videodisc developed by the Division, is being piloted in five school locations in their Business Education programs. This is one of several innovative technologies being tested in school settings to determine their effec-tiveness as instructional tools.

Pupil Services Programs

The Board passed COMAR 13A.05.05, Pupil Services Programs, in February of 1987. The bylaw, which states that each school system shall provide a coordinated program of pupil services for all students in the areas of guidance, school health services, school psychology, and pupil personnel, resulted in part from the Report of the Maryland Commission on Secondary Education, Student Services and Activities, Volume III and the Superinten-dent's Task Force on Pupil Services. Local school systems are preparing their coordinated Pupil Services Programs Plan for September 1, 1988 certification.

A.   Guidance

Implementation of the newly-enacted guidance program, COMAR 13A.05.05.02, was certified by all 24 local school system superintendents. In support of this bylaw, a variety of program and professional development initiatives were completed: 1) school guidance delivery and management systems were established in nine LEAs; 2) innovative elementary school guidance programs/procedures were estab-lished in 14 LEAs; 3) timely inservice activities were produced for more than 1,000 of Maryland's 1,350 school counselors; and 4) all local education agencies implemented activities to better meet the career guidance needs of handi-capped and disadvantaged students, including developing transition plan formulas.

B.   School Psychology

Fifteen regional inservice programs for local education agency school psychologists were completed this year. A framework for school psychologists to use in reassessing special education students was developed by local education agency school psychology representatives.

C.   Pupil Personnel

Continued coordination and support was given to the Maryland Interagency Committee on School Attendance, Inc. (MIGOSA). The Committee provided assistance to MSDE to help organize the Maryland Pupil Services Conference on Dropout Prevention held on November 9, 1987. A packet of school attendance and dropout public relations materials was prepared by MIGOSA for statewide distri-bution in February of 1988. These materials were funded by MSDE and the Governor's Employment and Training Council. MIGOSA provided assistance to MSDE for the First National Conference on Dropout Prevention, which was be held in

Winston-Salem, N.C. on March 27-29, 1988. The conference is jointly sponsored by MSDE and the North Carolina Department of Public Instruction.

D. School Health Services

The position of School Health Services Specialist has been established. A framework for school health services is being prepared to meet the requirements of COMAR 13A.05.05.05, Pupil Services Programs. The School Health Manual is being revised and a Health Services Framework is being developed. Both documents will assist LEAs in the further enhancement of their school health program. An update of the analysis of the proposed school health services standards is being prepared. Additionally, a survey of the status of school health services throughout the state is being completed in collaboration with the Department of Health and Mental Hygiene.

Initiatives on the teenage parenting issue begun in 1984 were continued by the Inter-departmental Committee on Teenage Pregnancy and Parenting in Maryland. This committee represents six state agencies (Education, Health, Economic and Employment Development, Human Resources, Juvenile Services, and the Office for Children and Youth).

Accomplishments this year include:

o   A state wide interagency conference, attended by 625 people, on the issues of teen pregnancy and parenting.

o   Distribution of $2,000 incentive grants to local jurisdictions who develop programs and services that use an interagency approach to address the issues surrounding teen pregnancy.

o   An update of the annual networking guide that identifies specific agency and community contacts dealing with the issues of teenage pregnancy.

o   A statewide meeting, composed of agency representatives who work with adolescents, that helped people focus on barriers to preventing teen pregnancy and ways to assist pregnant and parenting teens.

Additionally, the committee is working collaboratively with the Department of Health and Mental Hygiene to promote the "Campaign for Our Children."

E. Programs to Reduce Disruption in Schools

Efforts in 1987 to reduce disruption included the continuation of the Maryland "Disruptive Youth" Professional Development Academy and the adoption of programs in 18 local education agencies, with multiple schools involved in each county. All projects follow the guidelines established in ss7-303 and may be remedial or preventive. Projects generally fall into one of three categories:

1. Level A, for the most severely maladjusted students, which provides long-term services in alternative settings;

2. Level B, for students who are beginning to continually misbehave, which provides short-term direct services, such as pupil services, as alternatives to suspension and office referrals; and

3. Level C, for all students and staff, which provides long-term assistance to administrators and teachers who deal with disruptive and misbehaving students.

F. Maryland's Student Assistance Program

Maryland's Student Assistance Program is being piloted in seven schools in six jurisdictions: Baltimore City (two schools), Baltimore County, Calvert County, Kent County, Queen Anne's County, and Washington County. Through early identification, intervention, and referral, many of the young people who are at risk of not succeeding in school due to drug or alcohol abuse or related problems are being helped by trained school teams and local health department personnel.

The first training session was held in August. A school training session is being planned for the spring of 1988, to include six more schools. It is hoped that effectively functioning Student Assistance Teams will be operating in every state jurisdiction within three years.

With financial support provided by the Office of the Governor and the Masonic Charities of Maryland, Inc., this program is a model private/governmental cooperation.

G. The Volunteer Services Program (VSP)

MSDE promotes volunteer program development in local school systems and provides technical assistance, statewide dissemination of information, statewide data collection, and special recognition awards. Volunteers contributed 3,789,650 hours of service. Volunteers are parents, businesses, men and women, community citizens, and students who work in a variety of settings, providing instructional services to students ranging from the "at risk" to the "gifted." Estimates this year show that 148,980 volunteers provided instructional and support services to children, youth, and adults in Maryland schools in 1986-87.

SCHOOL PERSONNEL ENRICHMENT

Teacher Education and Teacher Quality

The National Teachers Examination has been validated for use as a requirement for beginning teacher certification. Approximately 1,000 college and public school personnel have examined actual test items. The validation studies have been completed by the Educational Testing Service of Princeton, New Jersey. Qualifying scores were announced by the State Superintendent on July 1, 1987. Beginning April 21, 1986 all new teacher candidates were required to take a battery of basic tests plus one in their specialty areas. Beginning July 1, 1987, all new teacher candidates were required to meet the qualifying scores.

The Teacher Assessment and Development Committee has gathered infor-mation to create a set of criteria for the evaluation of the teaching performance of student teachers. Field study of these criteria included 13 school systems, 30 administrators and supervisors, 168 class-room teachers, and 12 study teachers.

Training programs are being conducted to prepare classroom observers to use the criteria and to assist college and school personnel in planning staff development for student teachers. A Beginning Teacher Program is being piloted in five school systems, and two research reports to assist all school systems with beginning teachers have been prepared with the cooperation of Research for Better Schools.

The State Board of Education has created the State Coordinating Council on Field Experiences comprised of college and public school personnel and has charged it to study the following:

1. Characteristics of effective field experience programs.

2. Funding for training of college and school system supervisors of teacher preparation field experiences.

3. Funding to pay for public school teachers who supervise these field experiences.

A thorough study of the certification regulations to make them more consistent with approved college teacher preparation programs in Maryland has been initiated. Twenty-two committees have been appointed to work over the next 18 months and make recommendations to the Professional Standards and Teacher Education Advisory Board (PSTEAB) for the revision of the certification regulations.

Teacher Supply and Demand

Our most recent Teacher Supply and Demand report indicates a teacher shortage is projected for the next several years in many teaching fields. In September 1987, the State Board declared math, the physical sciences, trades and industry, industrial arts, and special education as areas of critical teacher shortage.

Three years ago this Board recommended and the General Assembly enacted a scholarship bill to attract able young people to teach in areas of critical shortage. It is working. Over the past three years there have been more than 200 awardees. One problem has been limited funds; applications are greatly outstripping resources.

Some liberal arts graduates without teacher training wish to become teachers. New programs designed to meet this need are presently approved at the University of Maryland, the University of Maryland Baltimore County, Western Maryland College, Bowie State College, and Coppin State College. A program, funded by the Council of Chief State School Officers, has been started by four area higher education institutions and the Baltimore City School Systems.

A program to recruit military personnel who are within two years of retirement has been launched. Those recruited will receive qualification training during those two years.

The Maryland Professional Development Academy

The nine institutes conducted in 1987 served 250 school principals and others. Focus was on the principal's leadership role in improving and assessing instruction, leadership styles, and team-building abilities and the relation of instruction to student disruption. Some 1,500 principals have attended these well-received institutes since they began ten years ago. There is growing evidence that it is the premier national model for administrative leadership.

The Internship Program

Since 1982, an important component in the Maryland Professional Development Academy (MPDA) has been the Internship Program in School Administration, a program designed to train prospective school leaders through a series of skill development institutes and supervised field experiences. The program is implemented through extensive training in conjunction with the MPDA summer institutes and other special sessions; a school-based, internship experience in administration, and by individual support action plans.

Fifteen participants are selected each year, with strong consideration given to candidates from school systems that do not have administrative training programs. Eighty participants completed the internship by June 30, 1987. Over 85 percent have been place in administrative positions in their school systems.

Maryland Assessment Center Program

The Maryland Assessment Center Program (MACP), based on the assessment center model developed by the National Association of Secondary School Principals, is part of a major initiative begun by the State Department of Education in October 1985 to improve the effectiveness of Maryland's school-based administrators. Currently serving nine-teen school systems in six regions of the state, the MACP helps school systems identify and develop candidates with potential success in school administration. To date, 330 candidates have been assessed. The assessment provides participants with information regarding their strengths and needs for improvement in administrative and inter-personal skills, gives the school administration an objective assessment of each participant's readiness to assume administrative responsibilities, and provides information useful to LEAs in planning inservice activities.

PROGRAMS FOR STUDENTS WITH SPECIAL NEEDS

Compensatory Education

During fiscal year 1987, $52,829,420 in federal funds were allocated for Chapter 1 programs in 402 elementary schools and five middle schools in Maryland's 23 counties and Baltimore City to help meet the special educational needs of disadvantaged children. The Chapter I program served 54,710 public school and 2,027 non-public school students. In addition, 29 local institutions for neglected or delinquent children provided Chapter I services to 977 students.

On average, Chapter I students received four hours of special instruction each week in small classes averaging ten students. Children from prekindergarten through 12th grade were helped, but 56 percent were in grades one through three. Supplementary instruction in reading was given to 83 percent of the participants and in mathematics to 60 percent. Language

arts, limited English, English-as-a-second-language, and guidance counseling were other services provided.

To help meet the special educational needs of neglected or delinquent children in state institutions, Chapter I funds in the amount of $1,014,158 were distributed to the Juvenile Services Administration and $224,995 to adult correction institutions. These programs provided a variety of services including remedial reading and math, GED instruction, and employment training and counseling.

State funds for compensatory education totaled $13,283,062. The program authorized a per child maximum of $70 to be distributed according to the same formula as that applied for Chapter I. State compensatory education funds supplemented Chapter I programs and were administered according to the Chapter I state and federal guidelines.

The Chapter I and state compensatory education funds paid for extra teachers, aides, equipment, materials, staff training, and promoted parental participation. During the past year, the Department continued to fund and assist the Maryland Chapter I Parent Advisory Council, an organization that helps parents become effective advocates for their children.

The following features of effective education are found in Maryland's compensatory education programs:

24

o   About three-fourths of all Chapter I
    and state compensatory education
    teachers provided instruction in
    groups of eight students or less, a
    group that is small enough potentially
    to improve academic achievement.

o   Almost all Chapter I elementary
    schools relied on teachers to provide
    instruction with the assistance of a
    classroom aide.

Gifted and Talented

    Maryland's 24 school systems served
almost 60,000 students in school year
programs, approximately nine percent of the
state's student population. To assure that
programs reflect the quality standards
targeted for the state, the systems
continue to focus on Criteria for
Excellence: Gifted and Talented Program
Guidelines and recommendations of the 1983
Superintendent's Task Force on Gifted and
Talented Education.

    Major activities include preparation
of materials to give better direction to
program development, materials to encourage
wider and more effective use of teaching
aids, a statewide conference to sharpen
planning skills, and program review and
technical assistance grant programs.

    Last summer, 2,600 Maryland students
participated in 115 programs in 60 courses
of study offered by the Department at 14
sites of the Maryland Summer Centers for
Gifted and Talented Students. Eligible

students took part in a wide range of
artistic, cultural, physical, environmental, scientific, mathematical, and scholarly
programs.

    The compilation below reflects major
program accomplishments for the Maryland
Summer Centers in 1987:

o   The first annual Summer Center Student
    Art Exhibit was held at the Maryland
    State House with Governor William
    Donald Schaefer, Lt. Governor Melvin
    Steinberg, and State Superintendent of
    Schools David Hornbeck addressing the
    audience and touring the student
    exhibit. A capacity crowd of Maryland
    Summer Center students and their
    families filled the state house in a
    display of interest and support.

o   The Summer Center for International
    Studies conducted an interstate
    computer-assisted simulation with the
    Pennsylvania Governor's School for
    International Studies. The culmin-
    ation of the program was a joint
    conference held at Hood College at
    which learning experiences and
    understandings concerning the
    formulation of public policy were
    exchanged.

o   The Summer Center for Mathematics and
    Technology implemented a cooperative
    learning and technical assistance
    program with the National Security
    Agency. The NSA personnel served as

mentors, guest speakers, and advisors to students.

o   A residential component to the Summer for Archaelogical Research was developed. The Center, operated in cooperation with the Maryland Historical Trust, extended its offering to include a Baltimore County residential program site.

o   The parent/child course piloted at the Summer Center for Science in 1986 was expanded based on its success and the interest of parents and students. The center, held in conjunction with the Maryland Science Center, offered two parent/child courses in 1987: Light and Photography and Observational Astronomy.

o   The Center for Critical and Creative Thinking enhanced its program by integrating cognitive and affective experiences. The classroom and field studies in thinking and problem solving were related in methodology to the residential Student Life and Evening programs. The result was a comprehensive experience in learning and living that may serve as a model for residential-type programs for gifted offered by the State, as well as local education agencies.

Migrant Education

Nine hundred ninety one children of migrant and seasonal farmworkers were enrolled in the Migrant Student Record Transfer System during the 1986-87 school year. Six hundred and five students received instructional services; 82 percent (496) of these youngsters attended one of the four summer migrant education program sites on the Eastern Shore.

The sites in Worcester, Dorchester, Somerset, and Queen Anne's counties served migrant students from infancy through age 21. All school aged children received instruction in reading, language development (including English for speakers of other languages) and/or mathematics. Supportive services, including social work, health and dental screenings, nutrition, and transportation were available at all sites. Reciprocal grants and agreements between local health and social services agencies and the sponsoring school systems funded migrant daycare and health services. Department of Human Resources grants for migrant daycare totaled $40,000, and was distributed to Dorchester, Queen Anne's, and Somerset counties. The East coast Migrant Headstart Project provided services to preschool youngsters in Caroline and Somerset counties.

Somerset County's migrant education program at Marion received national recognition from Secretary Bennett's Initiative to Improve the Education of Disadvantaged Children for its coordination of migrant services at a single site. All services--food stamps, WIC, health, social services, employment and education--were located within the school setting. This enabled families to receive comprehensive services at the time of school enrollment.

The Center for Human Services continued to fund staff for a GED program at Sudlersville. Community volunteers from the Girl Scouts, Boy Scouts, 4-H Clubs, and Foster Grandparents continued to assist students and teachers in the school.

Special Education

Last year the schools served 89,442 students from birth through 21 who needed special education programs. That figure has been fairly constant over the past several years.

MSDE continued to foster transition activities at both the state and local level. For FY 87 the following activities were selected:

o   Disseminating the MSDE Transition Guidelines state-wide to education and adult service agencies.

o   Conducting a symposium "Linking Technology for the Disabled" for area employers to highlight the accomplishments of disabled persons in the workplace, and encourage business/education partnerships.

o   Forming technical assistance teams to assist local education agencies in the development and implementation of transition programs.

o   Revising local level cooperative agreements committing Vocational-Technical Education, Vocational Rehabilitation, and Special Education to cooperative service delivery. These revised agreements reflect the requirements for transition planning in P.L. 98-199 and P.L. 94-457.

o   Developing and implementing a federally funded project for Learning Disabled high school students designed to provide vocational evaluation, skill training and job placement. Partners in this pilot program are MSDE, The Maryland Rehabilitation Center, Johns Hopkins University, and the Baltimore County Public Schools.

o   Developing and directing a Job Club Model designed to provide self advocacy training and pre-employment skills for students preparing to enter work study programs.

o   Completing a five program instructional television series to be used to train professionals in the transition process.

o   Beginning production of an instructional television series on Case Management.

o   Conducting parent and professional training programs on transition, networking, vocational skill development, and interagency cooperation. The Divisions of Special Education and

27

Support Services and Vocational-Technical Education have conducted a five-year follow-up study concerning handicapped and nonhandicapped students who graduated in 1981. This study found no significant differences between the success of the handicapped and the nonhandicapped students regarding work, post-secondary education, or independent living five years after graduating with a diploma from a Maryland high school.

During the past year, the Division of Special Education and Support Services (DSESS) continued to work with 17 local school systems in Maryland training parents to become more knowledgeable about public school programs for handicapped students. The project is organized and supported by the DSESS in cooperation with the Parent Educational Advocacy Training Center in Alexandria, Virginia. This organization, along with support from DSESS, assists parents to become effective advocates for their handicapped children. In addition, the DSESS continues to support and work with six local education agencies in Maryland that operate Parent Training Centers. The Centers, which are offices that operate under the leadership of a parent of a handicapped child, assist families that have a handicapped individual in the home and need special services, training services, training, or support.

The Maryland Learning Disabilities Initiative accomplished its three directives by (1) training educators in the diagnosis, (2) instruction of learning disabled students, and (3) identifying competencies for teachers of learning disabled students. Diagnostic and instructional manuals have been disseminated to teachers in all 24 of the state's LEAs. The Maryland Learning Disabilities Initiative continues its commitment to improving instruction for learning disabled students and is actively involved with the Johns Hopkins University and Kennedy Institute in developing computer-assisted instruction for mildly handicapped students. The interdisciplinary team has developed a Multi-Sensory Authoring Computer System (MACS-II) that addresses the learning area of language arts, with an emphasis on reading comprehension skills.

MSDE administers the American Printing House (APH) for the blind registration in Maryland, which mandates that a central registry of all legally blind students be centrally maintained and that the per capita allocation of APH federal funds be used to purchase necessary instructional materials. The number of children covered by this project has increased steadily over the years; it now covers 517 public and 233 nonpublic school children.

The Maryland Deaf-Blind Program, funded under the Education of the Handicapped Act (34 CFR Part 307), now in its fourteenth year, provides comprehensive support services to local education agencies, state-operated programs, and nonpublic schools serving children with hearing and visual impairments. Today, it serves over 80 deaf-blind children. The expanding emphasis for this year has been our two-week summer institute for teachers and students, as well as a seven-person statewide technical assistance team to provide assistance to teachers and staff across the state. As part of the state's leadership training activities, a curricular framework was developed to assist professionals and staff with the development of appropriate curricular activities for handicapped students.

During the past year, the Division of Special Education and Support Services has continued its leadership role in encouraging placement of handicapped children in the Least Restrictive Environment (LRE). Maryland now has pilot LRE initiatives in 17 of 24 LEAs. Activities range from pre-referral intervention programs to system-wide training of principals, supervisors, teachers, parents, and others in the least restrictive environment. This year the state will expand the pilot activities and instructional alternative and, in addition, sponsor the sixth annual statewide conference.

We continue for a sixth year the longitudinal study of the performance of handicapped students by grade, type of handicap, and LRE placement on Maryland's tests of reading, mathematics, writing, and citizenship skills.

In the same connection, the Department's Monitoring and Evaluation System is evaluating how each LEA incorporated the competency requirements into students' IEPs. Additionally, the Department is completing an 18-month federal Program Evaluation Project concerning effective teaching strategies for functional reading skills. "The findings indicated that increased time on tasks in grade 8 improved handicapped students' passing rates on the Maryland Functional Reading Test."

A cooperative agreement between MSDE and the National Cristina Foundation (NCF), a private nonprofit corporation founded to help handicapped individuals receive the benefits available through technology, was approved in October 1986 and will make available over the next 18 months 2,500 microcomputers for use by school-aged and adult disabled individuals in Maryland. A July 1, 1987, status report on this agreement indicates that 1,020 computers were deployed to LEAs throughout the State. Also, a statewide user group meeting was held at the MSDE/JHU Technology Center for the Disabled and a meeting of private businesses was held which was keynoted by the Governor.

Early childhood education has been a priority for MSDE. Technical assistance and inservice training, including a statewide conference entitled "Family Issues in Early Childhood/Special Education," was conducted during the year for early intervention staff. National outreach mode projects are being replicated, and the National Cristina computer/technology project for early childhood handicapped students is being implemented in the LEAs. An Early Childhood Service Questionnaire was disseminated throughout the 24 LEAs to document Maryland's early intervention programs.

The Department of Education has assisted the Governor's Office for Children and Youth in its role as lead agency for the planning phase of Part H, of Public Law 99-457, the Education of Handicapped Infants and Toddlers. This includes participating as a member of the Interagency Coordinating Council, data collection, sharing resources, developing the federal application, and collaborating with other agencies toward a family-centered, community-based, coordinated system of care for handicapped infants, toddlers and their families.

In 1986 Johns Hopkins University and the Maryland State Department of Education joined forces to form the Center for Technology in Human Disability. The aim of the collaborative enterprise is to promote the development and use of micro-computers and technological advances in home, school, vocational, and community settings for the benefit of persons with physical, learning, sensory, and multiple disabilities. The State Superintendent of Schools served as chairperson for the new organization for 1986 and 1987. The center, in conjunction with the Maryland State Department of Education, Division of Special Education and Support Services, conducted a multi-state computer camp for the disabled at the National Easter Seals Society Camp, Fairlee Manor. This two-week camp assisted individual disabled persons with needs related to the use of computer technology, as well as provided graduate credit for the staff working with these disabled persons through Johns Hopkins University and the University of Maryland, Easter Shore.

VOCATIONAL EDUCATION AND THE WORLD OF WORK

Over 225,000 students took advantage of the wide array of vocational education programs offered at all education levels during FY 87. Over 70,000 high school students enrolled in vocational programs for skills training; 60,000 community college students continued their occupational education; and 20,000 adults who wanted to upgrade their job skills chose vocational education. Students were enrolled in programs offered in 160 high schools, 32 vocational-technical centers, and 17 community colleges located in Maryland's 23 counties and Baltimore City. More than 1,130 inmates in Maryland correctional institutions received vocational certificates in 31 different program areas during the fiscal year. An additional 607 were enrolled in vocational education programs.

Programs and special initiatives were designed and put in place during FY 87 to address four goals: (a) equal access, (b) quality instruction, (c) quality support services, and (d) accountability.

Quality vocational education programs provided secondary, post-secondary, and adult students with basic education, technical expertise, and positive work attitudes necessary to enter employment and further their education. The results of several initiatives to promote linkages between the private and the public sectors are outlined in this section, as are the achievements of programs helping individuals, especially at-risk individuals, overcome persistent barriers to high-wage employment.

The successful placement of 2,242 handicapped secondary students in the mainstream of vocational education and 2,344 handicapped secondary students in separate programs has been accomplished. The Vocational Support Service Team (VSST) provided the opportunity for students in vocational education who have a handicapping condition to be placed in the least restrictive environment, assuring the provision of equal access. During 1987, a total of 69 VSSTs operated in 23 public school systems at the secondary school level. Most notable areas of improvement by students were in attendance, grades, and student behavior.

Four hundred forty-seven handicapped individuals were served in mainstream programs at the post-secondary level. Notable activities for the past year have included increased outreach and inservice activities, as well as the provision of necessary support services. For example, Essex Community College expanded its Vocational Support Services program for individuals with mental or physical disabilities who are experiencing difficulty in occupational programs.

Vocational Support Service Team members provided support services for 5,594 educationally disadvantaged secondary students who were enrolled in vocational programs. Approximately 69 teams provided such services as supplemental instruction, tutoring, study skills assistance, and career guidance activities. During the 1987 fiscal year, many teams initiated successful computer-assisted instruction services. Computer software in trade and related skills areas was used to supplement instruction. Support team members have been successful in designing and delivering inservice presentations to vocational faculty. Activities include involvement in vocational recruitment, vocational evaluation, and other career-related services. VSSTs also provided support services to 3,145 post-secondary disadvantaged students at 17 community colleges.

Support team personnel have reported improved student attendance and achievement and increased program completion as a result of providing vocational support services. Two hundred sixty-four secondary students with limited-English proficiency received additional services in mainstream programs. Vocational Support Service Team members report success in the use of bilingual vocational materials to enable students to succeed in their vocational programs.

31

More than 161 occupational programs at the post-secondary/adult level were improved, expanded, and modernized to meet the needs of the existing and future work force. Particular attention was given to strategies that raised employment competencies. Adult vocational courses were offered to 19,810 eligible students by 18 providers. Of those, twelve were community colleges and six were local school systems. Six community colleges, through their job placement offices and with assistance from other agencies, worked to place 1,410 vocational program graduates in occupations related to their vocational training.

Two post-secondary institutions were recognized through an award program provided by the Baltimore Gas and Electric Company. Prince George's Community College received recognition for its "demonstrated high degree of success in providing responsive occupational education programs that resulted in full-time employment for two-thirds of its 1985 graduates." Faculty members in the occupational programs of Parks Management at Frederick Community College and Allied Health at Essex Community College received cash awards from the Baltimore Gas and Electric Company in recognition of "innovative teaching and learning activities within their designated occupational program." The awards program was co-sponsored by the Maryland State Council on Vocational Education.

The Division of Vocational-Technical Education also funded customized business and industry training programs in which more than 300 Maryland private sector employees received technical training. Projects ranged from supervisory and management skills development to electronic assembly line procedures.

Ten programs were funded to serve adolescent single parents in Baltimore City, and Anne Arundel, Baltimore, Charles, Dorchester, Frederick, Howard, Prince George's, Queen Anne's, and Washington counties. Program services have been provided for 410 single parents. Services were provided in the program areas of entrepreneurship, trade and industry, home economics, health, and marketing education. Several local education agencies have sponsored conferences and seminars to assist teen parents in gaining employability skills. All programs were coordinated with the Local Interagency Committee on Teen Parenting, Teen Pregnancy, and Teen Pregnancy Prevention.

A high wage employment opportunities program was designed and started by Maryland New Directions, Inc. To prepare single parents and homemakers for entry into careers considered non-traditional for women and to provide appropriate support services to ensure active participation. Through assessment, counseling, group services, and support mechanisms, single parents and homemakers have been guided into training and education for non-traditional careers or placed in high wage employment. More than 24,500 vocational education administra-tors, faculty, staff, students, parents, and selected local business and industry personnel participated in programs sponsored to increase equal access for young women and men interested in pursuing vocational education programs non-traditional for their gender.

A vocational education-private sector initiative, "Beyond the Number," was conducted by the Prince George's County Public Schools. The title of the project refers to the fact that American educators are very good at counting. They know the number of black, white, Hispanic, male, female, physically challenged, exceptional, and nonexceptional students enrolled in Maryland schools. However, counting the actual number of student populations is only a part of implementing real educational equity. "Beyond the Numbers" brought together over 100 business, government, civic, and education leaders to share information about educational equity, to promote dialogue among diverse groups, to develop a common understanding of educational equity and excellence, and to develop action plans to be implemented by each participant. Presentations on the program were made at educational conferences throughout the United States in 1987.

Vocational educators were able to expand their programs through participation in a special project called "Intergrating Entrepreneurship Skills into the Vocational Classroom." Through this project, Open for Business, a DVTE video series, and Risks and Rewards, entrepreneurship resource materials from Ohio, were made available for classroom use throughout the state. Job placement and follow-up services were also expanded to place 12,210 secondary vocational program graduates in employment related to their training. An expanded feature of the job placement service was the development of a system to survey students and their employers at one-year and three-year intervals.

During FY 87, 275 sets of updated microfiche were distributed to the 24 local education agencies. Five workshops were conducted to assist counselors and other educational staff in the use of INFORM, a Maryland developed career information tool. More than 325,000 secondary students had access to the INFORM system. INFORM also provides career information to 17 community colleges, juvenile services and public libraries. Displace homemakers continued to use INFORM extensively through the single parent and homemaker programs at the community colleges.

Maryland public schools serve students who speak over 110 different languages. Guidance counselors have been particularly interested in helping these students understand the opportunities for high wage employment that are available to students who complete vocational technical programs. More than 135 counselors repre-senting all local education agencies participated in a two-day seminar to increase their skills in serving minority students. At the postsecondary level, 150 student services

33

personnel representing all Maryland community colleges attended "Access to Excellence," the major post-secondary statewide guidance conference in 1987.

Twenty-three local administrators with management responsibilities for vocational education participated in the Maryland Professional Development Academy Institute on Vocational-Technical Education. Administrators designed school-based computerized systems to manage vocational education. The systems addressed budget management and control, vocational information retrieval, accounting for expenditures from state categorical allocations, vocational record keeping, interchange of administrative information between central office and local schools, inventory control, analysis of follow-up data, and scheduling of vocational education programs.

The institutionalization of competency-based vocational education continued to be the top priority of curriculum efforts in 1987. Demonstrating a commitment for quality vocational education, MSDE formed a cadre of teachers who had demonstrated leadership in the use of competency-based vocational education materials. State technical committees were organized and have successfully completed three curriculum development efforts in the areas of building maintenance, residential electrician, and legal secretary. An additional curriculum activity was conducted for mathematics, science, and industrial arts/technology education

teachers to develop instructional strategies necessary to implement fundamental principles of mathematics and science through practical applications in the industrial arts/technology education program.

Public school systems used 240 films from the Maryland Vocational Curriculum Center media loan service. As a result of individual requests from teachers, 3,690 sets of curriculum materials were distributed to secondary and post-secondary institutions.

Vocational Student Organizations (VSOs) provided leadership development activities for more than 12,000 students. Advisors and officers of all six VSOs participated in organization development activities.

Community-based organizations provided programs to facilitate the entrance of youth into vocational education, employment, or other training. Career counseling services and skills development programs were provided for 84 individuals. The focus of the projects was to help young people return to school or gain employment. Project activities included individual counseling, education placement in GED or pre-employment training, job placement assistance, vocational skills training, development of individual vocational education action plans, and referrals to other agencies. Participants were served at Dundalk Community College and in Harford

County and Anne Arundel County Public Schools.

Maryland has provided state leadership, administrative and support services and activities, and information dissemination to ensure the quality and effectiveness of local consumer and homemaking, knowledge and skills in home economics, and improved options for successful family life. Emphasis was on assisting males and females assume their future roles of working both inside and outside the home.

The student and employer follow-up survey completed as a part of the proactive evaluation process indicated that 55 percent of the graduates who completed a vocational program were employed, 32 percent were attending school, and 6.6 percent were unemployed. Employers of vocationally prepared graduates were very satisfied with the students' skills, ability to learn, and work habits. Over 97 percent of the 1,581 employers who responded to the survey said they would hire other vocationally prepared graduates.

The Maryland Vocational-Technical Education Program Survey Report (FY 84-86) disclosed that:

o Over 77 percent of the students in vocational education were enrolled in the program of their first choice.

o More than 71 percent of the students said they like school better because of vocational education.

o Ninety-three percent of the instructors said program graduates had entry level skills.

o Ninety-seven percent of the students said they received guidance services.

o Ninety-six percent of the graduates who responded to the survey indicated that they were please with the quality of their instruction in the areas of reading, writing, and mathematics.

o Vocational students are succeeding in academic and vocational programs. For example, more than half reported that they were earning grades of A or B in their mathematics courses and two-thirds reported earning an A or B in their vocational programs.

In summary, more than 2,601 occupational, consumer and homemaking, and industrial arts/technology education programs were provided to over 220,000 students. There were 69 new programs and 313 improved programs. Federal vocational education funds made it possible for 575 guidance counselors from all Maryland public school systems to improve and expand vocational guidance services during FY 87. More than 7,400 vocational educators, administrators, and counselors at the secondary, postsecondary, and adult levels

35

participated in vocational education personnel development activities.

VOCATIONAL REHABILITATION

The Division of Vocational Rehabilitation (DVR) administers the state's Vocational Rehabilitation Program under the Rehabilitation Act of the Disability Determination Services (DDS) program of the Social Security Act. The mission of the DVR is to provide a program of rehabilitation services to handicapped citizens of Maryland and assist them in becoming independent, employed members of the community.

During the last fiscal year the Division, through the Office of Field Operations, delivered services to over 29,000 individuals. Of the number, 3,859 clients were rehabilitated--meaning these individuals achieved gainful employment as a result of the services provided or arranged by DVR staff. Sixty-two percent of those individuals rehabilitated were severely handicapped.

The Division conducted year-long comprehensive planning initiatives in an effort to expand and enhance vocational rehabilitation services to three target populations:

o persons with chronic mental illness,

o persons with traumatic head injury, and

o individuals who were transitioning from school to work.

As a direct result of those planning efforts, the Agency developed and initiated a Program Implementation Plan on a Division-wide basis that will facilitate and ensure the provision of meaningful and substantial services to those special populations.

The Division has completed its third year as an active partner in the Maryland Supported Employment Project (MSEP). MSEP is a statewide initiative to make system changes in state agencies, private non-profit service providers, and employers to improve the availability and the impact of Supported Employment. The project is an innovative service for individuals with severe disabilities funded under a five-year, $2.1 million project grant from the U.S. Department of Education.

Over the past year, the Division expanded its efforts relating to the administration of the state's Supported Employment Program. This program is designed to serve very severely handicapped individuals who, prior to availability of these services, were often ineligible for traditional vocational rehabilitation programming. Supported Employment ensures long-term, ongoing support services for individuals with very severe handicaps. It provides for paid employment in an integrated work setting of handicapped and non-handicapped workers; real jobs for real wages.

36

The Division administers the Independent Living Rehabilitation Services Program which serves individuals with severe handicaps who can benefit from rehabilitation services. The aim for such people is to often achieve or maintain independence in their families and their communities. This program includes:

o   Statewide service provision through the Division's field offices located in all subdivisions of the state;

o   The award and oversight of a contract to Maryland Citizens for Housing for the Disabled (MCHD) for the operation of a center for independent living services;

o   A contractual arrangement with the Greater Baltimore Medical Center and the University of Maryland Hospital for the provision of independent living services to older blind individuals.

The Maryland Rehabilitation Center (MRC) served 1,773 clients last year with an average daily census of 285, representing 95 percent of program capacity.   MRC is a comprehensive rehabilitation facility that provides multi-disciplinary services to individuals with handicaps, particularly those who are severely disabled.   MRC is designed to address the needs of individuals who will require multiple rehabilitation services and provides medical and therapeutic services, vocational evaluation and training, specialized recreational programming, and the services of a skilled nursing unit.   The MRC continued its widely recognized leadership role in the design and provision of innovative programming including:

o   Applied technology and rehabilitation engineering for individuals with very severe disabilities;

o   Case management and job placement/ training for individuals with traumatic head injuries;

o   Specialization of services for individuals with specific learning disabilities (SLD) transitioning from school to work.

Disability Determination Services (DDS) developed and adjudicated 48,316 claims for Social Security Disability Insurance and Supplemental Security Income payments.   DDS also referred 2,824 individuals for vocational rehabilitation services.   Examiner productivity increased by 50 percent over the previous year as processing time for claims and pending workloads were significantly reduced.   DDS was able to reduce the use of consultative examinations as medical evidence by 10 percent, resulting in a savings of $385,000.   Additionally, numerous presentations were made around the state to physicians, medical facilities, and advocacy groups to explain the claims development and adjudication process.

The Division of Vocational Rehabilitation was actively engaged in many other initiatives during the past year including:

o The study and implementation of programmatic changes resulting from the 1986 Amendments to the Rehabilitation Act;

o Presentation of the Annual Injured Workers Conference at MRC;

o Accreditation of additional community based rehabilitation facilities;

o Administration of the Attendant Care and Social Security Reimbursement Programs;

o Implementation of an on-line data collection system, both demographic and financial, for internal and external management information.

EQUITY

During 1987 the Department received grant awards from the U.S. Department of Education for the support of equity services to local education agencies.

Department-coordinated Maryland Women's History Month activities in 1987 included the development and dissemination of a 300-page curriculum resource packet to all Maryland schools. The packet, "Making a Difference: Maryland Women and Social Reform," was highlighted by the National Women's History Project at two national conferences.

A statewide Equity in Mathematics, Science, and Computer Science Network was convened to share ideas and projects in Maryland that have been developed and implemented to increase the participation of females and minorities in these areas. This Network has been asked to consult on equity issues related to the proposed state high school for math and science.

Increasing Student Achievement through Education Equity is a Maryland Professional Development Academy Institute designed to increase awareness and skills of current and potential school administrators. This year's participants came from 12 local school systems, representing the following areas: Instructional Supervision, Principal/Assistant Principal, Human Relation Specialist, Teacher Specialist, Teacher and Administrative Trainee. Topics that build awareness of how to promote educational equity for maximum student achievement and a positive school environment were explored.

Again, Department staff provided a 10-day training seminar and school year workshops designed to make teachers and administrators more sensitive to the importance of a multi-cultural approach to curriculum development and implementation. Thirty-five participants received the training and were provided program follow-up as they began the new school year.

38

A national origin policy framework to increase the effectiveness of service provisions to non-English proficient (NEP) and limited-English proficient (LEP) children in Maryland public schools is in the process for approval.

ADULT EDUCATION

Adult Education

A. Adult Literacy State Planning

Last spring the Department began work with the State Board of Community Colleges and Department of Human Resources on the development of a comprehensive interagency plan to virtually eliminate illiteracy among adults in Maryland by the year 2000.

The strategic plan, Literacy: An Action Plan for Maryland, reflects input from over 300 literacy providers and support groups from across the state. Key recommendations of the plan are:

o   To mandate literacy as a priority of Maryland;

o   To assign the Education Task Force of the Governor's Employment and Training Council the task of coordinating state policy and interagency collaboration;

o   To establish a Maryland Literacy Foundation to encourage private sector funding; to establish a statewide literacy center for data collection, information and referral, and technical assistance;

o   To form local literacy teams with membership from public and private sectors to coordinate local delivery systems;

o   To fix responsibility with the primary adult literacy provider for assuring a comprehensive educational delivery system for adult literacy;

o   To provide an assessment and referral center for all adult literacy students;

o   To assign local liaisons to work with local school boards, local literacy teams, literacy providers, and assessment/referral centers and to seek significant non-federal funding increases;

o   To refocus federal monies to support the performance standards of the Action Plan.

B. The Adult Basic Education Program (ABE)

1. Ongoing Programs

Approximately 900,000 adults in Maryland lack a high school diploma. Some 450,000 have completed eight years or less of schooling. This year 29,797 adults received basic education services through Department-sponsored programs. For each

$100 of federal money received, local school systems provided an average of $77.75 or 44 percent of the total program cost.

2. Special Projects

Six federally funded projects were conducted during 1987. Two focused on community collaboration strategies to enhance adult literacy education. Literacy providers and business and industry were surveyed to identify collaboration models that could be replicated throughout the state. These projects developed two major documents: A Training Guide for Building Employer-Education Literacy Partnerships, and a State Literacy Services Directory, as well as reports on community literacy partnerships and business literacy partnerships in Maryland. One grant was awarded to the state association for adult and community education to provide regional staff development for adult education teachers and administrators. Three projects focused on the further development and expansion of the Maryland Adult Performance Program (Project MAPP), a competency-based model to be integrated in local adult basic education programs by FY 89. Through these projects curriculum frameworks and assessment instruments were refined and revised with input from local teachers and administrators.

C. The Maryland Adult External High School Diploma Program (XD)

The Maryland Adult External High School Diploma Program is a competency-based, applied performance assessment system through which competent adults demonstrate functional life-related skills in the areas of reading, writing, computation, occupational preparedness, and consumer, scientific, aesthetic, self and social awareness. The 13 LEA XD sites graduated 706 students in FY 87.

D. Adult General Education Program (AGE)

Adult General Education is a state-funded program to support local adult education classes in GED instruction, career exploration, parenting, consumerism, functional skills, and English for speakers of other languages. Eighteen counties in Maryland conducted AGE programs serving 84,825 students.

E. The Evening High School Program (EHS)

The Evening High School Program is an extension of the regular day school program, offering original or review credit classes. Credits earned may be applied toward a high school diploma. Requirements for these subjects are the same as those for subjects in day school. As of September 1987, there were 3,056 enrollments in eight evening high schools.

F.   General Education Development Program
      (GED)

    GED instruction is offered in each
local education agency in the state.
Several activities were recently initiated
to increase participation in GED
instruction. A GED instructional
television series has been on the air since
January 1987, providing both an alternative
means to prepare for the GED and promoting
interest in GED classes. A campaign by
Dollar General Stores has increased
interest among GED students and persons who
wish to volunteer. Four regional
promotional projects are also currently
being conducted to promote high school
completion programs for adults. GED class
enrollments increased significantly in FY
87. The GED Program tested 12,207
individuals in FY 87 and awarded 6,828
diplomas.

Community Education

A.   The Multi-Service Community Center
      Program (MSCC)

    These centers in 11 local education
agencies serve the educational, vocational,
employment, recreational, and leisure needs
of youth and adults. Activities include
sponsorship of career and college nights,
small group seminars, and individual
counseling sessions. Major program
components include information and referral
services, career and vocational counseling
and assessment, and job referral. MSCCs

provided services to 48,220 clients in FY
87.

B.   The School-Community Centers Program
      (SCCP)

    This program makes use of school
facilities during non-school hours to
provide recreational and enrichment
activities for young people, ages 5-20
years. Local administration is provided by
school systems in cooperation with the
recreation and parks departments.
Activities offered include drop-in
recreation, math and reading tutoring,
cultural arts, computer studies, family
library nights, and activities especially
designed for physically and mentally
disabled youth and young adults. In FY 87,
over 116,000 hours of programming were
conducted in 555 schools located throughout the state. Overall, the program
enrolled a total of 123,299 registrants and
served another 524,000 persons on a drop-in
basis.

CORRECTIONAL EDUCATION

    While the Correctional Education
Program was settling into a new
organizational home within the Bureau of
Vocational Rehabilitation and Correctional
Education, the opening of Maryland's newest
correctional center represented the biggest
single priority project for the
correctional education staff during 1987.

    The Eastern Correctional Institution
includes extensive educational facilities

41

consisting of a school and library in each of two compounds as well as a satellite school in the restricted custody housing unit. Each of the two schools includes four vocational education laboratories. As the new schools and libraries were being equipped and staffed, planning was completed to organize the instructional and library service programs. A staff complement of 39 full and part-time staff persons was allowed for the operation of academic, vocational, and library programs during day and evening hours. A gradual hiring program resulted in one of two academic staffs being on board and providing instructional service by the end of 1987. Librarians, vocational instructors, and additional academic staff persons will be hired and their programs will begin during the early months of 1988.

An excellent facility, ample funding for supplies and materials, and a quality staff will combine to result in a flagship program in correctional education at the Eastern Correctional Institution. Special features include state of the art training in eight vocational program areas, extensive computer access and integration within both academic and vocational programs, instructional services for restricted housing inmates, day and night instructional programs, full use model adult education curriculum design, and well articulated academic and vocational instruction programs.

Education services throughout the correctional facilities continue to stress

the prison literacy challenge. Legislation enacted in 1987 requires the identification of illiterate inmates and their classification by correctional officials into school programs, and it requires reporting to the Parole Commission on the educational progress of these students. Both the corrections agency and the Department welcomed this affirmation of Maryland's long term priority of prison literacy instruction and service of targeted student inmates.

The legislation will require an extension of these services to more and more inmates. This follows from an expanded literacy standard (a higher academic threshold for mandatory enrollment) which is being phased in over three years beginning on January 1, 1988. "Literacy Labs," an innovative Maryland instructional approach recognized in a federal agency publication and honored by a personal visit by the wife of the Vice-President of the United States during 1987, were expanded further as program services are readied to meet the expanding challenge in literacy instruction.

The Department began an important planning process in collaboration with Secretary Bishop Robinson of the Department of Public Safety and Correctional Services and with assistance from the Departments of State Planning and General Services.

A proposal under review by the 1988 General Assembly includes a Metropolitan Transition Services Center in Baltimore

42

City where the Department would operate a major new occupational preparation program. The project proposal includes renovation of an existing facility near the Maryland Penitentiary for eight occupational skills training programs and for related client services including academic preparation, vocational counseling, vocational assessment, pre-release instruction, and job placement.

The Center will provide a unique opportunity for the involvement of private employers in the occupational preparation of inmates. Policy commitment has been made to this goal, and both the facility's location in the heart of the metropolitan region and the fact that participating inmates will be eligible for work release immediately upon completion of training should facilitate the accomplishment of this goal.

The emphasis on planning for occupational preparation services is complementary of the five-year "program of excellence" for vocational education already in process in the correctional education program. A comprehensive evaluation program was completed during 1987 that included on-site review teams using the Division of Vocational-Technical Education's structured program review format. As evaluation was completed, long range planning for improvement was initiated. Additional planning will occur during 1988 with implementation activities starting and running through the next three years of this five-year program of development.

Instructional services and library service programs continued to show progress in 1987. Program completion figures available in 1987 reflected progress in FY 87 as compared to the prior year. Academic enrollment rose from 1,968 in late FY 86 to 2,676 in late FY 87. Program completions (8th grade certificates, high school diplomas, and vocational certificates) increased from a total of 2,169 in FY 86 to 2,448 in FY 87. Also, enrollment as a proportion of the prison population rose from 28 percent to 30 percent from FY 86 to FY 87, continuing a long term trend toward expanding the proportion of inmates involved in education programs. Prospects for continued expansion are mixed. While the program at the new Eastern Shore facility represents an expansion in instructional resources, limitations of funds for evening contractual instruction constricts enrollment capacities in the other correctional schools. The Department continues to seek funding for contractual program expansion. It is hoped that at least by FY 90 appropriations will be available to provide for contractual program expansions in coordination with new construction at existing correctional institutions and to reverse the trend of curtailing the night schools.

ADMINISTRATION

Food Service Program

The Department administered seven child nutrition programs and the temporary emergency food assistance program, providing services to public and non-public schools, residential child care institutions, child care centers, summer camps, family day care homes, organized summer programs, charitable institutions, elderly individuals, and needy families. The year 1987 saw improvements and growth in each of those programs.

o   The school food service program continues to serve a greater number of children. Over 61 million meals were served last year in breakfast and lunch programs.

o   The fourth in a five-year series of courses for school level food service employees, "SuperVision," was distributed to all LEAs. The fifth course "Speakeasy" was developed and field tested.

o   A project was initiated and implemented to increase participation in the School Breakfast Program. Six LEAs, including Baltimore City, were provided special assistance to improve the efficiency and effectiveness of their program. Materials developed as a result of the project, "Be Better with Breakfast," have been provided to

all LEAs for use in elementary schools offering the School Breakfast Program.

o   Nutrimania, a multi-disciplinary nutrition education course, was developed and distributed to residential child care institutions.

Pupil Transportation

For FY 87 Maryland public school buses traveled over 79 million route miles, transporting approximately 447,000 pupils daily.

The Department is responsible for calculating the funding of pupil transportation for LEAs and for adopting rules and regulations for the safe transportation of pupils as specified in Section 5-203 of the Public School Laws of Maryland.

We take pride in the state's program, featuring training for both school bus driver instructors and school bus drivers. For FY 87 Maryland public school buses continued to increase the number of miles traveled per accident while increasing the level of service provided.

Public School Facilities

In 1987 over 70 locally funded projects were actively being planned or constructed in six local education agencies. The projects represent $300 million in capital improvements and range from small renovations and additions to major modernization and construction of new buildings. Local boards of education continue to request site reimbursement for a significant number of these projects.

The Department continues to monitor and compile energy use data. Energy consumption by Maryland public schools and school system buildings increased in 1986-1987 for the second year in a row. The average building used 79,417 BUT/GSF, up 2.3 percent from the previous year. Energy costs, however, showed a substantial decrease. The energy cost per FTE student averaged $115.84, down 7.2 percent from the 1986 report. (The cost reduction was due primarily to a decrease in the cost of No. 2 fuel oil.) School systems are continuing to acquire computerized mechanical controls and to design and specify energy conserving features in all major construction projects.

Indoor air quality continues to be identified by the Department as a public health problem. Less than adequate indoor air quality can lead to a higher risk of health problems, and increase in student and teacher absenteeism, diminished learning, and in extreme situations, a hazardous condition. A state Committee on Indoor Air Quality in Public Schools was established in the spring of 1986 with the goal to develop a school facility guide for distribution to local school systems, local health departments, architects, and engineers. This document was published in the fall of 1987, followed by workshops in January 1988. The purpose of this document and the subsequent workshops is to raise awareness of this topic and provide skills to prevent, assess, and solve indoor air quality problems. Our Office of School Facilities will be assisting all 24 school systems in the development of indoor air quality management programs.

The Asbestos Hazard Emergency Response Act (P.L. 99-519) was signed into law in October 1986 and directed the Environmental Protection Agency to promulgate regulations to provide a frame-work for addressing the asbestos problems in public and private elementary and secondary schools. These regulations will require school systems to conduct inspections for asbestos containing materials and develop management plans by October 1988 describing response actions that will be undertaken. The states, using an EPA model, must develop accreditation programs and may receive the management plans prepared by the school systems. The plans must be implemented by local school systems in a timely fashion beginning in July 1989. The requirements of these regulations will have a major financial impact on local systems. The comprehensiveness of the Asbestos Hazard Emergency Response Act has caused the Department of Education and the Department of the Environment to discontinue the development of standards under Article 7-418, Inspections for Asbestos.

In July, 1987, a Task Force on School Construction Finance was appointed to study and make recommendations concerning certain program aspects of the Public School

Construction Program and the future financing responsibilities for public elementary and secondary school construction in the state. At the writing of this report the Board of Public Works had adopted revisions to the rules, regulations, and procedures for the administration of the School Construction Program based on the task force recommendations. These revisions adjust the maximum state construction allocations to reflect the state and local sharing for all projects approved for local planning on or after February 11, 1987. The state share ranges from 50 to 75 percent of the eligible portion of a construction contract.

The Office of the Governor, with the approval of the General Assembly, increased funding for elementary and secondary education by $103,139,321, from $1,368,677,553 in FY 87 to $1,471,816,854 in FY 88.

The Current Expense Formula was increased from $1,651 per pupil to be shared between state and local governments in FY 87 to $1,846 to be shared in FY 88. This added $70,179,243 to the Current Expense and Compensatory Education Programs. In FY 88, $3.9 million of Basic Current Expense monies was set aside for expenditures in Vocational-Technical Education.

Special Education for Handicapped Children was increased by $8,466,447 of which $4,250,000 was added to the Current Expense Formula, which was the first increase in that program since FY 81. Most of the balance of $3,404,215 was added to the program that provides for the placement of severely handicapped students in private institutions bringing this program to a level of $16,900,000.

The Transportation Program for public school students was $113,379,689.

Fringe benefits such as retirement and social security increased from $354,955,646 in FY 87 to $385,594,023 in FY 88. Debt service for school construction was $169,958,643. The school construction and fringe benefit funding was, thereby, increased $25,228,736.

Total State Library funding increased from $16,314,055 to $17,905,529, an increase of $1,591,474. Part of these monies increased the per capita amount to be shared between state and local governments to $6.25.

Approximately $7,800,000 in state funds for innovative programs was provided to assist local school systems in the development of career educational services for students to fund projects designed to improve reading skills and to implement other projects. The state's program for funding services to four-year-old children in the Department's Elementary Education Program increased from $2,250,000 to $3,395,000, an increase of $1,045,000.

46

To increase the use of public school facilities during evenings and weekends which serve young people and adults in the 24 local school systems, the funding level was increased to $1.5 million.

The Gifted and Talented Program which provides services for those children who are above average, was funded at approximately $700,000.

Disruptive Youth initiatives received approximately $600,000.

Environmental Education had an increase of $103,000 bringing this program's funding to $253,000.

Adult Continuing Education, which benefits persons who are putting forth the effort to obtain a high school education, received $106,00, and Food Services which supplements meals for poor children received $6.8 million.

NON-PUBLIC SCHOOLS

The Department works with the 423 non-public schools that have received approval of the State Board of Education. In recent years the Department has assumed the responsibility for the approval of before and after school day care service, which has now been approved in 58 of these schools. In addition, the Department has assumed responsibility for the approval of educational programs operated by a non-public residential juvenile or child care facility licensed by the Juvenile Services

Administration or the Social Services Administration and for the approval of nursery school programs and kindergarten programs operating within a non-public group day care center licensed by the Department of Health and Mental Hygiene.

The Department has assumed responsibility for administering the Governor's program for the recognition of merit scholastic awards in non-public schools.

PUBIC INFORMATION AND PUBLICATIONS

The Public Information and Publications Office during 1987 performed a variety of functions to inform the public and broaden awareness and support for public education. These functions included the distribution of 28 press releases to newspapers, television stations, and radio stations throughout the state, as well as countless contacts by phone and in person with reporters and other representatives from these organizations. A related public information function was carried out with members of local school boards and education agencies through two department-wide newsletters and several other publications covering specific fields of education.

The Office frequently coordinated its activities with, and provided support for, the governor's Press Office. These activities included drafts of news releases and speeches, background information for news conferences, and taped interviews on

47

news conferences, and taped interviews on timely topics in public education for use by radio stations throughout Maryland.

The Department, with the editorial and production assistance of the Office, published more than 70 brochures, reports, guidelines, newsletters, posters, manuals, and packets. In the annual competition sponsored by the National Association of State Education Department Information Officers, the Department received seven awards, more than any other state. Awards of Excellence went to:

o   "Maryland Teacher of the Year"

o   "Diversify Your Interests"

o   "Standards for Library Media Programs in Maryland"

o   "Reading Ready Reference"

o   "The Business Disc: How to Start and Run a Small Business"

Awards of Distinction were won by:

o   "Maryland State Board of Education, 1986-87"

o   "Fact Book, 1985-86"

The Office directed the Maryland Teacher of the Year program to draw positive attention to the state's many fine teachers. Out of 17 teachers nominated by local school systems, Paul S. Schatz, a Harford County elementary school teacher, took top honors. Funding for the program was provided by the Maryland Elementary and Secondary Education Foundation.

TABLE

1

General Statistics About Maryland Public Schools: 1986-87

Population of Maryland (July 1, 1987)	4,499,000
Public School Enrollment	675,747
Average Daily Membership	671,570
Average Daily Attendance	618,463
Number of Public Schools	1,189
Number of High School Graduates	46,107
Total Staff Employed	72,930
Average Teacher Salary	$30,700
Local Education Budget from Federal, State, and Local Sources for Current Expenses	$3.0 Billion
Cost Per Pupil Belonging	$4,301

TABLE

2

Maryland's Rank Among the States

Category	Amount	United States Average	Rank
Pupils in Average Daily Membership per Teacher in Public Elementary and Secondary Schools, Fall 1986	17.33%	N/A	19
Estimated Average Salaries of Public School Teachers, 1986-87	$28,893	$26,551	8
Estimated Percent of Revenue for Public Elementary and Secondary Schools, 1986-87			
Local Governments	55.39%	43.58%	13
State Government	39.31%	50.14%	40
Federal Government	5.30%	6.28%	34
State and Local Government Expenditures for All Education as Percent of Total General Expenditures for All Functions, 1984-85	34.63%	34.77%	33
Estimated Current Expenditures per Public Elementary and Secondary Pupils, 1986-87			
in Average Daily Attendance	$4,660	$3,983	10
in Average Daily Membership	$4,283	N/A	12
Public School Revenue per Pupil in Average Daily Attendance, 1986-87	$5,120	$4,386	9

SOURCE: National Education Association, Rankings of the State, 1987

TABLE

3

Number of Maryland Public Schools: September 30, 1986

Local Unit	Grand Total	Elementary∕	Secondary* Total	Junior (Grades 7-9)	Jr.-Sr. (Grades 7-12)	Senior (Grades 9-12)	Other Total	Middle	Combined
Total State	1,189	745	245	63	21	161	199	130	69
Allegany	24	12	5	0	1	4	7	3	4
Anne Arundel	111	74	24	10	2	12	13	7	6
Baltimore City	179	120	30	6	1	23	29	17	12
Baltimore	145	95	22	0	3	19	28	25	3
Calvert	14	6	3	0	1	2	5	3	2
Caroline	9	4	4	2	0	2	1	0	1
Carroll	31	16	6	0	1	5	9	7	2
Cecil	25	14	5	0	2	3	6	4	2
Charles	27	15	4	0	0	4	8	6	2
Dorchester	11	5	2	0	0	2	4	2	2
Frederick	41	23	7	0	0	7	11	8	3
Garrett	17	10	2	0	0	2	5	2	3
Harford	42	25	9	0	1	8	8	7	1
Howard	44	25	8	0	0	8	11	10	1
Kent	8	3	1	0	0	1	4	3	1
Montgomery	156	103	41	18	4	19	12	4	8
Prince George's	171	115	47	25	0	22	9	2	7
Queen Anne's	9	5	1	0	0	1	3	3	0
St. Mary's	27	18	3	0	0	3	6	4	2
Somerset	13	7	2	0	2	0	4	2	2
Talbot	9	5	2	0	0	2	2	1	1
Washington	42	26	8	0	2	6	8	7	1
Wicomico	22	14	6	2	1	3	2	0	2
Worcester	12	5	3	0	0	3	4	3	1

Excludes vocational technical schools which have enrollment comprised of students from other secondary schools within the same local unit.
∕Includes one one-teacher school in Somerset.

TABLE

4

Fall Enrollment by Local Unit and Year: Maryland Public Schools: Fall 1976 to Fall 1986

Local Unit	1976	1977	1978	1979	1980	1981	1982	1983	1984	1985	1986
Total State	860,879	836,807	809,933	777,725	750,776	721,841	699,201	683,491	673,840	671,560	675,747
Allegany	15,638	15,153	14,644	14,044	13,472	12,888	12,563	12,272	11,772	11,675	11,554
Anne Arundel	77,049	75,653	74,031	71,989	69,845	67,422	65,621	64,520	63,685	63,576	64,006
Baltimore City	159,038	152,153	145,503	136,187	129,984	123,376	119,570	116,872	113,574	111,987	111,243
Baltimore	118,844	113,302	107,702	102,329	97,481	92,387	87,977	84,268	81,386	80,730	80,259
Calvert	7,236	7,406	7,722	7,835	7,865	7,799	7,781	7,897	8,032	8,138	8,499
Caroline	5,154	5,061	4,869	4,694	4,638	4,490	4,389	4,391	4,292	4,321	4,392
Carroll	19,829	20,202	20,318	20,296	20,167	19,808	19,447	19,287	19,470	19,693	20,147
Cecil	13,310	13,333	13,282	13,072	12,847	12,640	12,433	12,263	12,096	12,133	12,169
Charles	17,357	17,732	17,868	17,811	17,586	17,511	17,048	16,918	16,821	16,873	17,183
Dorchester	6,032	5,791	5,503	5,381	5,220	5,297	5,194	5,154	5,053	4,960	4,970
Frederick	22,958	23,483	23,658	23,642	23,459	23,364	23,164	23,173	23,435	23,790	24,678
Garrett	5,844	5,761	5,584	5,530	5,421	5,364	5,259	5,141	5,137	5,133	5,099
Harford	33,955	33,589	33,096	32,021	30,870	29,877	28,646	27,774	27,367	27,558	28,121
Howard	24,657	25,440	25,606	25,400	25,227	24,865	24,256	24,024	24,332	25,030	25,629
Kent	3,444	3,314	3,204	3,025	2,850	2,667	2,524	2,459	2,407	2,378	2,356
Montgomery	117,630	112,625	107,430	102,633	99,024	95,686	92,595	91,170	91,650	92,880	94,457
Prince George's	144,747	139,479	133,953	127,529	122,321	116,598	112,279	108,694	106,377	103,611	103,301
Queen Anne's	4,884	4,925	4,809	4,772	4,731	4,612	4,597	4,581	4,630	4,696	4,824
St. Mary's	12,159	12,311	12,560	12,652	12,281	11,704	11,317	11,075	11,088	11,253	11,604
Somerset	4,286	4,127	3,985	3,886	3,778	3,644	3,538	3,499	3,420	3,413	3,401
Talbot	4,500	4,465	4,270	4,145	3,996	3,852	3,783	3,657	3,679	3,667	3,784
Washington	22,814	22,386	21,759	20,919	20,320	19,315	18,777	18,139	17,817	17,566	17,308
Wicomico	13,313	13,133	12,762	12,352	11,991	11,593	11,473	11,300	11,304	11,387	11,622
Worcester	6,201	5,983	5,815	5,581	5,402	5,082	4,970	4,963	5,016	5,112	5,141

TABLE
5

Prekindergarten Enrollment: Maryland Public Schools: Fall 1976 to Fall 1986

Local Unit	1976	1977	1978	1979	1980	1981	1982	1983	1984	1985	198
Total State	4,130	3,955	4,626	4,955	5,668	6,351	7,306	7,315	8,002	8,710	9,3
Allegany	0	0	0	0	0	25	17	21	15	18	:
Anne Arundel	18	0	0	0	0	280	370	368	418	323	2:
Baltimore City	2,281	2,485	2,583	2,773	3,266	2,996	3,283	3,552	3,963	4,054	4,1:
Baltimore	18	37	128	72	143	169	254	337	422	750	1,0:
Calvert	114	0		34	68	87	104	122	111	109	1(
Caroline	0	0		0	0	0	24	29	0	20	:
Carroll	51	57		0	79	72	49	93	108	93	1(
Cecil	0	0		25	16	65	48	76	98	132	1:
Charles	48	49	6?	117	71	157	137	157	155	126	1:
Dorchester	0	0	0	52	80	112	135	114	162	163	1'
Frederick	16	0	3	0	0	21	42	32	39	57	(
Garrett	0	0	0	0	8	24	32	24	30	57	:
Harford	107	0	0	0	0	58	70	62	64	113	2:
Howard	0	0	0	0	0	62	61	88	73	99	(
Kent	0	0	0	0	0	10	2	0	0	7	(
Montgomery	792	615	622	711	787	1,055	1,437	1,037	1,068	1,165	1,2
Prince George's	214	177	340	317	340	477	532	527	560	664	7
Queen Anne's	0	0	0	0	8	8	0	8	11	14	
St. Mary's	86	20	196	235	235	260	277	287	346	327	3
Somerset	60	62	99	100	145	138	152	143	154	154	1
Talbot	0	0	0	0	0	0	25	0	0	0	
Washington	325	345	472	394	418	261	238	217	187	211	1
Wicomico	0	108	122	125	0	3	5	7	3	11	
Worcester	0	0	0	0	4	11	12	14	15	43	

TABLE
6

Kindergarten Enrollment: Maryland Public Schools: Fall 1976 to Fall 1986

Local Unit	1976	1977	1978	1979	1980	1981	1982	1983	1984	1985	1986
Total State	54,738	47,922	43,418	42,583	41,913	41,594	44,529	43,819	46,472	48,057	50,505
Allegany	1,091	948	834	819	814	768	841	830	794	836	839
Anne Arundel	5,168	4,559	4,269	4,248	4,037	3,962	4,308	4,174	4,304	4,475	4,734
Baltimore City	9,782	8,453	7,766	7,361	7,571	7,611	8,271	8,294	8,692	8,587	8,934
Baltimore	6,990	6,077	5,321	5,188	5,152	4,955	5,253	5,109	5,412	5,615	5,763
Calvert	486	475	434	508	418	531	549	571	617	651	680
Caroline	349	295	274	308	314	308	356	334	313	333	371
Carroll	1,441	1,276	1,182	1,202	1,305	1,247	1,259	1,243	1,404	1,478	1,625
Cecil	895	861	822	774	770	801	834	779	799	831	854
Charles	1,118	1,032	927	947	920	875	985	941	1,011	1,104	1,100
Dorchester	384	310	250	260	268	291	336	328	313	356	372
Frederick	1,671	1,631	1,476	1,614	1,510	1,585	1,699	1,717	1,798	1,875	2,116
Garrett	450	398	352	389	357	371	381	369	429	417	395
Harford	2,299	2,065	1,919	1,881	1,746	1,798	1,844	1,797	1,914	2,010	2,147
Howard	1,629	1,563	1,400	1,450	1,346	1,367	1,403	1,469	1,531	1,691	1,831
Kent	212	200	193	161	189	145	164	178	144	175	189
Montgomery	7,198	6,182	5,395	5,351	5,270	5,221	5,577	5,437	6,130	6,816	7,201
Prince George's	8,956	7,385	6,706	6,198	6,076	6,104	6,358	6,180	6,554	6,358	6,757
Queen Anne's	330	278	250	256	302	301	353	339	331	359	398
St. Mary's	968	859	856	913	804	751	780	810	874	924	976
Somerset	283	273	233	224	239	237	250	276	245	271	240
Talbot	249	250	220	200	205	224	247	251	289	280	352
Washington	1,548	1,409	1,307	1,226	1,202	1,099	1,248	1,238	1,327	1,350	1,312
Wicomico	882	827	723	778	805	751	839	778	850	856	930
Worcester	359	316	309	327	293	291	394	377	397	409	389

TABLE 7

Fall Enrollment by Grade and Organization: Maryland Public Schools: 1977 - 1986

Fall of	Grand Total	Kinder-garten*	1	2	3	4	5	6	7	8	9	10	11	12+	Ungraded Special	Ungraded Other
1977	836,807	51,877	51,903	52,288	51,265	51,710	53,223	55,980	68,854	72,182	71,980	72,111	64,196	57,788	18,823	42,627
1978	809,933	48,044	46,850	50,420	52,087	51,633	51,872	54,075	65,663	67,325	72,243	72,822	63,624	57,901	19,347	36,027
1979	777,725	47,538	44,223	45,533	51,258	52,998	52,594	52,197	61,188	62,484	67,109	70,701	62,918	56,419	22,951	27,614
1980	750,776	47,581	44,045	43,073	46,824	52,342	54,289	53,404	60,033	60,040	64,243	67,241	61,719	56,312	20,420	19,210
1981	721,841	47,945	43,951	42,491	43,210	47,015	52,189	54,817	58,409	57,251	60,196	63,456	57,526	55,981	23,931	13,473
1982	699,201	51,835	45,892	44,585	44,843	45,584	49,929	55,023	59,811	57,836	59,906	60,610	55,417	53,358	14,572	0
1983	683,491	51,134	49,426	43,815	44,734	44,805	45,462	49,593	57,931	58,133	60,299	57,991	53,697	51,546	14,925	0
1984	673,840	54,474	49,819	47,444	43,933	44,704	44,501	45,642	52,343	56,391	61,969	57,190	51,449	49,647	14,334	0
1985	671,560	56,767	53,071	48,372	47,830	44,812	44,874	45,527	48,583	51,196	61,848	57,357	50,764	48,250	12,309	0
1986	675,747	59,866	55,915	51,196	48,875	48,378	44,985	46,081	47,828	47,315	57,118	56,031	51,860	47,584	12,715	0
							Total Elementary									
1977	421,466	51,877	51,903	52,288	51,265	51,710	53,223	55,980	35	0	0	0	0	0	10,680	42,505
1978	402,609	48,044	46,850	50,420	52,087	51,633	51,872	54,075	32	0	0	0	0	0	11,631	35,508
1979	386,661	47,538	44,223	45,533	51,258	52,998	52,594	52,197	74	0	0	0	0	0	12,738	27,508
1980	372,828	47,581	44,045	43,073	46,824	52,342	54,289	53,404	28	0	0	0	0	0	12,111	19,131
1981	356,655	47,945	43,951	42,491	43,210	47,015	52,189	54,817	27	0	0	0	0	0	11,607	13,403
1982	344,147	51,835	45,892	44,585	44,843	45,584	49,929	55,023	0	0	0	0	0	0	6,456	0
1983	335,652	51,134	49,426	43,815	44,734	44,805	45,462	49,593	0	0	0	0	0	0	6,683	0
1984	337,510	54,474	49,819	47,444	43,933	44,704	44,501	45,642	0	0	0	0	0	0	6,993	0
1985	346,542	56,767	53,071	48,372	47,830	44,812	44,874	45,527	0	0	0	0	0	0	5,289	0
1986	360,902	59,866	55,915	51,196	48,875	48,378	44,985	46,081	0	0	0	0	0	0	5,606	0
							Total Secondary									
1977	415,341	0	0	0	0	0	0	0	68,819	72,182	71,980	72,111	64,196	57,788	8,143	122
1978	407,324	0	0	0	0	0	0	0	65,631	67,325	72,243	72,822	63,624	57,901	7,716	62
1979	391,064	0	0	0	0	0	0	0	61,114	62,484	67,109	70,701	62,918	56,419	10,213	106
1980	377,948	0	0	0	0	0	0	0	60,005	60,040	64,243	67,241	61,719	56,312	8,309	79
1981	365,186	0	0	0	0	0	0	0	58,382	57,251	60,196	63,456	57,526	55,981	12,324	70
1982	355,054	0	0	0	0	0	0	0	59,811	57,836	59,906	60,610	55,417	53,358	8,116	0
1983	347,839	0	0	0	0	0	0	0	57,931	58,133	60,299	57,991	53,697	51,546	8,242	0
1984	336,330	0	0	0	0	0	0	0	52,343	56,391	61,969	57,190	51,449	49,647	7,341	0
1985	325,018	0	0	0	0	0	0	0	48,583	51,196	61,848	57,357	50,764	48,250	7,020	0
1986	314,845	0	0	0	0	0	0	0	47,828	47,315	57,118	56,031	51,860	47,584	7,109	0

*Includes enrollment in prekindergarten classes.
+Includes postgraduates.

TABLE

8

ENROLLMENT BY RACE: MARYLAND PUBLIC SCHOOL: FALL 1986

Local Unit	Total Enrollment	American Indian/ Alaskan Native		Asian/Pacific Islander		Black		Hispanic		White and Others	
		Number	Percent	Number	Percent	Number	Percent	Number	Percent	Number	Percent
Total State	674,274	1,199	0.2	19,395	2.9	217,524	32.3	9,997	1.5	426,159	63.2
Allegany	11,554	17	0.2	32	0.3	223	1.9	11	0.1	11,271	97.5
Anne Arundel	63,926	63	0.1	982	1.5	9,208	14.4	312	0.5	53,361	83.5
Baltimore City	111,292	276	0.2	660	0.6	88,871	79.9	300	0.3	21,185	19.0
Baltimore	80,328	132	0.2	2,004	2.5	12,151	15.1	483	0.6	65,558	81.6
Calvert	8,495	3	*	25	0.3	1,987	23.4	13	0.2	6,467	76.1
Caroline	4,392	2	0.1	10	0.2	1,014	23.1	15	0.3	3,351	76.3
Carroll	20,113	12	0.1	107	0.5	383	1.9	61	0.3	19,550	97.2
Cecil	12,161	17	0.1	58	0.5	565	4.7	45	0.4	11,476	94.4
Charles	16,972	49	4.3	131	0.8	3,798	22.2	30	0.2	12,964	76.1
Dorchester	4,970	2	*	20	0.4	2,010	40.4	23	0.5	2,915	58.7
Frederick	24,575	11	0.5	180	0.7	1,481	6.0	107	0.4	22,796	92.8
Garrett	5,086	2	*	3	0.1	8	0.2	3	0.1	5,070	99.6
Harford	27,611	70	0.3	382	1.4	3,024	11.0	307	1.1	23,828	86.3
Howard	25,640	64	0.3	1,011	3.9	3,579	14.7	173	0.4	20,813	81.2
Kent	2,356	2	0.1	8	0.3	616	26.2	15	0.6	1,715	72.8
Montgomery	94,460	142	0.2	9,471	10.0	14,342	15.2	5,845	6.2	64,660	68.4
Prince George's	102,530	265	0.3	3,848	3.8	62,778	61.2	2,072	2.0	33,567	32.7
Queen Anne's	4,824	-	-	-	-	776	16.1	-	-	4,048	83.9
St. Mary's	11,596	53	0.5	171	1.5	2,132	18.4	89	0.8	9,151	78.9
Somerset	3,574	0	0.0	2	0.1	1,611	45.1	9	0.3	1,952	54.6
Talbot	3,784	3	0.1	7	0.2	1,101	29.1	3	0.1	2,670	70.6
Washington	17,271	8	0.1	111	0.6	627	3.6	46	0.3	16,479	95.4
Wicomico	11,620	3	*	131	1.1	3,547	30.5	17	0.2	7,922	68.2
Worcester	5,144	3	0.1	41	0.8	1,692	32.9	18	0.3	3,390	65.9

*Less Than 0.1%

TABLE
9

Public and Nonpublic School Enrollment by Grade: State of Maryland: September 30, 1986

Local Unit	Grand Total	Total Elementary	Pre Kinder-garten	Kinder-garten	Ungraded Special	1	2	3	4	5	6
Total State	811,184	450,122	35,956	61,055	6,776	65,755	60,152	57,364	56,647	52,668	53,74!
Allegany	13,410	7,074	507	964	76	1,013	914	929	887	876	90₤
Anne Arundel	74,576	40,525	3,087	5,644	1,016	5,788	5,256	5,073	5,078	4,677	4,90!
Baltimore City	134,472	80,075	5,858	10,778	424	12,640	11,278	10,666	10,133	9,091	9,20]
Baltimore	107,439	59,472	6,264	7,832	693	8,374	7,685	7,206	7,388	6,757	7,27]
Calvert	9,102	5,089	212	717	166	827	667	648	624	618	61₤
Caroline	4,719	2,558	105	378	56	332	335	355	378	319	30₤
Carroll	21,143	11,337	499	1,685	164	1,642	1,568	1,415	1,465	1,385	1,51₤
Cecil	13,710	7,468	383	989	30	1,102	1,015	1,000	1,007	978	96₤
Charles	18,929	10,176	224	1,302	207	1,642	1,433	1,374	1,390	1,275	1,32!
Dorchester	5,152	2,885	232	396	54	450	325	381	359	323	36!
Frederick	27,022	15,130	772	2,293	139	2,300	2,063	2,012	1,906	1,832	1,81]
Garrett	5,230	2,874	117	397	27	453	416	373	360	375	35₤
Harford	31,706	17,201	1,278	2,374	223	2,447	2,332	2,175	2,145	2,065	2,16]
Howard	29,806	16,769	2,114	2,175	295	2,216	2,054	2,090	1,957	1,945	1,92]
Kent	2,612	1,454	18	216	61	230	191	202	197	161	17₤
Montgomery	124,014	68,668	9,428	9,395	1,389	9,315	8,328	7,889	7,923	7,487	7,51₤
Prince George's	123,293	65,331	3,256	8,477	1,400	9,547	9,169	8,720	8,704	8,131	7,92]
Queen Anne's	5,070	2,784	109	400	7	408	371	382	376	371	36₤
St. Mary's	14,017	7,738	508	1,119	129	1,173	1,105	942	978	911	87]
Somerset	3,544	2,101	159	263	50	296	268	287	270	244	26₤
Talbot	4,611	2,695	234	406	18	409	373	345	325	281	30₤
Washington	19,518	10,292	249	1,409	113	1,600	1,512	1,454	1,379	1,244	1,33]
Wicomico	12,352	7,283	132	1,013	25	1,119	1,064	1,005	985	945	99!
Worcester	5,737	3,144	211	433	14	432	430	441	433	377	37]

Elementary

TABLE

9

Public and Nonpublic School Enrollment by Grade: State of Maryland: September 30, 1986

| Local Unit | Total Secondary | Ungraded Special | Secondary | | | | | |
			7	8	9	10	11	12
Total State	361,062	7,960	55,569	54,924	64,594	63,782	59,451	54,782
Allegany	6,336	76	893	941	1,040	1,097	1,178	1,111
Anne Arundel	34,052	448	5,323	5,427	6,280	6,1,01	5,746	4,727
Baltimore City	54,397	319	9,490	8,596	11,513	9,757	7,788	6,934
Baltimore	47,967	430	7,378	7,440	8,409	8,336	8,128	7,846
Calvert	4,013	229	631	578	656	710	642	567
Caroline	2,161	164	375	326	359	356	300	281
Carroll	9,806	135	1,427	1,476	1,673	1,824	1,688	1,583
Cecil	6,242	37	1,017	985	1,071	1,122	1,053	957
Charles	8,753	335	1,365	1,299	1,486	1,560	1,411	1,297
Dorchester	2,267	18	326	363	414	398	408	340
Frederick	11,892	309	1,864	1,900	1,994	2,066	2,001	1,758
Garrett	2,356	22	393	367	398	436	397	343
Harford	14,505	106	2,140	2,258	2,668	2,534	2,499	2,300
Howard	13,037	443	2,061	1,945	2,170	2,294	2,138	1,986
Kent	1,158	48	175	199	183	176	193	184
Montgomery	55,346	2,747	7,832	7,977	8,536	9,383	9,588	9,283
Prince George's	57,962	1,661	8,371	8,448	10,586	10,510	9,463	8,923
Queen Anne's	2,286	8	306	338	414	457	398	365
St. Mary's	6,279	217	963	901	1,119	1,065	1,034	980
Somerset	1,443	0	249	216	283	264	224	207
Talbot	1,916	32	306	297	350	310	327	294
Washington	9,226	107	1,380	1,427	1,663	1,707	1,540	1,402
Wicomico	5,069	53	904	810	863	887	863	689
Worcester	2,593	16	400	410	466	432	444	425

Total State	675,747	360,902	9,361	50,505	5,606	55,915	51,196	48,875	48,378	44,985	46,081
Allegany	11,554	5,786	26	839	76	890	790	809	772	766	818
Anne Arundel	64,006	32,918	213	4,734	986	5,040	4,552	4,451	4,496	4,108	4,338
Baltimore City	111,243	66,761	4,153	8,934	0	10,751	9,685	9,136	8,588	7,728	7,786
Baltimore	80,259	42,053	1,030	5,763	307	6,553	6,039	5,606	5,782	5,287	5,686
Calvert	8,499	4,644	107	680	166	773	615	592	577	568	566
Caroline	4,392	2,417	32	371	45	322	328	341	369	313	296
Carroll	20,147	10,499	106	1,625	160	1,558	1,488	1,363	1,410	1,325	1,464
Cecil	12,169	6,402	137	854	30	985	881	875	910	880	850
Charles	17,183	8,736	125	1,100	207	1,410	1,195	1,202	1,205	1,111	1,181
Dorchester	4,970	2,739	174	372	54	431	316	366	348	316	362
Frederick	24,678	13,309	62	2,116	138	2,124	1,887	1,843	1,768	1,681	1,690
Garrett	5,099	2,777	56	395	19	447	413	367	358	371	351
Harford	28,121	15,029	291	2,147	223	2,258	2,162	2,026	2,008	1,910	2,004
Howard	25,629	13,000	90	1,831	200	1,963	1,838	1,867	1,737	1,744	1,730
Kent	2,356	1,253	8	189	45	199	161	183	175	135	158
Montgomery	94,457	48,373	1,299	7,201	1,234	7,479	6,625	6,271	6,328	5,965	5,971
Prince George's	103,301	52,532	703	6,757	1,368	7,819	7,671	7,254	7,314	6,880	6,766
Queen Anne's	4,824	2,653	16	398	7	406	363	370	373	367	353
St. Mary's	11,604	6,326	339	976	129	996	900	747	792	725	722
Somerset	3,401	1,999	149	240	50	283	254	275	260	232	256
Talbot	3,784	2,094	0	352	18	345	309	293	275	237	265
Washington	17,308	9,174	190	1,312	105	1,436	1,343	1,290	1,216	1,102	1,180
Wicomico	11,622	6,667	10	930	25	1,040	981	940	909	885	947
Worcester	5,141	2,761	45	389	14	407	400	408	408	349	341

5,768	76	800	866	945	1,013	1,069	999
31,088	419	4,790	4,894	5,765	5,653	5,307	4,260
44,482	0	8,091	7,186	9,824	7,973	6,077	5,331
38,206	319	5,718	5,816	6,804	6,719	6,538	6,292
3,855	229	582	542	644	681	620	557
1,975	8	365	318	349	355	300	280
9,648	135	1,385	1,431	1,650	1,806	1,671	1,570
5,767	37	910	892	1,020	1,050	975	883
8,447	335	1,208	1,160	1,481	1,560	1,408	1,295
2,231	18	321	353	413	393	400	333
11,369	306	1,748	1,758	1,927	1,994	1,925	1,711
2,322	22	382	364	395	430	389	340
13,092	106	2,015	2,122	2,396	2,237	2,188	2,028
12,629	396	1,885	1,794	2,150	2,283	2,137	1,984
1,103	46	161	177	180	171	187	181
46,084	2,614	6,299	6,389	7,089	7,832	8,048	7,813
50,769	1,627	7,138	7,321	9,393	9,250	8,244	7,796
2,171	8	301	332	385	430	374	341
5,278	217	796	740	956	893	853	823
1,402	0	233	209	281	256	220	203
1,690	32	263	246	322	273	303	251
8,134	90	1,218	1,265	1,469	1,497	1,356	1,239
4,955	53	859	766	854	884	858	681
2,380	16	360	374	426	398	413	393

Total State	346,391	186,300	4,978	25,757	3,746	28,847	26,309	25,125	24,728	22,969	23,841
Allegany	5,907	3,032	17	430	49	484	407	407	386	412	440
Anne Arundel	32,981	16,978	116	2,403	674	2,605	2,306	2,247	2,284	2,102	2,241
Baltimore City	56,444	34,427	2,117	4,508	0	5,663	5,040	4,738	4,421	3,908	4,032
Baltimore	40,952	21,757	594	2,931	186	3,290	3,146	2,896	2,962	2,786	2,966
Calvert	4,386	2,423	59	345	109	412	319	326	264	290	299
Caroline	2,233	1,227	18	178	30	175	159	177	193	147	150
Carroll	10,327	5,388	59	790	104	833	729	675	733	703	762
Cecil	6,261	3,308	72	472	20	484	426	450	492	445	447
Charles	8,912	4,544	54	539	125	750	651	629	615	570	611
Dorchester	2,551	1,430	103	204	37	207	168	179	176	166	190
Frederick	12,731	6,856	41	1,069	87	1,106	990	932	911	840	880
Garrett	2,555	1,427	28	197	14	222	209	197	168	200	192
Harford	14,521	7,725	148	1,101	140	1,170	1,088	1,046	1,033	980	1,019
Howard	13,116	6,700	54	922	144	1,004	946	958	927	873	872
Kent	1,198	641	6	98	28	109	83	94	79	68	76
Montgomery	48,539	24,892	716	3,735	860	3,827	3,305	3,227	3,207	2,957	3,058
Prince George's	53,248	27,209	375	3,475	927	4,011	4,010	3,678	3,737	3,494	3,502
Queen Anne's	2,466	1,354	12	211	4	205	185	186	187	191	173
St. Mary's	5,932	3,256	178	491	77	511	462	396	393	374	374
Somerset	1,717	1,023	77	125	30	148	125	133	138	120	127
Talbot	1,939	1,089	0	180	13	173	139	160	137	126	161
Washington	8,908	4,778	98	678	62	738	705	667	631	583	616
Wicomico	5,930	3,426	6	471	19	514	508	514	468	454	472
Worcester	2,637	1,410	30	204	7.	206	203	213	186	180	181

160,091	4,773	24,648	24,238	29,239	28,355	25,682	23,156
2,875	45	390	416	505	481	537	501
16,003	268	2,488	2,525	2,974	2,917	2,742	2,089
22,017	0	4,212	3,679	5,018	3,940	2,801	2,367
19,195	184	2,960	3,016	3,427	3,334	3,252	3,022
1,963	163	290	284	324	327	313	262
1,006	5	188	152	194	174	154	139
4,939	97	672	750	863	919	829	809
2,953	20	490	444	514	535	509	441
4,368	232	609	605	765	781	697	679
1,121	9	165	192	195	193	198	169
5,875	214	899	925	1,030	1,025	939	843
1,128	14	195	179	199	214	174	153
6,796	58	1,058	1,106	1,236	1,183	1,115	1,040
6,416	274	936	899	1,077	1,152	1,065	1,013
557	27	69	80	96	104	94	87
23,647	1,795	3,186	3,196	3,535	3,995	4,090	3,850
26,039	1,093	3,789	3,763	4,901	4,670	4,066	3,757
1,112	2	163	178	199	227	170	173
2,676	158	413	355	469	453	411	417
694	0	112	113	143	135	102	89
850	18	137	131	166	149	120	129
4,130	55	621	662	753	767	655	617
2,504	33	439	399	432	452	415	334
1,227	9	167	189	224	228	234	176

s

Total State	329,356	174,602	4,383	24,748	1,000	27,000	24,001	25,190	25,090	22,010	22,240
Allegany	5,647	2,754	9	409	27	406	383	402	386	354	378
Anne Arundel	31,025	15,940	97	2,331	312	2,435	2,246	2,204	2,212	2,006	2,097
Baltimore City	54,799	32,334	2,036	4,426	0	5,088	4,645	4,398	4,167	3,820	3,754
Baltimore	39,307	20,296	436	2,832	121	3,263	2,893	2,710	2,820	2,501	2,720
Calvert	4,113	2,221	48	335	57	361	296	266	313	278	267
Caroline	2,159	1,190	14	193	15	147	169	164	176	166	146
Carroll	9,820	5,111	47	835	56	725	759	688	677	622	702
Cecil	5,908	3,094	65	382	10	501	455	425	418	435	403
Charles	8,271	4,192	71	561	82	660	544	573	590	541	570
Dorchester	2,419	1,309	71	168	17	224	148	187	172	150	172
Frederick	11,947	6,453	21	1,047	51	1,018	897	911	857	841	810
Garrett	2,544	1,350	28	198	5	225	204	170	190	171	159
Harford	13,600	7,304	143	1,046	83	1,088	1,074	980	975	930	985
Howard	12,513	6,300	36	909	56	959	892	909	810	871	858
Kent	1,158	612	2	91	17	90	78	89	96	67	82
Montgomery	45,918	23,481	583	3,466	374	3,652	3,320	3,044	3,121	3,008	2,913
Prince George's	50,053	25,323	328	3,282	441	3,808	3,661	3,576	3,577	3,386	3,264
Queen Anne's	2,358	1,299	4	187	3	201	178	184	186	176	180
St. Mary's	5,672	3,070	161	485	52	485	438	351	399	351	348
Somerset	1,684	976	72	115	20	135	129	142	122	112	129
Talbot	1,845	1,005	0	172	5	172	170	133	138	111	104
Washington	8,400	4,396	92	634	43	698	638	623	585	519	564
Wicomico	5,692	3,241	4	459	6	526	473	426	441	431	475
Worcester	2,504	1,351	15	185	7	201	197	195	222	169	160

154,194	2,330	23,180	23,077	27,879	27,676	26,178	24,428
2,893	31	410	450	440	532	532	498
15,085	151	2,302	2,369	2,791	2,736	2,565	2,171
22,465	0	3,879	3,507	4,806	4,033	3,276	2,964
19,011	135	2,758	2,800	3,377	3,385	3,286	3,270
1,892	66	292	258	320	354	307	295
969	3	177	166	155	181	146	141
4,709	38	713	681	787	887	842	761
2,814	17	420	448	506	515	466	442
4,079	103	599	555	716	779	711	616
1,110	9	156	161	218	200	202	164
5,494	92	849	833	897	969	986	868
1,194	8	187	185	196	216	215	187
6,296	48	957	1,016	1,160	1,054	1,073	988
6,213	122	949	895	1,073	1,131	1,072	971
546	19	92	97	84	67	93	94
22,437	819	3,113	3,193	3,554	3,837	3,958	3,963
24,730	534	3,349	3,558	4,492	4,580	4,178	4,039
1,059	6	138	154	186	203	204	168
2,602	59	383	385	487	440	442	406
708	0	121	96	138	121	118	114
840	14	126	115	156	124	183	122
4,004	35	597	603	716	730	701	622
2,451	20	420	367	422	432	443	347
1,153	7	193	185	202	170	179	217

s

TABLE
13
Nonpublic School Enrollment, Number of Schools and Teachers: State of Maryland: September 30, 1986

| | | Enrollment | | | | | Number of Schools | | | | | | Total |
| | | | | Elementary | | | | Prekinder- | | | | | |
Local Unit	Grand Total	Total	Pre-kinder-garten	Kinder-garten	Grades 1-6	Grades 7-12	Grand Total	garten and/or Kgn. Only	Ele-mentary	Secon-dary	Middle	Com-bined	Teacher (F.T.E.)
Total State	135,437	89,220	26,595	10,550	52,075	46,217	858	345	300	70	9	134	8,595.
Allegany	1,856	1,288	481	125	682	568	15	7	5	1	0	2	95.
Anne Arundel	10,570	7,606	2,874	910	3,822	2,964	68	34	19	3	0	12	592.
Baltimore City	23,229	13,314	1,705	1,844	9,765	9,915	107	24	49	12	6	16	1,483.
Baltimore	27,180	17,419	5,234	2,069	10,116	9,761	143	61	45	13	2	22	1,827.
Calvert	603	445	105	37	303	158	7	3	1	0	0	3	53.
Caroline	327	141	73	7	61	186	7	3	1	0	0	3	31.
Carroll	996	838	393	60	385	158	9	3	4		0	2	47.
Cecil	1,541	1,066	246	135	685	475	14	5	4	1	0	4	125.
Charles	1,746	1,440	99	202	1,139	306	12	2	9	0	0	1	79.
Dorchester	182	146	58	24	64	36	5	1	2	1	0	1	16.
Frederick	2,344	1,821	710	177	934	523	19	9	5	1	0	4	186.
Garrett	131	97	61	2	34	34	6	1	1	1	0	3	14.
Harford	3,585	2,172	987	227	958	1,413	27	14	8	1	0	4	151.
Howard	4,177	3,769	2,024	344	1,401	408	45	29	11	0	0	5	196.
Kent	256	201	27	27	164	55	4	1	1	0	0	2	25.
Montgomery	29,557	20,295	8,129	2,194	9,972	9,262	204	101	65	19	0	19	2,103.
Prince George's	19,992	12,799	2,553	1,720	8,526	7,193	102	31	48	12	0	12	1,071.
Queen Anne's	246	131	93	2	36	115	4	2		1	0	1	23.
St. Mary's	2,413	1,412	169	143	1,100	1,001	19	6	11	1	1	2	132.
Somerset	143	102	10	23	69	41	2	6		1	0	1	13.
Talbot	827	601	234	54	313	226	8	5	1	0	0	2	72.
Washington	2,210	1,118	59	97	962	1,092	15	1	4	3	0	7	158.
Wicomico	730	616	122	83	411	114	9	1	5	0	0	3	54.
Worcester	596	383	166	44	173	213	7	3	1	0	0	3	40.

TABLE
14

Catholic School Enrollment, Number of Schools and Teachers: State of Maryland: September 30, 1986

| | Enrollment | | | | | | Number of Schools | | | | | | Total |
| | | | Elementary | | | | | Prekinder- | | | | | |
Local Unit	Grand Total	Total	Pre-kinder-garten	Kinder-garten	Grades 1-6	Grades 7-12	Grand Total	garten and/or Kgn. Only	Ele-mentary	Secon-dary	Middle	Com-bined	Teachers (F.T.E.)
Total State	60,215	33,006	664	3,800	28,542	27,209	183	1	135	35	7	5	3,143.8
Allegany	1,213	742	56	103	583	471	6	1	4	1	0	0	57.4
Anne Arundel	4,101	2,416	0	327	2,089	1,685	7		5	2	0	0	182.4
Baltimore City	14,633	7,391	198	989	6,204	7,242	47		30	11	5	1	771.3
Baltimore	12,021	6,705	74	785	5,846	5,316	33	0	25	6	1	1	663.1
Calvert	107	80	0	0	80	27	1		1	0	0	0	6.2
Caroline	167	11	0	0	11	156	2		1			1	20.4
Carroll	224	179	0	0	179	45	1		1			0	9.8
Cecil	578	470	21	69	380	108	3		3			0	34.7
Charles	1,427	1,156	13	170	973	271	4	0	4	0	0	0	55.5
Dorchester	0	0	0	0	0	0	0	0	0	0	0	0	0.0
Frederick	959	597	0	34	563	362	4		3	1			60.4
Garrett	0	0	0	0	0	0	0		0	0			0.0
Harford	1,496	410	0	40	370	1,086	3		2	1			19.2
Howard	1,291	1,026	0	90	936	265	5	0	5	0	0	0	61.8
Kent	0	0	0	0	0	0	0	0	0	0	0		0.0
Montgomery	8,579	4,901	192	533	4,176	3,678	27		21	5	0	1	516.8
Prince George's	10,475	5,405	102	493	4,810	5,070	28		22	6	0	0	518.3
Queen Anne's	0	0	0	0	0	0	0		0	0	0	0	.0
St. Mary's	1,779	876	8	80	788	903	8	0	6	1	1	0	93.0
Somerset	0	0	0	0	0	0	0	0	0	0	0		0.0
Talbot	354	177		22	155	177	1		0	0		1	29.0
Washington	536	240		30	210	296	2		1	1			30.5
Wicomico	275	224		35	189	51	1	0	1	0	0		13.0
Worcester	0	0	0	0	0	0	0		0	0	0		0.0

Local Unit	Grand Total	Elementary Total	Elementary Pre-kinder-garten	Elementary Kinder-garten	Elementary Grades 1-6	Grades 7-12	Grand Total	Prekinder-garten and/or Kgn. Only	Ele-mentary	Secon-dary	Middle	Com-bined	Tota Teach (F.T.
Total State	75,222	56,214	25,931	6,750	23,533	19,008	675	344	165	35	2	129	5,45
Allegany	643	546	425	22	99	97	9	6	1	0	0	2	3
Anne Arundel	6,469	5,190	2,874	583	1,733	1,279	61	34	14	1	0	12	40
Baltimore City	8,596	5,923	1,507	855	3,561	2,673	60	24	19	1	1	15	71
Baltimore	15,159	10,714	5,160	1,284	4,270	4,445	110	61	20	7	1	21	1,16
Calvert	496	365	105	37	223	131	6	3	0	0	0	3	4
Caroline	160	130	73	7	50	30	5	3	0	0	0	2	1
Carroll	772	659	393	60	206	113	8	3					
Cecil	963	596	225	66	305	367	11	5					
Charles	319	284	86	32	166	35	8	2					
Dorchester	182	146	58	24	64	36	5	1					
Frederick	1,385	1,224	710	143	371	161	15	9	2	0	0	4	12
Garrett	131	97	61	2	34	34	6	1					1
Harford	2,089	1,762	987	187	588	327	24	14					13
Howard	2,886	2,743	2,024	254	465	143	40	29					13
Kent	256	201	10	27	164	55	4	1					2
Montgomery	20,978	15,394	7,937	1,661	5,796	5,584	177	101	44	14		18	1,58
Prince George's	9,517	7,394	2,451	1,227	3,716	2,123	74	31	25	6		12	55
Queen Anne's	246	131	93	2	36	115	4	2	0	1		1	2
St. Mary's	634	536	161	63	312	98	11	4	5	0	0	2	3
Somerset	143	102	10	23	69	41	2	0	1	0	0	1	1
Talbot	473	424	234	32	158	49	7	5	1			1	4
Washington	1,674	878	59	67	752	796	13	1	3	2		7	12
Wicomico	455	392	122	48	222	63	8	1	4		0	3	4
Worcester	596	383	166	44	173	213	7	3	1	0	0	3	4

TABLE
16

Nonpublic School Enrollment by Grade: State of Maryland: September 30, 1986

Local Unit	Grand Total	Total Elementary	Pre-Kinder-garten	Kinder-garten	Ungraded Special & Regular	1	2	3	4	5	6
Total State	135,437	89,220	26,595	10,550	1,170	9,840	8,956	8,489	8,269	7,683	7,668
Allegany	1,856	1,288	481	125	0	123	124	120	115	110	90
Anne Arundel	10,570	7,606	2,874	910	30	748	704	622	582	569	567
Baltimore City	23,229	13,314	1,705	1,844	424	1,889	1,593	1,530	1,545	1,363	1,421
Baltimore	27,180	17,419	5,234	2,069	386	1,821	1,646	1,600	1,606	1,470	1,587
Calvert	603	445	105	37	0	54	52	56	47	50	44
Caroline	327	141	73	7	11	10	7	14	9	6	4
Carroll	996	838	393	60	4	84	80	52	55	60	50
Cecil	1,541	1,066	246	135	0	117	134	125	97	98	114
Charles	1,746	1,440	99	202	0	232	238	172	185	164	148
Dorchester	182	146	58'	24	0	19	9	15	11	7	3
Frederick	2,344	1,821	710	177	1	176	176	169	138	151	123
Garrett	131	97	61	2	8	6	3	6	2	4	5
Harford	3,585	2,172	987	227	0	189	170	149	137	155	158
Howard	4,177	3,769	2,024	344	95	253	216	223	220	201	193
Kent	256	201	10	27	16	31	30	19	22	26	20
Montgomery	29,557	20,295	8,129	2,194	155	1,836	1,703	1,618	1,595	1,522	1,543
Prince George's	19,992	12,799	2,553	1,720	32	1,728	1,498	1,466	1,390	1,251	1,161
Queen Anne's	246	131	93	2	0	2	8	12	3	4	7
St. Mary's	2,413	1,412	169	143	0	177	205	195	186	186	151
Somerset	143	102	10	23	0	13	14	12	10	12	8
Talbot	827	601	234	54	0	64	64	52	50	44	39
Washington	2,210	1,118	59	97	8	164	169	164	163	142	152
Wicomico	730	616	122	83	0	79	83	65	76	60	48
Worcester	596	383	166	44	0	25	30	33	25	28	32

TABLE
16

Nonpublic School Enrollment by Grade: State of Maryland: September 30, 1986

| Local Unit | Total Secondary | Ungraded Special & Regular | Secondary | | | | | |
			7	8	9	10	11	12
Total State	46,217	851	7,741	7,609	7,476	7,751	7,591	7,19
Allegany	568	0	93	75	95	84	109	11
Anne Arundel	2,964	29	533	533	515	448	439	46
Baltimore City	9,915	319	1,399	1,410	1,689	1,784	1,711	1,60
Baltimore	9,761	111	1,660	1,624	1,605	1,617	1,590	1,55
Calvert	158	0	49	36	12	29	22	1
Caroline	186	156	10	8	10	1	0	
Carroll	158	0	42	45	23	18	17	1
Cecil	475	0	107	93	51	72	78	7
Charles	306	0	157	139	5	0	3	
Dorchester	36	0	5	10	1	5	8	
Frederick	523	3	116	142	67	72	76	4
Garrett	34	0	11	3	3	6	8	
Harford	1,413	0	125	136	272	297	311	27
Howard	408	47	176	151	20	11	1	
Kent	55	2	14	22	3	5	6	
Montgomery	9,262	133	1,533	1,588	1,447	1,551	1,540	1,47
Prince George's	7,193	34	1,233	1,127	1,193	1,260	1,219	1,12
Queen Anne's	115	0	5	6	29	27	24	2
St. Mary's	1,001	0	167	161	163	172	181	15
Somerset	41	0	16	7	2	8	4	
Talbot	226	0	43	51	28	37	24	4
Washington	1,092	17	162	162	194	210	184	16
Wicomico	114	0	45	44	9	3	5	
Worcester	213	0	40	36	40	34	31	3

TABLE
17

Catholic School Enrollment by Grade: State of Maryland: September 30, 1986

Local Unit	Grand Total	Total Elementary	Pre-Kinder-garten	Kinder-garten	Ungraded Special & Regular	1	2	3	4	5	6
Total State	60,215	33,006	664	3,800	76	5,188	4,926	4,683	4,757	4,502	4,410
Allegany	1,213	742	56	103	0	104	112	97	101	93	76
Anne Arundel	4,101	2,416	0	327	0	390	363	339	344	332	321
Baltimore City	14,633	7,391	198	989	45	1,247	1,050	991	1,011	910	950
Baltimore	12,021	6,705	74	785	20	1,065	1,017	946	985	878	935
Calvert	107	80	0	0	0	5	15	21	15	18	6
Caroline	167	11	0	0	11	0	0	0	0	0	0
Carroll	224	179	0	0	0	32	31	27	26	35	28
Cecil	578	470	21	69	0	70	77	64	53	55	61
Charles	1,427	1,156	13	170	0	192	197	149	153	147	135
Dorchester	0	0	0	0	0	0	0	0	0	0	0
Frederick	959	597	0	34		97	109	99	82	102	74
Garrett	0	0	0	0		0	0	0	0	0	0
Harford	1,496	410	0	40		55	69	52	53	66	75
Howard	1,291	1,026	0	90	0	153	143	160	167	151	162
Kent	0	0	0	0	0	0	0	0	0	0	0
Montgomery	8,579	4,901	192	533		726	705	669	721	677	678
Prince George's	10,475	5,405	102	493		839	796	838	810	805	731
Queen Anne's	0	0	0	0		0	0	0	0	0	0
St. Mary's	1,779	876	8	80	0	119	138	137	140	146	108
Somerset	0	0	0	0	0	0	0	0	0	0	0
Talbot	354	177	0	22		34	35	25	24	19	18
Washington	536	240	0	30		35	35	34	39	37	30
Wicomico	275	224	0	35	0	36	34	35	33	31	22
Worcester	0	0	0	0	0	0	0	0	0	0	0

TABLE
17

Catholic School Enrollment by Grade: State of Maryland: September 30, 1986

Local Unit	Total Secondary	Ungraded Special & Regular	Secondary					
			7	8	9	10	11	
Total State	27,209	281	4,550	4,442	4,362	4,600	4,558	4
Allegany	471	0	77	53	84	72	88	
Anne Arundel	1,685	0	296	302	288	266	263	
Baltimore City	7,242	125	1,000	991	1,296	1,310	1,293	1
Baltimore	5,316	0	969	974	824	857	822	
Calvert	27	0	12	15	0	0	0	
Caroline	156	156	0	0	0	0	0	
Carroll	45	0	24	21	0	0	0	
Cecil	108	0	58	50	0	0	0	
Charles	271	0	145	126	0	0	0	
Dorchester	0	0	0	0	0	0	0	
Frederick	362	0	78	106	38	48	52	
Garrett	0	0	0	0	0	0	0	
Harford	1,086	0	54	55	224	253	263	
Howard	265	0	137	128	0	0	0	
Kent	0	0	0	0	0	0	0	
Montgomery	3,678	0	659	679	535	602	632	
Prince George's	5,070	0	820	711	842	934	897	
Queen Anne's	0	0	0	0	0	0	0	
St. Mary's	903	0	127	128	157	161	176	
Somerset	0	0	0	0	0	0	0	
Talbot	177	0	20	31	24	35	24	
Washington	296	0	50	45	50	62	48	
Wicomico	51	0	24	27	0	0	0	
Worcester	0	0	0	0	0	0	0	

TABLE
18

Nonpublic Non-Catholic School Enrollment by Grade: State of Maryland: September 30, 1986

Local Unit	Grand Total	Total Elementary	Pre-Kinder-garten	Kinder-garten	Ungraded Special & Regular	1	2	3	4	5	6
Total State	75,222	56,214	25,931	6,750	1,094	4,652	4,030	3,806	3,512	3,181	3,258
Allegany	643	546	425	22	0	19	12	23	14	17	14
Anne Arundel	6,469	5,190	2,874	583	30	358	341	283	238	237	246
Baltimore City	8,596	5,923	1,507	855	379	642	543	539	534	453	471
Baltimore	15,159	10,714	5,160	1,284	366	756	629	654	621	592	652
Calvert	496	365	105	37	0	49	37	35	32	32	38
Caroline	160	130	73	7	0	10	7	14	9	6	4
Carroll	772	659	393	60	4	52	49	25	29	25	22
Cecil	963	596	225	66	0	47	57	61	44	43	53
Charles	319	284	86	32	0	40	41	23	32	17	13
Dorchester	182	146	58	24	0	19	9	15	11	7	3
Frederick	1,385	1,224	710	143	1	79	67	70	56	49	49
Garrett	131	97	61	2	8	6	3	6	2	4	5
Harford	2,089	1,762	987	187	0	134	101	97	84	89	83
Howard	2,886	2,743	2,024	254	95	100	73	63	53	50	31
Kent	256	201	10	27	16	31	30	19	22	26	20
Montgomery	20,978	15,394	7,937	1,661	155	1,110	998	949	874	845	865
Prince George's	9,517	7,394	2,451	1,227	32	898	702	628	580	446	430
Queen Anne's	246	131	93	2	0	2	8	12	3	4	7
St. Mary's	634	536	161	63	0	58	67	58	46	40	43
Somerset	143	102	10	23	0	13	14	12	10	12	8
Talbot	473	424	234	32		30	29	27	26	25	21
Washington	1,674	878	59	67	8	129	134	130	124	105	122
Wicomico	455	392	122	48	0	45	49	30	43	29	26
Worcester	596	383	166	44	0	25	30	33	25	28	32

TABLE
18

Nonpublic Non-Catholic School Enrollment by Grade: State of Maryland: September 30, 1986

Local Unit	Total Secondary	Ungraded Special & Regular	Secondary 7	8	9	10	11	12
Total State	19,008	570	3,191	3,167	3,114	3,151	3,033	2,7
Allegany	97	0	16	22	11	12	21	
Anne Arundel	1,279	29	237	231	227	182	176	1
Baltimore City	2,673	194	399	419	393	474	418	3
Baltimore	4,445	111	691	650	781	760	768	6
Calvert	131	0	37	21	12	29	22	
Caroline	30	0	10	8	10	1	0	
Carroll	113	0	18	24	23	18	17	
Cecil	367	0	49	43	51	72	78	
Charles	35	0	12	13	5	0	3	
Dorchester	36	0	5	10	1	5	8	
Frederick	161	3	38	36	29	24	24	
Garrett	34	0	11	3	3	6	8	
Harford	327	0	71	81	48	44	48	
Howard	143	47	39	23	20	11	1	
Kent	55	2	14	22	3	5	6	
Montgomery	5,584	133	874	909	912	949	908	8
Prince George's	2,123	34	413	416	351	326	322	2
Queen Anne's	115	0	5	6	29	27	24	
St. Mary's	98	0	40	33	6	11	5	
Somerset	41	0	16	7	2	8	4	
Talbot	49	0	23	20	4	2	0	
Washington	796	17	112	117	144	148	136	1
Wicomico	63	0	21	17	9	3	5	
Worcester	213	0	40	36	40	34	31	

TABLE
19

Students Receiving Special Education Services in Maryland: By Level: 1986-87

Local Unit	Total	I Diagnostic/ Prescriptive	II Itinerant	III Resource Rooms	IV Self-Contained Classes	V-Special School or Center-Day Public*	V-Special School or Center-Day Nonpublic	VI Residential Public*	VI Residential Nonpublic	VII Home and Hospital
Total State	90,606	5,787	29,962	17,270	24,207	10,538	1,239	796	254	553
Allegany	1,448	129	553	466	265	19	1	0	0	15
Anne Arundel	8,130	759	3,219	2,143	1,481	479	10	0	39	0
Baltimore City	19,034	217	3,243	3,298	9,186	2,341	628	0	44	77
Baltimore	9,514	409	3,194	925	2,977	1,817	145	0	22	25
Calvert	977	25	352	178	350	62	0	0	2	8
Caroline	931	92	457	219	125	33	0	0	5	0
Carroll	2,640	430	1,199	404	475	95	2	0	5	30
Cecil	1,498	144	511	381	332	122	1	0	7	0
Charles	2,614	163	749	892	586	220	0	0	0	4
Dorchester	713	91	312	204	76	21	0	0	2	7
Frederick	3,710	450	1,692	715	314	492	0	0	2	45
Garrett	774	91	278	227	159	4	0	0	0	15
Harford	3,634	370	1,577	868	525	228	4	0	10	52
Howard	3,217	257	1,156	848	589	290	11	0	14	52
Kent	294	16	161	34	62	20	0	0	1	0
Montgomery	10,793	841	4,466	1,242	1,967	1,833	262	85	63	34
Prince George's	11,330	566	2,901	2,341	3,335	1,815	165	53	24	130
Queen Anne's	498	14	152	158	151	8	0	0	1	14
St. Mary's	1,847	17	860	428	394	113	0	0	0	34
Somerset	559	82	243	123	71	40	0	0	0	0
Talbot	391	40	236	51	59	0	0	0	4	1
Washington	2,975	486	1,502	463	324	187	8	0	3	2
Wicomico	1,372	50	709	367	129	110	2	0	5	0
Worcester	549	48	194	188	73	38	0	0	0	8
State Operated	1,164	0	46	107	202	151	0	658	0	0

*Includes nonpublic placements not requiring state approval.
NOTE: Students receiving services in Maryland public schools, state-approved nonpublic schools, and state-operated programs.

TABLE
20

Handicapping Conditions of Students Receiving Special Education Services in Maryland: 1986-87

Local Unit	Total	Mentally Retarded	Hearing Impaired	Deaf	Speech Impaired	Visually Handi- capped	Emotion- ally Disturbed	Orthope- dically Impaired	Other Health Impaired	Specific Learning Disability	Multiple Handicap	Deaf/ Blind
Total State	90,606	6,720	754	625	26,718	630	3,764	878	1,275	45,634	3,534	74
Allegany	1,448	139	7	0	498	7	65	10	42	658	22	0
Anne Arundel	8,130	331	66	4	2,146	26	427	76	195	4,634	225	0
Baltimore City	19,034	1,713	125	31	5,564	100	780	76	128	9,954	563	0
Baltimore	9,514	1,026	71	21	3,028	44	218	90	58	4,537	421	0
Calvert	977	70	12	0	304	1	36	8	3	520	23	0
Caroline	931	60	3	2	348	6	7	1	3	440	60	1
Carroll	2,640	191	21	2	1,296	13	63	38	13	952	51	0
Cecil	1,498	119	8	0	328	1	41	9	10	947	35	0
Charles	2,614	410	25	1	549	14	74	13	39	1,449	40	0
Dorchester	713	41	5	2	305	2	11	3	9	268	67	0
Frederick	3,710	279	60	4	1,064	6	207	29	73	1,764	221	3
Garrett	774	45	13	4	271	4	48	8	26	342	13	0
Harford	3,634	459	22	9	1,171	21	70	48	46	1,723	65	0
Howard	3,217	141	34	11	1,088	20	378	55	136	1,255	99	0
Kent	294	59	2	0	103	1	1	4	0	117	7	0
Montgomery	10,793	522	107	115	3,083	100	749	89	33	5,254	729	12
Prince George's	11,330	249	134	68	2,198	63	302	184	276	7,169	685	2
Queen Anne's	498	52	1	1	185	3	2	8	13	227	5	1
St. Mary's	1,847	212	11	2	725	9	71	31	67	698	20	1
Somerset	559	59	0	0	199	0	4	6	6	275	10	0
Talbot	391	47	3	0	175	1	1	5	1	149	9	0
Washington	2,975	226	15	2	1,412	10	41	33	70	1,122	44	0
Wicomico	1,372	168	6	4	395	2	20	20	6	698	52	1
Worcester	549	58	3	1	265	1	0	10	9	192	10	0
State Operated	1,164	44	0	341	18	175	148	24	13	290	58	53

NOTE: Students receiving services in Maryland public schools, state-approved nonpublic schools, and state-operated programs.

TABLE
21

Pupil Withdrawals by Grade: Maryland Public Schools: 1986-87
Terminations - Including Death·

Local Unit	Grand Total	Total Elem.	Prekg.	Kgn.	1	2	3	4	5	6	Spec. Educ.	Un-graded	Total Secd.	7	8	9	10	11	12	Spec. Educ.
L STATE	18,436	2,368	774	609	245	117	131	119	122	191	3ᴇ	24	16,068	534	862	4,456	4,088	3,339	2,665	124
GANY	99	5	0	4	0	0	0	1			0	0	94	4	3	16	27	27	15	
ARUNDEL	1,551	52	0	25	1	0	2	2		2	0	20	1,499	19	67	375	470	387	171	1
[MORE CITY	8,572	1,652	512	394	207	99	112	93	10	135	0	0	6,920	379	473	2,214	1,623	1,037	1,194	
[MORE	1,789	134	53	29	7	1	5	6	0	24	0	4	1,655	61	146	415	404	380	249	2
ERT	152	12	3	5	0	0	0	1	0	0	3	0	140	1	0	33	42	34	30	0
LINE	107	0	0	0	0	0	0	0	0	0	0		107	3	6	31	23	23	17	
DLL	277	17	12	2	1	1	0	0	1	0	0		260	0	3	42	72	64	74	
L	312	38	9	17	2	2	1	1	1	3	2		274	4	22	56	71	70	51	
LES	228	13	10	2	0	0	0	0	1	0	0		215	2	4	62	75	51	21	4
HESTER	92	16	7	4	0	0	0	0	0	4	1	0	76	6	7	19	14	21	9	8
ERICK	321	13	0	3		3	0		1	0	6	0	308	4	11	63	75	82	71	2
ETT	64	11	8	2		0			0	1	0	0	53	2	4	10	20	11	6	0
ORD	496	17	13	3		0		0	1	0	0	0	479	5	26	161	90	119	77	1
RD	197	4	0	1	0	1		0	1	0	0	0	193	0	0	39	58	57	39	0
	16	1	0	1	0	0		0	0	0	0	0	15	0	1	3	2	3	2	4
GOMERY	1,373	198	52	57	2	8	1	13	9	15	10	0	1,175	23	30	188	322	343	268	1
CE GEORGE'S	1,823	94	53	19		1		0	2	3	13	0	1,729	13	28	471	493	418	235	71
ANNE'S	77	2	1	1		0		0	0	0	0	0	75	0	1	20	22	21	9	2
MARY'S	251	29	18	10	0	0		0	0	1	0	0	222	0	5	79	40	48	35	15
BSET	57	8	5	1	0			0	1	0	1	0	59	2	4	25	13	8	7	0
YT	61	4	0	1		1	0	1	0	1		0	57	0	3	27	11	10	6	0
NGTON	264	29	17	11	0		0	0	1	0		0	235	2	5	55	63	66	38	6
IICO	191	18	0	17		0	0	0	0	1		0	173	3	13	39	46	39	32	1
ISTER	56	1	1	0		0	0	0	0	0	0	0	55	1	0	13	12	20	9	0

ncludes Prekg., 499 and Kgn., 264 withdrawals due to immaturity.

TABLE
22

Pupil Withdrawals: Cause of Termination: Maryland Public Schools: September-June 1986-87: Grades Prek-6

Local Unit	Total Include Death	Total Exclude Death	Illness	Employ- ment	Mar- riage	Military Service	Incom- patibility with School *	Court Action	Econ- omic	Special Cases - Superintendent's Approval Expul- sion +	Immatu- rity #	Other	Parent Teach. Program	Undeter- mined	Expul- sion @	Preg- nancy	Death
TOTAL STATE	2,368	2,319	15	0	0	2	6	9	1	35	784	24	23	1,419	1	0	49
ALLEGANY	5	4	0	0	0	0	0	0	0	0	4	0		0	0	0	1
ANNE ARUNDEL	52	45	4	0	0	0	0	0	0	1	38	1		1	0	0	7
BALTIMORE CITY	1,652	1,652	0	0	0	0	0	0	0	0	424			1,222	0	0	0
BALTIMORE	134	128	1	0	0	0	2	2	0	28	71	0	0	17	0	0	6
CALVERT	12	10	1	0	0	0	1	1	0	0	7	0	0	0	0	0	2
CAROLINE	0	0	0	0	0	0	0			0	0	0		0		0	
CARROLL	17	17	0	0	0	0	0	0	0	0	14	0		0		0	0
CECIL	38	37	1	0	0	0	0	0	0	0	16	0		14		0	0
CHARLES	13	12	0	0	0	0	0	0	0	0	8	3	0	1	0	0	1
DORCHESTER	16	15	1	0	0	0	0	0	0	3	10	1		0	0	0	1
FREDERICK	13	12	0	0	0	0	0			1	1	1	6	3			1
GARRETT	11	11	0	0	0	0	0			1	7	0		2			0
HARFORD	17	16	0	0	0	0	0			0	15	0		0			1
HOWARD	4	3	0	0	0	0	0	0	0	0	0	0	0	3	0	0	1
KENT	1	1	0	0	0	0	0	0	0	0	1	0		0	0	0	0
MONTGOMERY	198	193	2	0	0	0	0	3	0	0	23	4	6	15			5
PRINCE GEORGE'S	94	75	2	0	0	2	3	2	0	0	65	0	1				19
QUEEN ANNE'S	2	2	0	0	0	0	0	0	0	0	2	0	0		0		0
ST. MARY'S	29	28	0	0	0	0	0	0	0	0	27	1	0		0		1
SOMERSET	8	8	1	0	0	0	0	0	1	1	5	0	0	0		0	1
TALBOT	4	4	0	0	0	0	0	0	0	0	1	0	2	1	0	0	0
WASHINGTON	29	28	2	0	0	0	0	0	0	0	26	0	0	0	0	0	1
WICOMICO	18	17	0	0	0	0	0	0	0	1	17	0	0	0	0	0	1
WORCESTER	1	1	0	0	0	0	0	0	0	0	1	0	0	0	0	0	0

* Incompatibility between school and pupil (16 years of age and older).
+ Expulsion for disciplinary reasons (under 16 years of age).
# Under compulsory attendance age.
@ Expulsion - 16 years and older

TABLE

22

Pupil Withdrawals: Cause of Termination: Maryland Public Schools: September-June 1986-87: Grades 7-12

ocal Unit	Total Include Death	Total Exclude Death	Illness	Employ-ment	Mar-riage	Military Service	Incom-patibility with School *	Court Action	Econ-omic	Special Cases - Superintendent's Approval Expul-sion +	Immatu-rity #	Other	Parent Teach. Program	Undeter-mined	Expul-sion @	Preg-nancy	Death
L STATE	16,068	15,977	4	763	42	33	11,789	143	113	607	6	329	6	1,762	312	32	91
GANY	94	91	2	4	2	0	49	5	1	1		9	0	1	1	6	3
ARUNDEL	1,499	1,488	11	79	3	1	1,204	9		88		59	0	0	32	2	11
IMORE CITY	6,920	6,920	0	0	18	3	5,161	0		0		69	0	1,669	0	0	0
IMORE	1,655	1,645	1	13	1	0	1,042	12	1	353	0	25	0	5	189	4	10
ERT	140	139	1	0	0	0	132	2	0	0	0	0	0	0	2	2	1
LINE	107	105	0	41	0	0	46	1	0	10	0	0	0	0	7	0	2
OLL	260	255	2	2	0	0	236	0	0	5	0	7	1	2	0	0	5
L	274	271	9	0	2	0	202	14	1	4	0	25	0	11	1	2	3
LES	215	214	1	33	1	1	170	0	0	5	0	0	1	2	0	0	1
HESTER	76	74	0	0	0	0	54	2	0	11	0	3	0	0	4	0	2
ERICK	308	303	1	55	3	4	200	4	2	11	2	16		5	0	0	5
ETT	53	53	0	0	1	0	41	2	0	3	0	3		0	1	2	0
ORD	479	476	2	21	0	0	376	1	2	45	3	17	0	0	9	0	3
RD	193	189	0	1	0	0	184	1	0	0	1	0		2	0	0	4
	15	15	0	2	0	0	12	0	0	0	0	0		0	1	0	0
GOMERY	1,175	1,164	4	251	3	3	789	22		3	0	18	0	6	4	2	11
CE GEORGE'S	1,729	1,710	1	239	4	20	1,182	59	9	39	0	28	1		36	5	19
N ANNE'S	75	74	0	0	0	0	65	0		4	0	5	0		0	0	1
MARY'S	222	220	1	6	0	1	175	5	0	10	0	2	3	6	14	3	2
RSET	59	59	0	1	0	0	46	0	0	4	0	7	0		1	0	0
OT	57	55	1		0		44	0	0	0	0	1	0	0	0	0	2
INGTON	235	231	1		4		177	2	0	3	0	33	0	0	1	3	4
ICO	173	171	0		0	0	165	1	0	1	0	0	0	0	4	0	2
ESTER	55	55	2	0	0	0	37	1	0	7	0	2	0	0	5	1	0

:ompatibility between school and pupil (16 years of age and older).
pulsion for disciplinary reasons (under 16 years of age).
ier compulsory attendance age.
pulsion - 16 years and older

TABLE
23

Pupil Withdrawals: By Transfer: Maryland Public Schools: September-June 1986-87: Grades PreK-6

TOTAL STATE	50,414	26,549	11,283	9,311	1,840	311	182	938
ALLEGANY	468	263	41	137	23	0	0	4
ANNE ARUNDEL	3,839	1,726	765	1,156	85	37	16	54
BALTIMORE CITY	15,459	9,578	4,896	0	930	0	0	55
BALTIMORE	4,540	1,931	1,492	800	153	51	28	85
CALVERT	509	191	141	126	34	7	2	8
CAROLINE	275	79	99	89	3	2	0	3
CARROLL	665	258	190	193	6	4	4	10
CECIL	673	323	54	259	18	0	4	5
CHARLES	840	285	266	235	29	8	4	15
DORCHESTER	216	86	70	51	2	5	2	0
FREDERICK	1,253	562	232	380	41	4	0	34
GARRETT	209	112	29	66	1	0	1	0
HARFORD	3,687	2,699	279	609	26	19	10	45
HOWARD	1,493	646	336	319	45	96	4	47
KENT	86	27	13	42	2	1	0	1
MONTGOMERY	4,787	2,349	542	1,266	176	23	62	369
PRINCE GEORGE'S	8,043	4,024	1,187	2,454	156	32	39	151
QUEEN ANNE'S	190	33	109	41	2	1	0	4
ST. MARY'S	969	358	128	408	56	2	1	16
SOMERSET	135	41	51	34	3	3	1	2
TALBOT	162	38	65	48	5	1	2	3
WASHINGTON	954	525	84	299	27	3	0	16
WICOMICO	722	374	124	199	16	1	1	7
WORCESTER	240	41	80	100	1	11	3	4

* In another state or territory of the United States, or a United States overseas dependent school.

TABLE

23

Pupil Withdrawals: By Transfer: Maryland Public Schools: September-June 1986-87: Grades 7-12

Local Unit	Total	TO PUBLIC SCHOOL			TO NONPUBLIC SCHOOL			Other Programs
		In the Same Local Unit	Outside the Local Unit		In the Same Local Unit	Outside the Local Unit		
			In Maryland	Other State *		In Maryland	Other State *	
'AL STATE	42,801	26,545	6,571	5,962	899	351	231	2,242
.EGANY	199	90	26	68	9	0	0	6
IE ARUNDEL	2,929	1,303	541	660	45	44	32	304
.TIMORE CITY	20,039	15,546	2,799	0	400	0	0	294
.TIMORE	2,482	837	792	516	71	45	25	195
.VERT	356	133	88	99	12	12	4	8
IOLINE	122	7	54	48	1	3	1	8
IROLL	462	233	88	89	2	10	6	35
:IL	336	116	49	145	12	0	2	12
IRLES	645	219	138	160	8	9	3	108
ICHESTER	89	15	27	33	7	1	1	5
:DERICK	1,006	418	173	261	17	10	9	118
IRETT	75	12	16	36	0	0	2	9
IFORD	2,788	2,124	224	358	14	15	8	45
IARD	1,116	398	271	266	12	130	16	23
IT	42	1	11	27	0	1	0	2
ITGOMERY	2,936	1,199	325	847	142	24	77	322
NCE GEORGE'S	5,364	2,267	606	1,740	104	35	29	583
IEN ANNE'S	85	4	44	24	2	2	1	8
MARY'S	653	222	105	278	23	0	7	17
IERSET	57	8	22	11	3	0	0	13
IBOT	78	13	23	23	1	2	0	16
HINGTON	587	290	61	134	10	1	5	86
OMICO	240	81	47	85	3	2	3	19
CESTER	115	9	40	54	1	4	1	6

another state or territory of the United States, or a United States overseas dependent school.

TABLE
24

Nonpromotions by Number and Percent: Maryland Public Schools: June Net Roll 1987 :   Grades Prek.-12

TOTAL STATE	662,791	628,366	34,425	5.2	362,220	348,326	13,894	3.8	300,571	280,040	20,531	6.8
ALLEGANY	11,425	11,291	134	1.2	5,652	5,578	74	1.3	5,773	5,713	60	1.0
ANNE ARUNDEL	62,755	59,114	3,641	5.8	33,049	32,543	506	1.5	29,706	26,571	3,135	10.6
BALTIMORE CITY	106,016	91,481	14,535	13.7	65,542	58,598	6,944	10.6	40,474	32,883	7,591	18.8
BALTIMORE	78,908	76,082	2,826	3.6	42,537	41,350	1,187	2.8	36,371	34,732	1,639	4.5
CALVERT	8,534	8,336	198	2.3	4,742	4,603	139	2.9	3,792	3,733	59	1.6
CAROLINE	4,247	4,102	145	3.4	2,366	2,334	32	1.	1,881	1,768	113	6.0
CARROLL	19,982	19,519	463	2.3	10,654	10,501	153	1.	9,328	9,018	310	3.3
CECIL	11,940	11,585	355	3.0	6,460	6,247	213	3.	5,480	5,338	142	2.6
CHARLES	16,854	16,669	185	1.1	8,566	8,458	108	1.	8,288	8,211	77	0.9
DORCHESTER	4,885	4,614	271	5.5	2,727	2,610	117	4.4	2,158	2,004	154	7.1
FREDERICK	24,248	23,945	303	1.2	13,237	12,991	246	1.9	11,011	10,954	57	0.5
GARRETT	5,021	4,846	175	3.5	2,764	2,651	113	4.1	2,257	2,195	62	2.7
HARFORD	27,895	27,073	822	2.9	15,254	14,888	366	2.4	12,641	12,185	456	3.6
HOWARD	24,625	24,137	488	2.0	12,657	12,549	108	0.9	11,968	11,588	380	3.2
KENT	2,344	2,227	117	5.0	1,267	1,211	56	4.4	1,077	1,016	61	5.7
MONTGOMERY	94,421	91,551	2,870	3.	49,662	48,554	1,108	2.2	44,759	42,997	1,762	.9
PRINCE GEORGE'S	101,687	96,924	4,763	4.	53,429	51,968	1,461	2.7	48,258	44,956	3,302	.8
QUEEN ANNE'S	4,800	4,690	110	2.	2,675	2,632	43	1.6	2,125	2,058	67	.2
ST. MARY'S	11,357	10,851	506	4.0	6,340	6,124	216	3.4	5,017	4,727	290	.8
SOMERSET	3,363	3,196	167	5.0	1,982	1,880	102	5.1	1,381	1,316	65	4.7
TALBOT	3,726	3,449	277	7.	2,079	1,907	172	8.3	1,647	1,542	105	6.4
WASHINGTON	17,192	16,732	460	2.	9,129	8,945	184	2.0	8,063	7,787	276	3.4
WICOMICO	11,454	10,922	532	4.	6,678	6,450	228	3.4	4,776	4,472	304	6.4
WORCESTER	5,112	5,030	82	1.6	2,772	2,754	18	0.6	2,340	2,276	64	2.7

TABLE

25

Public High School Graduates: State of Maryland: . 1976-77 - 1986-87

Year/	High School Graduates		
Local Unit	Total	Boys	Girls
1976-77	55,503	26,606	28,897
1977-78	55,880	27,109	28,771
1978-79	55,276	26,333	28,943
1979-80	54,491	25,963	28,528
1980-81	54,050	26,138	27,912
1981-82	54,621	26,483	28,138
1982-83	52,446	25,374	27,072
1983-84	50,684	24,620	26,064
1984-85	48,299	23,472	24,827
1985-86	46,700	22,474	24,226
1986-87	46,107	22,453	23,654
By Local Unit - 1986-87			
Allegany	974	489	485
Anne Arundel	4,213	2,050	2,163
Baltimore City	4,802	2,053	2,749
Baltimore	6,049	2,877	3,172
Calvert	622	303	319
Caroline	260	122	138
Carroll	1,500	740	760
Cecil	840	399	441
Charles	1,305	681	624
Dorchester	317	158	159
Frederick	1,661	820	841
Garrrett	331	156	175
Harford	1,956	985	971
Howard	1,959	1,038	921
Kent	176	85	91
Montgomery	8,046	4,038	4,008
Prince George's	7,298	3,604	3,694
Queen Anne's	329	161	168
St. Mary's	781	396	385
Somerset	193	80	113
Talbot	232	118	114
Washington	1,227	613	614
Wicomico	649	320	329
Worcester	387	167	220

TABLE
26

Average Number of Pupils Belonging per Teacher and Principal: Maryland Public Schools: 1986-87

Local Unit	Total	Elementary	Secondary
Total State	15.1	16.9	13.4
Allegany	15.7	15.6	15.9
Anne Arundel	15.4	16.1	14.7
Baltimore City	16.2	18.3	13.8
Baltimore	13.7	16.3	11.6
Calvert	16.5	18.1	14.9
Caroline	14.4	15.6	13.1
Carroll	16.1	19.6	13.5
Cecil	14.9	17.5	12.8
Charles	15.7	17.8	14.1
Dorchester	14.9	18.0	12.2
Frederick	16.1	18.7	13.7
Garrett	15.7	18.5	13.3
Harford	15.8	19.0	13.2
Howard	14.2	16.3	12.6
Kent	13.5	19.7	9.9
Montgomery	14.1	14.4	13.7
Prince George's	15.8	17.2	14.6
Queen Anne's	15.8	22.3	11.7
St. Mary's	13.9	16.2	11.9
Somerset	13.9	19.9	9.8
Talbot	14.2	20.9	10.1
Washington	14.8	16.5	13.3
Wicomico	15.5	17.3	13.6
Worcester	12.8	18.0	9.5

TABLE
27

Average Number of Pupils Belonging: Maryland Public Schools: 1986-87: Grades Prek.-12

| Local Unit | Grand Total | ELEMENTARY | | | | SECONDARY |
		Total	Prekindergarten	Kindergarten	Grades 1-6	
TOTAL STATE	671,570.0	362,511.4	8,760.7	50,187.4	303,563.3	309,058.6
ALLEGANY	11,490.8	5,670.9	0.0	828.6	4,842.3	5,819.9
ANNE ARUNDEL	63,857.0	33,160.4	0.0	4,770.3	28,390.1	30,696.6
BALTIMORE CITY	110,073.2	66,663.3	4,191.4	8,970.9	53,501.0	43,409.9
BALTIMORE	80,017.9	42,657.3	1,149.1	5,796.3	35,711.9	37,360.6
CALVERT	8,516.2	4,702.2	98.8	689.1	3,914.3	3,814.0
CAROLINE	4,319.9	2,392.7	0.0	371.3	2,021.4	1,927.2
CARROLL	19,523.7	10,011.1	0.0	1,634.9	8,376.2	9,512.6
CECIL	11,924.6	6,327.4	119.7	848.3	5,359.4	5,597.2
CHARLES	16,585.3	8,227.8	85.0	563.4	7,579.4	8,357.5
DORCHESTER	4,933.6	2,733.1	174.9	374.2	2,184.0	2,200.5
FREDERICK	24,525.2	13,327.7	0.0	2,090.5	11,237.2	11,197.5
GARRETT	5,027.2	2,759.0	58.8	392.3	2,307.9	2,268.2
HARFORD	28,247.2	15,276.3	275.8	2,240.1	12,760.4	12,970.9
HOWARD	25,795.3	13,194.6	0.0	1,827.9	11,366.7	12,600.7
KENT	2,339.2	1,259.7	10.7	186.9	1,062.1	1,079.5
MONTGOMERY	94,461.4	49,174.4	1,032.9	7,295.9	40,845.6	45,287.0
PRINCE GEORGE'S	102,496.5	53,305.9	815.9	6,700.9	45,789.1	49,190.6
QUEEN ANNE'S	4,806.7	2,648.7	0.0	399.5	2,249.2	2,158.0
ST. MARY'S	11,516.5	6,383.9	354.1	981.0	5,048.8	5,132.6
SOMERSET	3,395.0	1,984.3	148.0	248.6	1,587.7	1,410.7
TALBOT	3,760.1	2,089.2	0.0	353.3	1,735.9	1,670.9
WASHINGTON	17,265.8	9,105.0	191.6	1,314.5	7,598.9	8,160.8
WICOMICO	11,554.5	6,684.7	6.4	919.6	5,758.7	4,869.8
WORCESTER	5,137.2	2,771.8	47.6	389.1	2,335.1	2,365.4

TABLE 28

Average Number of Pupils Attending: Percent of Attendance: Maryland Public Schools: 1986-87; Grades Prek.-12

TOTAL STATE	618,463.2	339,921.2	7,766.1	46,407.4	285,747.7	278,542.0	92.0	93.7	88.6	92.4	94.1	90.1
ALLEGANY	10,806.1	5,388.2	0.0	778.7	4,609.5	5,417.9	94.0	95.	0.0	94.0	95.1	93.1
ANNE ARUNDEL	59,765.6	31,417.0	0.0	4,444.9	26,972.1	28,348.6	93.6	94.0	0.0	93.2	95.0	92.4
BALTIMORE CITY	94,773.7	59,834.5	3,654.3	7,939.1	48,241.1	34,939.2	86.1	89.8	87.2	88.5	90.1	80.5
BALTIMORE	74,920.0	40,324.0	1,047.1	5,389.7	33,887.2	34,596.0	93.6	94.5	91.1	93.0	94.8	92.6
CALVERT	8,006.6	4,450.7	89.9	645.7	3,715.1	3,555.9	94.0	94.7	91.0	93.7	94.9	93.2
CAROLINE	4,068.1	2,287.2	0.0	351.	1,936.2	1,780.9	94.2	95.6	0.	94.5	95.7	92.4
CARROLL	18,301.8	9,494.3	0.0	1,524.	7,970.0	8,807.5	93.7	94.8	0.	93.2	95.1	92.6
CECIL	10,954.1	5,952.8	110.1	787.	5,055.2	5,001.3	91.9	94.1	92.	92.8	94.3	89.4
CHARLES	15,489.9	7,817.0	-76.8	519.	7,220.4	7,672.9	93.4	95.0	90.	92.3	95.2	91.8
DORCHESTER	4,634.7	2,582.6	163.6	348.	2,070.4	2,052.1	93.9	94.5	93.	93.2	94.7	93.3
FREDERICK	22,802.2	12,679.0	0.0	1,978.2	10,700.8	10,123.2	93.0	95.1	0.0	94.6	95.2	90.4
GARRETT	4,736.3	2,612.5	52.5	365.1	2,194.9	2,123.8	94.2	94.7	89.3	93.1	95.1	93.6
HARFORD	26,583.9	14,519.8	253.3	2,106.2	12,160.3	12,064.1	94.1	95.0	91.8	94.0	95.2	93.0
HOWARD	24,370.9	12,636.9	0.0	1,746.0	10,890.9	11,734.0	94.5	95.8	0.0	95.5	95.8	93.1
KENT	2,199.1	1,201.8	9.4	176.5	1,015.9	997.3	94.0	95.4	87.9	94.4	95.6	92.4
MONTGOMERY	87,935.	46,437.4	908.5	6,803.	38,725.1	41,498.	93.1	94.	88.0	93.3	94.8	91.6
PRINCE GEORGE'S	94,155.	50,264.9	721.0	6,193.	43,350.4	43,890.	91.9	94.	88.4	92.4	94.6	89.2
QUEEN ANNE'S	4,501.	2,505.3	0.0	373.	2,132.0	1,996.	93.7	94.	0.0	93.4	94.7	92.5
ST. MARY'S	10,754.	6,041.0	328.6	915.	4,796.7	4,713.	93.4	94.	92.8	93.3	95.0	91.8
SOMERSET	3,151.	1,857.1	132.6	229.	1,495.5	1,294.	92.8	93.6	89.6	92.1	94.1	91.8
TALBOT	3,539.4	1,989.9	0.0	334.7	1,655.2	1,549.	94.1	95.2	0.0	94.7	95.3	92.7
WASHINGTON	16,258.0	8,641.1	171.1	1,225.2	7,244.8	7,616.	94.2	94.9	89.3	93.2	95.3	93.3
WICOMICO	10,897.5	6,355.2	4.7	863.9	5,487.6	4,541.	94.3	95.1	73.4	93.9	95.2	93.3
WORCESTER	4,855.7	2,630.0	42.6	367.0	2,220.4	2,225.	94.5	94.9	89.5	94.3	95.0	94.1

TABLE
29

Number of Maryland Public Elementary Schools* by Pupil Membership: September 30, 1986

cal Unit	Total Schools	Less Than 100	100-199	200-299	300-399	400-499	500-599	600-699	700-799	800 or or More
					Pupil Membership					
tal State	814	40	50	106	192	188	125	64	31	18
legany	16	0	1	4	6	2	2	0	1	0
ne Arundel	80	4	7	13	19	12	15	5	4	1
ltimore City	132	5	6	11	25	32	16	21	7	9
ltimore	98	1	1	21	40	22	10	3	0	0
lvert	8	2	0	0	0	0	2	1	2	1
roline	5	0	0	0	2	1	1	1	0	0
rroll	18	2	1	0	3	3	0	5	4	0
cil	16	0	1	5	4	3	2	1	0	0
arles	17	2	0	2	2	3	3	4	0	1
rchester	7	0	2	1	1	2	1	0	0	0
ederick	26	2	2	2	5	5	2	5	2	1
rrett	13	4	4	3	0	1	1	0	0	0
rford	26	0	2	2	2	9	6	1	1	3
ward	26	0	1	1	6	9	8	1	0	0
nt	4	0	1	3	0	0	0	0	0	0
ntgomery	111	6	4	9	30	24	23	9	6	0
ince George's	122	2	8	6	29	40	28	6	3	0
een Anne's	5	0	0	3	0	1	0	0	1	0
. Mary's	20	2	3	5	6	3	1	0	0	0
merset	9	4	3	0	1	1	0	0	0	0
lbot	6	0	1	2	1	1	1	0	0	0
shington	27	1	2	10	7	5	2	0	0	0
comico	16	2	0	3	1	6	1	1	0	2
rcester	6	1	0	0	2	3	0	0	0	0

ides combined schools which are not specifically middle schools.

TABLE
30

Number of Maryland Public Secondary Schools* by Pupil Membership: September 30, 1986

Local Unit	Total Schools	Less Than 400	400-599	600-799	800-999	1000-1199	1200-1399	1400-1599	1600-1799	1800-1999	2000 or more
Total State	375	38	77	76	54	36	40	15	13	15	11
Allegany	8	1	1	4	1	1	0	0	0	0	0
Anne Arundel	31	1	1	8	9	3	1	4	1	1	2
Baltimore City	47	8	5	7	5	3	7	4	3	4	1
Baltimore	47	3	6	12	8	3	9	1	3	1	0
Calvert	6	1	2	1		0	2	0	0	0	0
Caroline	4	1	2	0	1	0	0	0	0	0	0
Carroll	13	2	2	3	0	2	2	0	0	0	1
Cecil	9	1	5	0		2	1	0	0	0	0
Charles	10	1	2	2	1	0	2	1	1	0	0
Dorchester	4	1	1	1	0	1	0	0	0	0	0
Frederick	15	0	4	3	5	0	2	1	0	0	0
Garrett	4	1	1	1	0	1	0	0	0	0	0
Harford	16	0	2	2	6	3	3	0	0	0	0
Howard	18	0	7	3	2	5	1	0	0	0	0
Kent	4	3		1	0	0	0	0	0	0	0
Montgomery	45	2	6	10	7	5	5	1	3	5	1
Prince George's	49	5	13	10	1	3	3	2	2	4	6
Queen Anne's	4	0	1	1	0	0	0	1	0	0	0
St. Mary's	7		3	1		2	1	0	0	0	0
Somerset	4	1	2	1	0	0	0	0	0	0	0
Talbot	3	1	0	1	1	0	0	0	0	0	0
Washington	15	3	6	2	2	1	1	0	0	0	0
Wicomico	6	0	1	3	2	1	0	0	0	0	0
Worcester	6	1	4		1	0	0	0	0	0	0

*Includes midddle schools.

TABLE
31

California Achievement Test Results*: Maryland Public Schools: 1986-87

Local Unit	Reading Comprehension Grade Level			Language Total Grade Level			Mathematics Total Grade Level		
	3	5	8	3	5	8	3	5	8
Total State	3.7	6.1	10.0	3.8	7.3	10.2	3.5	6.0	9.8
Allegany	3.5	5.7	8.8	3.7	6.4	8.8	3.3	5.3	8.7
Anne Arundel	3.7	6.2	10.0	3.9	7.3	9.5	3.5	5.9	9.6
Baltimore City	2.9	5.3	8.4	3.1	5.8	8.9	3.2	5.6	8.8
Baltimore	4.0	6.5	10.0	4.2	8.1	10.0	3.6	6.2	9.9
Calvert	4.0	6.9	10.9	4.5	8.4	11.8	4.0	6.7	10.0
Caroline	3.7	6.1	9.3	4.4	7.7	9.6	3.6	6.2	9.0
Carroll	3.9	6.5	10.3	4.0	7.6	10.1	3.5	6.0	10.0
Cecil	3.7	6.2	10.0	3.6	7.1	9.1	3.4	5.9	9.0
Charles	3.5	5.7	9.5	3.7	7.1	9.9	3.3	5.5	9.6
Dorchester	3.3	5.4	8.0	3.6	6.8	8.5	3.4	5.4	8.4
Frederick	3.7	6.3	10.1	4.2	7.8	10.1	3.6	6.3	9.5
Garrett	3.5	5.7	9.3	3.5	6.7	9.5	3.3	5.5	8.9
Harford	4.0	6.6	10.6	3.9	7.5	10.4	3.6	6.0	10.0
Howard	4.1	7.3	12.0	4.6	8.5	11.6	3.9	6.7	11.1
Kent	3.6	5.8	9.7	4.5	6.6	10.8	3.7	5.6	9.5
Montgomery	4.2	7.3	11.3	4.9	8.8	11.6	4.0	6.8	12.5
Prince George's	3.4	5.4	8.8	3.8	6.6	10.2	3.5	5.5	9.1
Queen Anne's	3.5	5.7	9.5	3.6	6.2	8.8	3.4	5.6	8.7
St. Mary's	3.4	5.8	9.3	3.4	6.6	9.3	3.3	5.4	9.0
Somerset	3.0	5.3	8.4	3.2	6.1	8.8	3.0	5.0	8.2
Talbot	4.0	6.7	9.7	3.9	7.3	9.9	3.4	5.6	9.2
Washington	3.6	6.0	9.1	3.6	6.7	9.2	3.3	5.5	9.0
Wicomico	3.6	5.8	9.5	3.6	6.4	9.1	3.4	5.5	8.9
Worcester	3.9	5.9	10.0	4.2	7.0	10.3	3.6	5.7	9.5

*Average grade equivalent scores on required subtests of the California Achievement Tests. The first digit represents the grade and the second digit the month within the grade.

SOURCE: Maryland Accountability Testing Program Annual Report, School Year 1986-87

TABLE
32

Statistics about Maryland Pupil Transportation: 1986-87

| Local Unit | Number of Vehicles | | Number of Miles | | Pupils Transported | | | | |
| | Publicly-Owned | Contract | Regular | Handicapped | Number | | | | |
					Regular	Handicapped	Percent	Expenditures*	State Aid
Total State	2,492	2,644	56,221,965	23,228,568	426,710	20,652	66.2%	$152,024,147	$113,379,689
Allegany	32	119	853,911	287,208	7,920	158	69.9	2,857,234	2,604,004
Anne Arundel	59	379	5,914,956	1,620,141	44,098	1,306	70.9	14,171,587	11,076,815
Baltimore City	41	299	438,648	3,233,078	27,143	5,591	29.4	13,534,687	9,453,303
Baltimore	512	38	5,252,282	3,468,247	48,634	2,614	63.9	15,140,939	13,629,401
Calvert	0	72	1,495,452	206,933	8,403	70	99.7	2,219,363	1,862,098
Caroline	7	49	2,711,160	169,632	3,939	79	91.5	1,328,716	1,322,630
Carroll	12	189	732,888	589,920	18,410	455	93.6	4,863,677	4,190,465
Cecil	9	103	1,435,628	244,314	10,321	192	86.4	2,492,520	2,371,906
Charles	4	176	2,864,574	610,961	15,424	179	90.8	4,506,311	4,538,010
Dorchester	5	53	789,498	80,100	4,388	92	90.1	1,358,239	1,340,587
Frederick	170	74	3,166,013	546,120	20,345	365	83.9	5,269,082	4,194,145
Garrett	0	86	959,310	64,481	5,278	35	+104.2	1,674,693	1,730,853
Harford	50	205	3,188,438	343,350	22,076	327	79.7	6,164,245	5,578,654
Howard	0	227	2,682,963	1,340,292	17,525	643	70.9	6,698,380	4,957,734
Kent	8	39	535,078	60,822	1,801	36	78.0	971,889	897,242
Montgomery	750	19	5,818,500	5,067,754	54,666	4,501	62.6	28,188,898	12,210,502
Prince George's	727	3	8,882,675	4,112,390	67,901	3,049	68.7	26,553,423	17,623,390
Queen Anne's	16	59	1,186,902	60,660	4,749	31	99.1	1,586,429	1,477,663
St. Mary's	6	113	1,971,999	401,476	10,842	362	96.6	3,083,197	2,999,158
Somerset	0	46	568,656	86,040	2,668	39	79.6	1,090,106	1,043,625
Talbot	3	41	575,964	61,188	2,502	44	67.3	902,161	840,689
Washington	81	69	1,926,486	306,449	13,959	319	82.5	3,282,818	3,407,625
Wicomico	0	115	1,309,243	152,100	9,193	103	80.0	2,503,540	2,504,410
Worcester	0	71	960,741	114,912	4,525	62	89.2	1,582,013	1,524,780

*Includes fixed charges
+includes students transported to Allegany County

TABLE
33

Professional Staff Employed in Instructional Function: Prek.-12: Maryland Public Schools: 1976-77 - 1986-87

Local Unit	1976-77	1977-78	1978-79	1979-80	1980-81	1981-82	1982-83	1983-84	1984-85	1985-86	1986-87
Total State	48,545.8	48,279.9	48,303.3	47,419.6	46,405.4	44,705.8	42,971.3	42,530.0	42,841.4	43,336.0	44,505.0
Allegany	837.5	834.5	847.0	843.0	839.0	816.0	789.0	764.0	737.0	732.9	730.0
Anne Arundel	4,199.0	4,208.9	4,231.9	4,185.5	4,197.7	4,062.8	3,998.7	4,037.8	4,033.9	4,089.3	4,141.4
Baltimore City	9,144.0	8,990.3	8,579.9	8,362.8	8,055.2	7,423.0	7,103.5	6,812.0	7,028.2	6,813.0	6,806.8
Baltimore	7,011.6	7,057.3	6,932.3	6,683.2	6,540.3	6,315.5	6,037.7	6,031.6	5,791.3	5,794.1	5,856.1
Calvert	404.1	432.8	448.5	479.3	504.5	467.3	477.8	465.6	480.5	494.6	515.5
Caroline	293.0	291.8	288.8	298.3	289.8	292.0	288.5	290.0	295.0	296.0	300.4
Carroll	1,035.3	1,058.2	1,103.7	1,118.8	1,139.2	1,133.9	1,136.3	1,151.5	1,169.0	1,187.0	1,213.6
Cecil	658.2	693.0	728.5	753.7	768.5	778.0	794.0	789.0	788.5	804.9	797.9
Charles	900.9	960.0	1,013.5	1,049.0	1,079.7	1,043.0	1,029.5	1,014.9	1,016.0	1,022.8	1,055.4
Dorchester	349.5	371.3	376.2	376.0	354.6	350.0	305.0	300.5	326.5	328.6	332.1
Frederick	1,123.4	1,245.5	1,333.5	1,334.8	1,379.6	1,368.3	1,403.1	1,399.2	1,437.8	1,461.2	1,527.9
Garrett	317.5	320.1	327.2	339.2	352.1	341.0	318.7	332.2	336.0	326.2	319.6
Harford	1,847.6	1,889.3	1,900.6	1,909.1	1,864.6	1,760.1	1,707.1	1,662.6	1,659.1	1,691.4	1,787.3
Howard	1,394.5	1,440.5	1,503.5	1,540.0	1,524.5	1,524.4	1,515.3	1,532.3	1,558.2	1,723.0	1,811.5
Kent	204.7	201.0	199.8	204.0	193.5	174.7	178.4	171.5	171.1	168.1	173.0
Montgomery	6,962.0	6,728.9	6,728.7	6,541.7	6,382.9	6,227.4	6,074.0	6,007.3	6,122.4	6,504.0	6,717.5
Prince George's	7,921.1	7,653.0	7,823.1	7,373.9	6,965.5	6,748.9	6,034.2	6,008.5	6,102.4	6,055.1	6,467.4
Queen Anne's	255.0	270.0	276.0	277.5	282.0	300.0	303.5	303.5	307.0	297.8	303.9
St. Mary's	680.7	686.0	721.9	736.4	751.4	720.1	703.4	711.6	728.8	746.5	826.2
Somerset	242.0	252.5	245.0	245.5	219.5	238.0	225.0	232.5	232.0	229.0	243.4
Talbot	301.0	296.0	294.0	272.0	263.0	271.4	271.5	260.9	257.5	264.7	264.7
Washington	1,291.0	1,226.0	1,221.0	1,335.4	1,298.0	1,212.0	1,176.5	1,177.5	1,166.0	1,163.9	1,167.0
Wicomico	770.5	781.5	782.0	775.8	762.8	749.2	721.5	712.0	723.2	742.2	744.6
Worcester	401.7	391.4	387.2	384.7	397.5	388.8	379.1	361.5	374.0	399.7	401.8

TABLE
34

Professional Staff Employed in Instructional Function: Prek.-6: Maryland Public Schools: 1976-77 - 1986-87

Local Unit	1976-77	1977-78	1978-79	1979-80	1980-81	1981-82	1982-83	1983-84	1984-85	1985-86	1986-87
Total State	23,476.9	22,668.4	22,670.0	22,117.4	21,756.5	21,265.4	19,672.8	19,387.2	19,806.7	20,515.6	21,462.1
Allegany	379.0	381.0	389.5	388.0	389.5	376.5	361.0	348.5	319.5	386.1	364.2
Anne Arundel	2,015.5	1,859.6	1,952.9	1,873.2	2,065.6	1,996.3	1,859.8	1,941.7	1,955.1	1,992.3	2,059.0
Baltimore City	4,930.0	4,565.5	4,432.3	4,271.2	4,159.5	3,843.0	3,649.7	3,395.6	3,493.7	3,647.5	3,651.3
Baltimore	3,037.9	3,045.7	2,987.8	2,921.8	2,866.7	2,830.2	2,622.8	2,479.1	2,496.3	2,562.1	2,622.9
Calvert	187.6	228.1	204.5	216.3	226.8	219.2	217.0	232.8	216.0	232.4	259.8
Caroline	143.8	142.9	141.4	150.4	141.1	144.1	139.8	140.5	145.5	148.0	153.2
Carroll	501.4	443.2	467.1	468.1	465.8	491.7	445.2	453.8	466.3	492.6	511.3
Cecil	331.8	318.0	371.2	386.0	345.0	379.7	387.9	408.4	391.0	368.5	362.1
Charles	400.0	422.0	457.0	446.5	446.7	499.0	481.9	472.5	456.9	447.3	462.5
Dorchester	173.1	185.0	187.9	176.0	176.6	184.0	212.0	210.5	211.7	143.4	151.5
Frederick	599.5	709.5	709.8	714.3	677.5	665.7	659.0	665.4	749.8	671.3	713.1
Garrett	180.7	183.7	182.7	190.6	197.8	190.1	179.0	179.8	176.9	149.2	149.2
Harford	906.2	895.9	856.8	873.4	814.7	840.2	729.2	701.9	715.6	759.5	804.6
Howard	638.2	630.7	668.0	682.0	607.5	594.4	508.9	634.9	644.8	755.0	808.5
Kent	107.5	108.0	105.5	108.0	69.2	64.8	75.9	92.9	77.0	56.6	64.0
Montgomery	3,069.1	2,944.9	2,862.3	2,726.3	2,770.5	2,702.8	2,528.6	2,514.7	2,712.8	3,216.0	3,423.8
Prince George's	4,028.4	3,808.4	3,883.2	3,704.8	3,500.2	3,517.8	2,908.9	2,822.6	2,861.2	2,733.0	3,096.0
Queen Anne's	130.5	131.2	137.1	135.5	136.0	147.0	151.0	151.0	154.0	110.6	118.7
St. Mary's	315.9	323.0	334.7	342.3	345.9	326.8	315.0	311.0	322.2	341.9	395.2
Somerset	103.0	111.5	128.5	102.5	109.0	113.0	115.5	125.0	134.5	137.2	99.6
Talbot	128.0	121.5	118.5	108.5	79.5	99.4	107.5	114.3	99.5	97.7	100.
Washington	598.0	536.5	524.0	609.7	624.0	523.5	498.5	483.8	476.0	542.9	551.
Wicomico	370.4	381.3	379.8	368.9	365.9	355.9	350.1	348.0	356.4	375.9	385.0
Worcester	201.4	191.3	187.5	153.1	175.5	160.3	168.6	158.5	174.0	148.6	154.8

TABLE
35

Professional Staff Employed in Instructional Function: Grades 7-12: Maryland Public Schools: 1976-77 - 1986-87

Local Unit	1976-77	1977-78	1978-79	1979-80	1980-81	1981-82	1982-83	1983-84	1984-85	1985-86	1986-87
Total State	25,068.9	25,611.5	25,633.3	25,302.2	24,648.9	23,440.4	23,298.5	23,171.3	23,034.7	22,820.4	23,042.9
Allegany	458.5	453.5	457.5	455.0	449.5	439.5	428.0	415.5	417.5	346.8	365.8
Anne Arundel	2,183.5	2,349.3	2,279.0	2,312.3	2,132.1	2,066.5	2,138.9	2,096.1	2,078.8	2,097.0	2,082.4
Baltimore City	4,214.0	4,424.9	4,147.6	4,091.6	3,895.7	3,580.0	3,453.8	3,511.4	3,534.5	3,165.5	3,155.5
Baltimore	3,973.7	4,011.6	3,944.5	3,761.4	3,673.6	3,485.3	3,414.9	3,457.5	3,295.0	3,232.0	3,233.2
Calvert	216.5	204.7	244.0	263.0	277.7	248.1	260.8	232.8	264.5	262.2	255.7
Caroline	149.2	148.9	147.4	147.9	148.7	147.9	148.7	149.5	149.5	148.0	147.2
Carroll	533.9	615.0	636.6	650.7	673.4	642.2	691.1	697.7	702.7	694.4	702.3
Cecil	326.4	375.0	357.3	367.7	423.5	398.3	406.1	409.1	397.5	436.4	435.8
Charles	500.9	538.0	556.5	602.5	633.0	544.0	547.6	542.4	559.1	575.5	592.9
Dorchester	176.4	186.3	188.3	200.0	178.0	166.0	93.0	90.0	114.8	185.2	180.6
Frederick	523.9	536.0	623.7	620.5	702.1	702.6	744.1	733.8	688.0	789.9	814.8
Garrett	136.8	136.4	144.5	148.6	154.3	150.9	139.7	152.4	159.1	177.0	170.4
Harford	941.4	993.4	1,043.8	1,035.7	1,049.9	919.9	977.9	960.7	943.5	931.9	982.7
Howard	756.3	809.8	835.5	858.0	917.0	930.0	1,006.4	897.4	913.4	968.0	1,003.0
Kent	97.2	93.0	94.3	96.0	124.3	109.9	102.5	78.6	94.1	111.5	109.0
Montgomery	3,892.9	3,784.0	3,866.4	3,815.4	3,612.4	3,524.6	3,545.4	3,492.6	3,409.6	3,288.0	3,293.7
Prince George's	3,892.7	3,844.6	3,939.9	3,669.1	3,465.3	3,231.1	3,125.3	3,185.9	3,241.2	3,322.1	3,371.4
Queen Anne's	124.5	138.8	138.9	142.0	146.0	153.0	152.5	152.5	153.0	187.2	185.2
St. Mary's	364.8	363.0	387.2	394.1	405.5	393.3	388.4	400.6	406.6	404.6	431.0
Somerset	139.0	141.0	126.0	143.0	110.5	125.0	109.5	107.5	97.5	91.8	143.8
Talbot	173.0	174.5	175.5	163.5	183.5	172.0	164.0	146.6	158.0	167.0	164.7
Washington	693.0	689.5	697.0	725.7	674.0	688.5	678.0	693.7	690.0	621.0	615.1
Wicomico	400.1	400.2	402.2	406.9	396.9	393.3	371.4	364.0	366.8	366.3	359.0
Worcester	200.3	200.1	199.7	231.6	222.0	228.5	210.5	203.0	200.0	251.1	247.7

TABLE
36

Staff Employed in all Functions: Prek.-12: Maryland Public Schools: October, 1986

Local Unit	Grand Total	Secretaries and clerks	Noninstructional				Instructional				
			Total	Superintendents, Associates, and Assistant Superintendents	Directors, Coordinators, and Supervisors	Others	Total	Principals, Vice-Principals, Admin. Assts.	Teachers	Guidance, Media, and Psychological Staff	Aides
Total State	72,930.1	4,637.4	17,540.8	98.0	1,604.8	15,838.0	50,751.9	2,295.6	39,530.5	2,678.9	6,246.9
Allegany	1,197.4	61.0	322.4	2.0	30.0	290.4	814.0	32.0	652.0	46.0	84.0
Anne Arundel	6,268.2	477.8	1,138.5	8.0	164.0	966.5	4,651.9	222.0	3,656.7	262.7	510.5
Baltimore City	11,263.2	495.2	2,681.6	11.0	307.3	2,363.3	8,086.4	367.5	6,123.5	315.8	1,279.6
Baltimore	9,456.6	664.7	2,532.7	14.0	219.9	2,298.8	6,259.2	353.3	5,070.8	432.0	403.1
Calvert	861.9	58.0	178.6	3.0	23.0	152.6	625.3	29.0	453.1	33.4	109.8
Caroline	489.5	29.0	116.1	3.0	8.5	104.6	344.4	16.5	262.9	21.0	44.0
Carroll	1,843.4	99.1	386.1	3.0	43.7	339.4	1,358.2	56.5	1,092.6	64.5	144.6
Cecil	1,204.2	75.4	253.0	3.0	23.1	226.9	875.8	39.4	718.0	40.5	77.9
Charles	1,636.7	104.8	327.3	3.0	38.5	285.8	1,204.6	49.0	934.4	72.0	149.2
Dorchester	575.2	47.8	128.1	2.0	12.1	114.0	399.3	19.8	288.3	24.0	67.2
Frederick	2,541.2	157.6	661.9	3.0	73.5	585.4	1,721.7	80.5	1,370.5	76.9	193.8
Garrett	572.3	33.8	107.4	3.0	9.5	94.9	431.1	19.5	288.1	12.0	111.5
Harford	2,822.4	160.0	650.1	2.0	53.0	595.1	2,012.3	95.0	1,585.6	106.7	225.0
Howard	2,989.2	210.5	616.2	3.0	78.6	534.6	2,162.5	85.0	1,606.5	120.0	351.0
Kent	307.7	17.8	86.6	1.0	6.1	79.5	203.3	11.0	152.2	9.8	30.3
Montgomery	11,536.6	812.8	2,864.1	8.0	203.0	2,653.1	7,859.7	307.0	5,952.0	458.5	1,142.2
Prince George's	10,988.7	696.6	3,063.0	13.0	159.1	2,890.9	7,229.1	308.0	5,802.8	361.6	761.7
Queen Anne's	492.2	39.5	109.0	1.0	14.6	93.4	343.7	15.0	272.8	16.1	39.8
St. Mary's	1,252.9	90.5	251.5	1.0	24.0	226.5	910.9	41.6	735.0	49.6	84.7
Somerset	395.3	31.5	91.4	2.0	13.9	75.5	272.4	17.0	216.3	10.1	29.0
Talbot	418.9	24.5	89.3	3.0	9.0	77.3	305.1	16.0	236.7	12.0	40.4
Washington	1,947.5	133.0	496.8	1.0	46.0	449.8	1,317.7	60.0	1,030.0	77.0	150.7
Wicomico	1,226.3	79.5	260.8	3.0	28.5	229.3	886.0	40.0	676.9	27.7	141.4
Worcester	642.6	37.0	128.3	2.0	15.9	110.4	477.3	20.0	352.8	29.0	75.5

TABLE
37

Staff Employed in all Functions: Prek-12: Maryland Public Schools: October, 1986

Local Unit	Grand Total All Instructional Staff	PROFESSIONAL STAFF							
		Total	Principals, Vice-Principals, Admin. Assts.	Teachers	Librarians and other Educational Media Staff	Guidance Counselors	Psycho-logical Staff	Aides	Secretaries and Clerks
Total State	53,676.3	44,505.0	2,295.6	39,530.5	1,033.7	1,371.1	274.1	6,246.9	2,924.4
Allegany	851.0	730.0	32.0	652.0	23.0	19.0	4.0	84.0	37.0
Anne Arundel	4,997.0	4,141.4	222.0	3,656.7	87.7	145.0	30.0	510.5	345.1
Baltimore City	8,387.0	6,806.8	367.5	6,123.5	108.6	153.1	54.1	1,279.6	300.6
Baltimore	6,699.7	5,856.1	353.3	5,070.8	164.5	236.0	31.5	403.1	440.5
Calvert	659.3	515.5	29.0	453.1	11.0	18.4	4.0	109.8	34.0
Caroline	361.4	300.4	16.5	262.9	9.0	10.0	2.0	44.0	17.0
Carroll	1,423.4	1,213.6	56.5	1,092.6	29.4	29.0	6.1	144.6	65.2
Cecil	923.3	797.9	39.4	718.0	17.5	20.0	3.0	77.9	47.5
Charles	1,265.4	1,055.4	49.0	934.4	24.5	39.5	8.0	149.2	60.8
Dorchester	430.1	332.1	19.8	288.3	9.0	12.0	3.0	67.2	30.8
Frederick	1,804.0	1,527.9	80.5	1,370.5	36.7	36.2	4.0	193.8	82.3
Garrett	447.6	319.6	19.5	288.1	2.0	8.0	2.0	111.5	16.5
Harford	2,119.3	1,787.3	95.0	1,585.6	40.2	57.5	9.0	225.0	107.0
Howard	2,315.5	1,811.5	85.0	1,606.5	58.0	46.0	16.0	351.0	153.0
Kent	213.3	173.0	11.0	152.2	3.8	5.0	1.0	30.3	10.0
Montgomery	8,328.8	6,717.5	307.0	5,952.0	176.0	236.5	46.0	1,142.2	469.1
Prince George's	7,672.1	6,467.4	303.0	5,802.8	129.0	202.6	30.0	761.7	443.0
Queen Anne's	364.2	303.9	15.0	272.8	3.7	9.0	3.4	39.8	20.5
St. Mary's	965.4	826.2	41.6	735.0	30.1	18.5	1.0	84.7	54.5
Somerset	290.9	243.4	17.0	216.3	4.0	4.1	2.0	29.0	18.5
Talbot	320.1	264.7	16.0	236.7	5.0	6.0	1.0	40.4	15.0
Washington	1,399.7	1,167.0	60.0	1,030.0	43.0	28.0	6.0	150.7	82.0
Wicomico	939.5	744.6	40.0	676.9	7.0	17.7	3.0	141.4	53.5
Worcester	498.3	401.8	20.0	352.8	11.0	14.0	4.0	75.5	21.0

TABLE
38

Staff Employed in Instructional Function: Prek-6: Maryland Public Schools: October, 1986

Local Unit	Grand Total All Instructional Staff	Total	Principals, Vice-Principals, Admin. Assts.	Teachers	Librarians and other Educational Media Staff	Guidance Counselors	Psycho-logical Staff	Aides	Secretaries and Clerks
				PROFESSIONAL STAFF					
Total State	26,984.2	21,462.1	1,116.8	19,175.6	611.3	301.8	256.6	4,231.5	1,290.6
Allegany	454.2	364.2	17.0	322.2	14.0	7.0	4.0	74.0	16.0
Anne Arundel	2,590.2	2,059.0	108.0	1,833.3	55.7	32.0	30.0	377.0	154.2
Baltimore City	4,677.0	3,651.3	199.5	3,329.5	60.6	8.6	53.1	861.6	164.1
Baltimore	3,057.1	2,622.9	195.7	2,212.3	93.0	90.9	31.0	222.9	211.3
Calvert	347.1	259.8	14.0	232.4	6.0	3.4	4.0	72.8	14.5
Caroline	189.7	153.2	6.5	139.7	5.0	1.0	1.0	31.5	5.0
Carroll	649.8	511.3	25.5	462.3	16.4	1.0	6.1	114.5	24.0
Cecil	456.0	362.1	16.4	332.2	8.5	2.0	3.0	74.9	19.0
Charles	595.5	462.5	20.0	409.0	14.5	11.0	8.0	100.7	32.3
Dorchester	218.8	151.5	7.7	135.8	5.0	0.0	3.0	54.5	12.8
Frederick	872.9	713.1	34.5	651.9	21.7	1.0	4.0	121.8	38.0
Garrett	226.7	149.2	11.5	135.7	0.0	0.0	2.0	70.0	7.5
Harford	1,023.6	804.6	49.0	712.9	24.2	16.5	2.0	183.0	36.0
Howard	1,110.5	808.5	36.0	722.5	32.0	2.0	16.0	240.0	62.0
Kent	88.0	64.0	4.5	57.2	1.3	0.0	1.0	21.0	3.0
Montgomery	4,319.5	3,423.8	154.0	3,052.3	114.5	62.0	41.0	709.3	186.4
Prince George's	3,758.0	3,096.0	122.0	2,812.9	81.0	52.1	28.0	463.0	199.0
Queen Anne's	143.9	118.7	5.0	107.5	0.8	2.0	3.4	19.2	6.0
St. Mary's	487.4	395.2	18.0	355.1	20.1	1.0	1.0	71.7	20.5
Somerset	137.1	99.6	10.0	86.6	1.0	0.0	2.0	26.0	11.5
Talbot	137.0	100.0	5.0	94.0	1.0	0.0	0.0	30.0	7.0
Washington	707.9	551.9	28.0	485.9	29.0	3.0	6.0	126.0	30.0
Wicomico	528.1	385.6	23.0	355.3	1.0	3.3	3.0	118.0	24.5
Worcester	208.2	154.1	6.0	137.1	5.0	2.0	4.0	48.1	6.0

TABLE

39

Staff Employed in Instructional Function: 7-12: Maryland Public Schools: October, 1986

Local Unit	Grand Total All Instructional Staff	PROFESSIONAL STAFF							Secretaries and Clerks
		Total	Principals, Vice-Principals, Admin. Assts.	Teachers	Librarians and other Educational Media Staff	Guidance Counselors	Psycho-logical Staff	Aides	
Total State	26,692.1	23,042.9	1,178.8	20,354.9	422.4	1,069.3	17.5	2,015.4	1,633.8
Allegany	396.8	365.8	15.0	329.8	9.0	12.0	0.0	10.0	21.0
Anne Arundel	2,406.8	2,082.4	114.0	1,823.4	32.0	113.0	0.0	133.5	190.9
Baltimore City	3,710.0	3,155.5	168.0	2,794.0	48.0	144.5	1.0	418.0	136.5
Baltimore	3,642.6	3,233.2	157.6	2,858.5	71.5	145.1	0.5	180.2	229.2
Calvert	312.2	255.7	15.0	220.7	5.0	15.0	0.0	37.0	19.5
Caroline	171.7	147.2	10.0	123.2	4.0	9.0	1.0	12.5	12.0
Carroll	773.6	702.3	31.0	630.3	13.0	28.0	0.0	30.1	41.2
Cecil	467.3	435.8	23.0	385.8	9.0	18.0	0.0	3.0	28.5
Charles	669.9	592.9	29.0	525.4	10.0	28.5	0.0	48.5	28.5
Dorchester	211.3	180.6	12.1	152.5	4.0	12.0	0.0	12.7	18.0
Frederick	931.1	814.8	46.0	718.6	15.0	35.2	0.0	72.0	44.3
Garrett	220.9	170.4	8.0	152.4	2.0	8.0	0.0	41.5	9.0
Harford	1,095.7	982.7	46.0	872.7	16.0	41.0	7.0	42.0	71.0
Howard	1,205.0	1,003.0	49.0	884.0	26.0	44.0	0.0	111.0	91.0
Kent	125.3	109.0	6.5	95.0	2.5	5.0	0.0	9.3	7.0
Montgomery	4,009.3	3,298.7	153.0	2,899.7	61.5	174.5	5.0	432.9	282.7
Prince George's	3,914.1	3,371.4	181.0	2,989.9	48.0	150.5	2.0	298.7	244.0
Queen Anne's	220.3	185.2	10.0	165.3	2.9	7.0	0.0	20.6	14.5
St. Mary's	478.0	431.0	23.6	379.9	10.0	17.5	0.0	13.0	34.0
Somerset	153.8	143.8	7.0	129.7	3.0	4.1	0.0	3.0	7.0
Talbot	183.1	164.7	11.0	142.7	4.0	6.0	1.0	10.4	8.0
Washington	691.8	615.1	32.0	544.1	14.0	25.0	0.0	24.7	52.0
Wicomico	411.4	359.0	17.0	321.6	6.0	14.4	0.0	23.4	29.0
Worcester	290.1	247.7	14.0	215.7	6.0	12.0	0.0	27.4	15.0

TABLE
40

Staff Employed in Noninstructional Function: Maryland Public Schools: October, 1986

		Administration			Pupil Personnel		Health Services	
Local Unit	Total	Superin-tendents. Assoc., and Assistant Superin-tendents	Directors and Supervisors	Other Staff	Directors and Supervisors	Other	Director and Supervisors	Other
Total State	19,253.8	98.0	1,186.0	725.4	231.9	4.0	6.5	136.5
Allegany	346.4	2.0	21.0	8.0	4.0	-	-	-
Anne Arundel	1,271.2	8.0	113.7	50.0	37.0	-	-	-
Baltimore City	2,876.2	11.0	270.3	148.4	25.0	1.0	-	-
Baltimore	2,756.9	14.0	154.8	59.9	34.0	-	1.0	51.5
Calvert	202.6	3.0	15.3	2.0	5.0	-	-	-
Caroline	128.1	3.0	5.0	1.0	1.0	-	-	-
Carroll	420.0	3.0	33.4	19.1	5.3	-	-	8.0
Cecil	280.9	3.0	18.1	7.0	3.0	-	-	3.0
Charles	371.3	3.0	23.8	12.0	7.0	1.0	-	-
Dorchester	145.1	2.0	8.7	1.0	1.5	-	-	2.0
Frederick	737.2	3.0	58.0	2.0	4.0	-	0.5	-
Garrett	124.7	3.0	5.5	1.0	2.0	-	-	-
Harford	703.1	2.0	37.0	14.0	8.0	-	-	38.0
Howard	673.7	3.0	47.5	31.3	5.0	2.0	3.0	2.0
Kent	94.4	1.0	5.3	3.1	0.3	-	-	1.0
Montgomery	3,207.8	8.0	154.0	248.0	24.0	-	-	-
Prince George's	3,316.6	13.0	103.1	78.0	47.0	-	2.0	5.0
Queen Anne's	128.0	1.0	9.8	2.0	2.8	-	-	5.0
St. Mary's	287.5	1.0	17.0	2.0	4.0	-	-	-
Somerset	104.4	2.0	11.3	-	2.0	-	-	2.0
Talbot	98.8	3.0	6.0	1.0	1.0	-	-	-
Washington	547.8	1.0	37.0	27.0	5.0	-	-	-
Wicomico	286.8	3.0	18.3	7.0	3.0	-	-	13.0
Worcester	144.3	2.0	12.1	0.6	1.0	-	-	6.0

TABLE

40

Staff Employed in Noninstructional Function: Maryland Public Schools: October, 1986

Local Unit	Food Services		Operation of Plant		Maintenance of Plant		Pupil Transportation		Secretaries and Clerks
	Directors and Supervisors	Other	Directors and Supervisors	Other	Directors and Supervisors	Other	Directors and Supervisors	Other	
Total State	28.9	3,326.1	51.0	7,181.3	41.1	1,654.2	59.4	2,810.5	1,713.0
Allegany	1.0	99.7	1.0	134.0	1.0	20.0	2.0	28.7	24.0
Anne Arundel	-	-	3.3	677.7	3.0	130.0	7.0	108.8	132.7
Baltimore City	5.0	728.0	3.0	1,166.9	1.0	204.0	3.0	115.0	194.6
Baltimore	4.0	6.0	8.0	1,377.3	9.1	241.9	9.0	562.2	224.2
Calvert	0.2	41.4	0.5	76.9	0.5	26.1	1.5	6.2	24.0
Caroline	1.0	50.4	0.5	41.4	-	4.0	1.0	7.8	12.0
Carroll	1.0	101.4	1.0	146.8	1.0	41.0	2.0	23.1	33.9
Cecil	-	70.1	-	103.0	-	33.6	2.0	10.2	27.9
Charles	2.0	78.8	1.4	167.2	1.5	22.0	2.8	4.8	44.0
Dorchester	-	51.5	-	45.0	1.0	6.5	0.9	8.0	17.0
Frederick	-	177.7	3.0	239.0	4.0	40.0	4.0	126.7	75.3
Garrett	-	44.0	-	39.3	1.0	9.6	1.0	1.0	17.3
Harford	2.0	190.7	2.0	227.5	-	63.0	4.0	61.9	53.0
Howard	3.3	203.0	11.3	227.0	5.2	66.3	3.3	3.0	57.5
Kent	-	35.9	-	24.0	-	9.5	0.5	6.0	7.8
Montgomery	6.0	413.5	8.0	895.6	5.0	335.0	6.0	761.0	343.7
Prince George's	1.0	620.1	3.0	1,040.6	2.0	284.0	1.0	863.2	253.6
Queen Anne's	-	29.8	-	39.7	1.8	6.5	0.2	10.4	19.0
St. Mary's	-	69.6	0.5	106.9	0.5	39.0	2.0	12.0	36.0
Somerset	-	34.5	-	30.5	-	6.0	0.6	2.5	13.0
Talbot	-	32.3	-	39.0	1.0	5.0	1.0	-	9.5
Washington	1.0	110.8	1.0	190.0	-	33.0	2.0	89.0	51.0
Wicomico	0.4	90.2	3.0	99.9	2.0	18.2	1.8	1.0	26.0
Worcester	1.0	46.7	0.5	46.1	0.5	10.0	0.8	1.0	16.0

TABLE
41

Number and Percent of Staff by Race and Sex: Maryland Public Schools: OCTOBER, 1986
Total Professional Staff

Local Unit	Grand Total	White				Black				Other (AM.IND, ASIAN, HISPANIC)			
		Total				Total				Total			
		No.	%	Male	Female	No.	%	Male	Female	No.	%	Male	Female
Total State	47,110	36,398	77.3	11,678	24,720	10,210	21.7	2,062	8,148	502	1.1	124	378
Allegany	762	759	99.6	314	445	2	0.3	1	1	1	0.1	0	1
Anne Arundel	4,381	3,747	85.5	1,125	2,622	608	13.9	125	483	26	0.6	7	19
Baltimore City	7,207	2,261	31.4	798	1,463	4,883	67.8	888	3,995	63	0.9	20	43
Baltimore	6,230	5,712	91.7	2,020	3,692	465	7.5	116	349	53	0.9	12	41
Calvert	542	416	76.8	141	275	125	23.1	28	97	1	0.2	0	1
Caroline	312	261	83.7	83	178	51	16.3	13	38	0	0.0	0	0
Carroll	1,290	1,259	97.6	393	866	27	2.1	8	19	4	0.3	2	2
Cecil	838	807	96.3	264	543	29	3.5	10	19	2	0.2	1	1
Charles	1,106	837	75.7	244	593	262	23.7	47	215	7	0.6	3	4
Dorchester	350	275	78.6	85	190	73	20.9	20	53	2	0.6	0	2
Frederick	1,648	1,568	95.1	484	1,084	68	4.1	17	51	12	0.7	6	6
Garrett	339	338	99.7	123	215	0	0.0	0	0	1	0.3	0	1
Harford	1,877	1,741	92.8	606	1,135	128	6.8	21	107	8	0.4	4	4
Howard	1,911	1,627	85.1	506	1,121	261	13.7	67	194	23	1.2	5	18
Kent	183	148	80.9	50	98	35	19.1	11	24	0	0.0	0	0
Montgomery	7,226	6,274	86.8	1,835	4,439	742	10.3	171	571	210	2.9	49	161
Prince George's	6,753	4,757	70.4	1,423	3,334	1,933	28.6	398	1,535	63	0.9	9	54
Queen Anne's	322	272	84.5	93	179	49	15.2	14	35	1	0.7	0	1
St. Mary's	871	746	85.6	206	540	111	12.7	25	86	14	1.6	2	12
Somerset	258	175	67.8	56	119	81	31.4	17	64	2	0.8	0	2
Talbot	277	225	81.2	75	150	52	18.8	13	39	0	0.0	0	0
Washington	1,223	1,198	98.0	429	769	19	1.6	6	13	6	0.5	4	2
Wicomico	781	652	83.5	208	444	128	16.4	28	100	1	0.1	0	1
Worcester	423	343	81.1	117	226	78	18.4	18	60	2	0.5	0	2

TABLE
41

Number and Percent of Staff by Race and Sex: Maryland Public Schools: OCTOBER, 1986

Teachers

Total

Local Unit	Grand Total	White				Black				Other (AM.IND, ASIAN, HISPANIC)			
		Total No.	%	Male	Female	Total No.	%	Male	Female	Total No.	%	Male	Female
Total State	39,449	30,376	77.0	8,884	21,492	8,641	21.9	1,588	7,053	432	1.1	103	329
Allegany	644	642	99.7	243	399	1	0.2	1	0	1	0.2	0	1
Anne Arundel	3,621	3,089	85.3	819	2,270	513	14.2	87	426	19	0.5	5	14
Baltimore City	6,139	1,832	29.8	605	1,227	4,252	69.3	721	3,531	55	0.9	18	37
Baltimore	5,068	4,638	91.5	1,549	3,089	386	7.6	93	293	44	0.9	11	33
Calvert	442	337	76.2	102	235	104	23.5	18	86	1	0.2	0	1
Caroline	257	214	83.3	60	154	43	16.7	9	34	0	0.0	0	0
Carroll	1,092	1,066	97.6	301	765	23	2.1	7	16	3	0.3	2	1
Cecil	722	698	96.4	202	494	25	3.5	8	17	1	0.1	0	1
Charles ·	921	699	75.9	184	515	217	23.6	34	183	5	0.5	2	3
Dorchester	289	227	78.5	61	166	60	20.8	15	45	2	0.7	0	2
Frederick	1,391	1,329	95.5	388	981	55	4.0	13	42	7	0.5	3	4
Garrett	287	286	99.7	88	198	0	0.0	0	0	1	0.3	0	1
Harford	1,588	1,480	93.2	463	1,017	101	6.4	14	87	7	0.4	4	3
Howard	1,577	1,358	86.1	375	983	196	12.4	40	156	23	1.5	5	18
Kent	148	120	81.1	36	84	28	18.9	7	21	0	0.0	0	0
Montgomery	6,052	5,314	87.8	1,439	3,875	558	9.2	120	438	180	3.0	8	142
Prince George's	5,731	4,039	70.5	1,101	2,938	1,633	28.5	314	1,319	59	1.0	9	50
Queen Anne's	265	222	83.8	68	154	42	15.8	10	32	1	0.4	0	1
St. Mary's	732	620	84.7	166	454	98	13.4	20	78	14	1.9	2	12
Somerset	210	138	65.7	35	103	70	33.3	13	57	2	1.0	0	2
Talbot	232	188	81.0	52	136	44	19.0	9	35	0	0.0	0	0
Washington	1,019	997	97.8	321	676	17	1.7	6	11	5	0.5	4	1
Wicomico	673	566	84.1	159	407	106	15.8	18	88	1	0.1	0	1
Worcester	349	279	79.9	87	192	69	19.8	11	58	1	0.3	0	1

TABLE 41

Number and Percent of Staff by Race and Sex: Maryland Public Schools: OCTOBER, 1986

Principals

Total

Local Unit	Grand Total	White				Black				Other (AM.IND, ASIAN, HISPANIC)			
		Total No.	%	Male	Female	Total No.	%	Male	Female	Total No.	%	Male	Female
Total State	1,206	912	75.6	625	287	288	23.9	113	175	6	0.5	3	3
Allegany	22	22	100.0	15	7	0	0.0	0	0	0	0.0	0	0
Anne Arundel	113	93	82.3	63	30	18	15.9			2	1.8	1	
Baltimore City	180	46	25.6	26	20	134	3.	3		1	0.6	1	
Baltimore	147	136	92.5	86	50		6.			1	0.7	0	
Calvert	14	11	78.6	10	1		21.			0	0.0	0	
Caroline	11	9	81.8	8	1	2	18.2	2	0	0	0.0	0	0
Carroll	30	29	96.7	23		1	3.3	1		0	0.0	0	0
Cecil	26	22	84.6	20						0	0.0	0	
Charles	27	20	74.1	15		1				0	3.7	1	0
Dorchester	12	7	58.3	4						0	0.0		
Frederick	40	39	97.5	24	15	1	2.5	1	0	0	0.0	0	0
Garrett	17	17	100.0	12	5	0	0.0	0	0	0	0.0	0	0
Harford	42	39	92.9	35	4		7.1	2		0	0.0		
Howard	46	37	80.4	30	7		19.6	4		0	0.0		
Kent	7	5	71.4	4	1		28.6	2		0	0.0		
Montgomery	162	133	82.1	82	51	28	17.3	12	16	1	0.6	0	1
Prince George's	181	133	73.5	90	43	48	26.5	22	26	0	0.0	0	0
Queen Anne's	7	5	71.4	5	0	2	28.6	2	0	0	0.0	0	
St. Mary's	25	22	88.0	12	10	3	12.0	0	3	0	0.0	0	
Somerset	12	9	75.0	5	4	3	25.0	1	2	0	0.0	0	
Talbot	10	9	90.0	7	2	1	10.0	1	0	0	0.0	0	0
Washington	41	41	100.0	3	1			0		0	0.0	0	0
Wicomico	21							3					
Worcester	13					1		2					

TABLE
42

TOTAL CERTIFIED PROFESSIONAL STAFF AT SCHOOL LEVEL
BY PREPARATION
MARYLAND PUBLIC SCHOOLS: OCTOBER, 1986

LOCAL UNIT	TOTAL	DOCTOR'S DEGREE		MASTER'S DEGREE PLUS 30 HOURS		MASTER'S DEGREE		BACH.'S DEGREE PLUS 30 HOURS		BACHELOR'S DEGREE		2 - 3 YEARS COLLEGE		LESS THAN 2 YRS COLLEGE	
		NUMBER	PCT.	NUMBER	PCT.	NUMBER	PCT.	NUMBER	PCT.	NUMBER	PCT.	NUMBER	PCT.	NUMBER	PCT.
TOTAL STATE	44,559	495	1.1	7,892	17.7	12,554	28.2	15,252	34.2	8,068	18.1	144	0.3	154	0.3
ALLEGANY	726	2	0.3	49	6.7	357	49.2	235	32.4	81	11.2	1	0.1	1	0.1
ANNE ARUNDEL	4,159	34	0.8	365	8.8	1,590	38.2	1,523	36.6	623	15.0	8	0.2	16	0.4
BALTIMORE CITY	6,705	43	0.6	1,443	21.5	1,342	20.0	2,709	40.4	1,056	15.7	22	0.3	90	1.3
BALTIMORE	5,938	58	1.0	2,030	34.2	1,167	19.7	2,139	36.0	542	9.1	2	0.0	0	0.0
CALVERT	503	6	1.2	12	2.4	173	34.4	180	35.8	128	25.4	0	0.0	4	0.8
CAROLINE	297	2	0.7	9	3.0	74	24.9	106	35.7	103	34.7	1	0.3	2	0.7
CARROLL	1,230	7	0.6	129	10.5	321	26.1	507	41.2	253	20.8	0	0.0	13	1.1
CECIL	796	2	0.3	68	8.5	214	26.9	256	32.2	249	31.3	6	0.8	1	0.1
CHARLES	1,048	5	0.5	8	0.8	472	45.0	261	24.9	296	28.2	2	0.2	4	0.4
DORCHESTER	330	6	1.8	50	15.2	106	32.1	112	33.9	50	15.2	3	0.9	3	0.9
FREDERICK	1,563	12	0.8	179	11.5	415	26.6	501	32.1	444	28.4	11	0.7	1	0.1
GARRETT	292	0	0.0	24	8.2	123	42.1	72	24.7	72	24.7	1	0.3	0	0.0
HARFORD	1,812	11	0.6	335	18.5	705	38.9	420	23.2	332	18.3	9	0.5	4	0.2
HOWARD	1,763	20	1.1	205	11.6	653	37.0	338	19.2	537	30.5	6	0.3	0	0.0
KENT	172	1	0.6	12	7.0	49	28.5	0	0.0	109	63.4	1	0.6	0	0.0
MONTGOMERY	6,868	165	2.4	1,994	29.0	1,293	18.8	2,443	35.6	957	13.9	15	0.2	1	0.0
PRINCE GEORGE'S	6,454	99	1.5	773	12.0	2,194	34.0	2,391	37.0	970	15.0	27	0.4	0	0.0
QUEEN ANNE'S	298	2	0.7	7	2.3	105	35.2	102	34.2	81	27.2	1	0.3	0	0.0
ST. MARY'S	805	9	1.1	32	4.0	244	30.3	0	0.0	515	64.0	5	0.6	0	0.0
SOMERSET	234	1	0.4	5	2.1	53	22.6	96	41.0	78	33.3	1	0.4	0	0.0
TALBOT	262	0	0.0	3	1.1	40	15.3	39	14.9	178	67.9	1	0.4	1	0.4
WASHINGTON	1,166	8	0.7	90	7.7	455	39.0	440	37.7	163	14.0	10	0.9	0	0.0
WICOMICO	742	1	0.1	50	6.7	246	33.2	282	38.0	146	19.7	5	0.7	12	1.6
WORCESTER	396	1	0.3	20	5.1	163	41.2	100	25.3	105	26.5	6	1.5	1	0.3

TABLE
43

TOTAL CERTIFIED PROFESSIONAL STAFF AT ELEMENTARY SCHOOL LEVEL
BY PREPARATION
MARYLAND PUBLIC SCHOOLS: OCTOBER, 1986

LOCAL UNIT	TOTAL	DOCTOR'S DEGREE		MASTER'S DEGREE PLUS 30 HOURS		MASTER'S DEGREE		BACH.'S DEGREE PLUS 30 HOURS		BACHELOR'S DEGREE		2 - 3 YEARS COLLEGE		LESS THAN 2 YRS COLLEGE	
		NUMBER	PCT.	NUMBER	PCT.	NUMBER	PCT.	NUMBER	PCT.	NUMBER	PCT.	NUMBER	PCT.	NUMBER	PCT.
TOTAL STATE	20,085	185	0.9	3,021	15.0	5,695	28.4	7,078	35.2	4,093	20.4	6	0.0	7	0.0
ALLEGANY	285	0	0.0	13	4.9	136	51.3	90	34.0	26	9.8	0	0.0	0	0.0
ANNE ARUNDEL		14	0.7	129	6.7	751	38.9	708	36.7	327	16.9	2	0.1	0	0.0
BALTIMORE CITY		21	0.7	588	18.5	614	19.4	1,366	43.2	574	18.1	2	0.1	0	0.0
BALTIMORE		25	1.0	690	28.9	513	21.5	870	36.5	286	12.0	0	0.0	0	0.0
CALVERT		3	1.3	3	1.3	71	31.6	88	39.1	58	25.8	0	0.0		0.9
CAROLINE	151	1	0.7	4	2.6	39	25.8	55	36.4	51	33.8	0	0.0	1	0.7
CARROLL			0.2	41	8.1	140	27.7	219		105	20.8	0	0.0	0	0.0
CECIL			0.0	16	4.4	96	26.4	125		125	34.4		0.0		0.3
CHARLES			0.7	1	0.2	195	46.1	01		123	29.1		0.0		0.0
DORCHESTER			2.9	17	12.3	45	32.6	45		26	18.8		0.0		0.7
FREDERICK	726	3	0.4	82	11.3	203	28.0	229	31.5	209	28.8	0	0.0	0	0.0
GARRETT	143	0	0.0	14	9.8	60	42.0	32	22.4	37	25.9		0.0		0.0
HARFORD	789		0.3	116	14.7	329	41.7	210	26.6	132	16.7		0.0		0.0
HOWARD	724		0.4	85	11.7	255	35.2	126	17.4	255	35.2		0.0		0.0
KENT	64		0.0	5	7.8	16	25.0	0	0.0	43	67.2		0.0		0.0
MONTGOMERY	3,285	64	1.9	837	25.5	649	19.8	1,161	35.3	573	17.4	0	0.0	1	0.0
PRINCE GEORGE'S	3,	29	0.9	308	9.9	996	32.2	1,183	38.2	578	18.7	0	0.1	0	0.0
QUEEN ANNE'S		0	0.0	3	2.7	35	31.5	45	40.5	28	25.2		0.0		
ST. MARY'S		2	0.5	14	3.6	127	32.6	0	0.0	246	63.2		0.0		.
SOMERSET		1	1.6	1	1.6	14	22.6	33	53.2	13	21.0		0.0		.
TALBOT		0	0.0	0	0.0	13	13.3	13	13.3	72	73.5	0	0.0	0	0.0
WASHINGTON			1.0	31		215	41.9	191	37.2	68	13.3				
WICOMICO			0.	21		126	32.7	156	40.5	82	21.3				.
WORCESTER			0.	4	.	57	38.0	32	21.3	56	37.3				.

TABLE

44

TOTAL CERTIFIED PROFESSIONAL STAFF AT SECONDARY SCHOOL LEVEL
BY PREPARATION
MARYLAND PUBLIC SCHOOLS: OCTOBER, 1986

LOCAL UNIT	TOTAL	DOCTOR'S DEGREE		MASTER'S DEGREE PLUS 30 HOURS		MASTER'S DEGREE		BACH.'S DEGREE PLUS 30 HOURS		BACHELOR'S DEGREE		2 - 3 YEARS COLLEGE		LESS THAN 2 YRS COLLEGE	
		NUMBER	PCT.	NUMBER	PCT.	NUMBER	PCT.	NUMBER	PCT.	NUMBER	PCT.	NUMBER	PCT.	NUMBER	PCT.
OTAL STATE	16,151	228	1.4	3,501	21.7	4,326	26.8	5,436	33.7	2,381	14.7	133	0.8	146	0.9
LLEGANY	243	2	0.8	17	7.0	110	45.3	83	34.2	29	11.9	1	0.4	1	0.4
NNE ARUNDEL	1,564	16	1.0	184	11.8	581	37.1	577	36.9	184	11.8	6	0.4	16	1.0
ALTIMORE CITY	2,524	14	0.6	625	24.8	520	20.6	956	37.9	302	12.0	19	0.8	88	3.5
ALTIMORE	2,063	22	1.1	830	40.2	321	15.6	739	35.8	150	7.3	1	0.0	0	0.0
ALVERT	146	1	0.7	4	2.7	52	35.6	46	31.5	41	28.1	0	0.0	2	1.4
AROLINE	94	1	1.1	4	4.3	17	18.1	34	36.2	37	39.4	0	0.0	1	1.1
ARROLL	407	3	0.7	54	13.3	107	26.3	148	36.4	82	20.1	0	0.0	13	3.2
ECIL	304	2	0.7	34	11.2	74	24.3	98	32.2	90	29.6	6	2.0	0	0.0
HARLES	359	2	0.6	3	0.8	166	46.2	90	25.1	92	25.6	2	0.6	4	1.1
ORCHESTER	113	1	0.9	21	18.6	33	29.2	41	36.3	12	10.6	3	2.7	2	1.8
REDERICK	488	6	1.2	59	12.1	142	29.1	145	29.7	124	25.4	11	2.3	1	0.2
ARRETT	84	0	0.0	5	6.0	33	39.3	22	26.2	23	27.4	1	1.2	0	0.0
ARFORD	633	7	1.1	137	21.6	228	36.0	119	18.8	133	21.0	9	1.4	0	0.0
OWARD	575	11	1.9	73	12.7	214	37.2	112	19.5	156	27.1	5	0.9	4	0.7
ENT	54	0	0.0	1	1.9	19	35.2	0	0.0	33	61.1	1	1.9	0	0.0
ONTGOMERY	3,158	89	2.8	1,044	33.1	545	17.3	1,162	36.8	303	9.6	15	0.5	0	0.0
RINCE GEORGE'S	2,067	47	2.3	320	15.5	739	35.8	743	35.9	193	9.3	25	1.2	0	0.0
UEEN ANNE'S	96	0	0.0	2	2.1	38	39.6	21	21.9	34	35.4	1	1.0	0	0.0
T. MARY'S	235	3	1.3	15	6.4	63	26.8	0	0.0	149	63.4	5	2.1	0	0.0
OMERSET	91	0	0.0	1	1.1	21	23.1	36	39.8	33	36.3	0	0.0	0	0.0
ALBOT	89	0	0.0	3	3.4	18	20.2	8	9.0	58	65.2	1	1.1	1	1.1
ASHINGTON	363	0	0.0	36	9.9	139	38.3	130	35.8	48	13.2	10	2.8	0	0.0
ICOMICO	263	1	0.4	23	8.7	82	31.2	91	34.6	49	18.6	5	1.9	12	4.6
ORCESTER	138	0	0.0	6	4.3	64	46.4	35	25.4	26	18.8	6	4.3	1	0.7

TABLE 45

TOTAL CERTIFIED PROFESSIONAL STAFF AT MIDDLE AND COMBINED SCHOOL LEVEL
BY PREPARATION
MARYLAND PUBLIC SCHOOLS: OCTOBER, 1986

LOCAL UNIT	TOTAL	DOCTOR'S DEGREE		MASTER'S DEGREE PLUS 30 HOURS		MASTER'S DEGREE		BACH.'S DEGREE PLUS 30 HOURS		BACHELOR'S DEGREE		2 - 3 YEARS COLLEGE		LESS THAN 2 YRS COLLEGE	
		NUMBER	PCT.	NUMBER	PCT.	NUMBER	PCT.	NUMBER	PCT.	NUMBER	PCT.	NUMBER	PCT.	NUMBER	PCT.
TOTAL STATE	8,323	82	1.0	1,370	16.5	2,533	30.4	2,738	32.9	1,594	19.2	5	0.1	1	0.0
ALLEGANY	218	0	0.0	19	8.7	111	50.9	62	28.4	26	11.9	0	0.0	0	0.0
ANNE ARUNDEL		4	0.6	52	7.8	258	38.9	238	35.8	112	16.9	0	0.0	0	0.0
BALTIMORE CITY	1,	8	0.8	232	22.8	208	20.5	387	38.1	180	17.7		0.1		0.1
BALTIMORE	1,	11	0.7	510	34.2	333	22.3	530	35.5	106	7.1		0.1		0.0
CALVERT		2	1.5	5	3.8	50	37.9	46	34.8	29	22.0		0.0		0.0
CAROLINE	52	0	0.0	1	1.9	18	34.6	17	32.7	15	28.8	1	1.9	0	0.0
CARROLL	3??		0.9	34	10.7	74	23.3	140	44.2	66	20.8	0	0.0	0	0.0
CECIL	2		0.0	18	14.0	44	34.1	33	25.6	34	26.4	0	0.0	0	0.0
CHARLES			0.0	4	1.5	111	41.7	70	26.3	81	30.5	0	0.0	0	0.0
DORCHESTER			1.3	12	15.2	28	35.4	26	32.9	12	15.2	0	0.0	0	0.0
FREDERICK	348	3	0.9	38	10.9	70	20.1	127	36.4	111	31.8	0	0.0	0	0.0
GARRETT			0.0	5	7.7	30	46.2	18	27.7	12	18.5	0	0.0	0	0.0
HARFORD	2		0.5	82	21.0	148	37.9	91	23.3	67	17.2		0.0		0.0
HOWARD	4		1.3	47	10.1	184	39.7	100	21.6	128	27.2		0.2		0.0
KENT			1.9	6	11.1	14	25.9	0	0.0	33	61.1		0.0		0.0
MONTGOMERY	425	12	2.8	113	26.6	99	23.3	120	28.2	81	19.1	0	0.0	0	0.0
PRINCE GEORGE'S	1,291	23	1.8	145	11.2	459	35.6	465	36.0	199	15.4	0	0.0	0	0.0
QUEEN ANNE'S		2	2.2	2	2.2	32	35.2	36	39.6	19	20.9		0.0		
ST. MARY'S	1	4	2.2	3	1.7	54	29.8	0	0.0	120	66.3		0.0		
SOMERSET	-	0	0.0	3	3.7	18	22.2	27	33.3	32	39.5		1.2		
TALBOT	75	0	0.0	0	0.0	9	12.0	18	24.0	48	64.0	0	0.0	0	0.0
WASHINGTON	290	0	0.0	23	7.9	101	34.8	119	41.0	47	16.2	0	0.0	0	0.0
WICOMICO	94	0	0.0	6	6.4	38	40.4	35	37.2	15	16.0		0.0		
WORCESTER	108	0	0.0	10	9.3	42	38.9	33	30.6	23	21.3		.		.

TABLE
46

TOTAL NEW CERTIFIED PROFESSIONAL STAFF AT SCHOOL LEVEL
BY PREPARATION
MARYLAND PUBLIC SCHOOLS: OCTOBER, 1986

OCAL UNIT	TOTAL	DOCTOR'S DEGREE		MASTER'S DEGREE PLUS 30 HOURS		MASTER'S DEGREE		BACH.'S DEGREE PLUS 30 HOURS		BACHELOR'S DEGREE		2 - 3 YEARS COLLEGE		LESS THAN 2 YRS COLLEGE	
		NUMBER	PCT.	NUMBER	PCT.	NUMBER	PCT.	NUMBER	PCT.	NUMBER	PCT.	NUMBER	PCT.	NUMBER	PCT.
AL STATE	2,420	23	1.0	78	3.2	556	23.0	105	4.3	1,642	67.9	5	0.2	11	0.5
EGANY	12	0	0.0	0	0.0	4	33.3	0	0.0	8	66.7	0	0.0	0	0.0
E ARUNDEL	234	3	1.3	4	1.7	63	26.9	18	7.7	141	60.3	0	0.0	5	2.1
TIMORE CITY	252	2	0.8	11	4.4	47	18.7	18	7.1	172	68.3	0	0.0	2	0.8
TIMORE	319	3	0.9	31	9.7	108	33.9	23	7.2	154	48.3	0	0.0	0	0.0
VERT	33	0	0.0	0	0.0	11	33.3	2	6.1	19	57.6	0	0.0	1	3.0
OLINE	23	1	4.3	0	0.0	3	13.0	4	17.4	14	60.9	0	0.0	1	4.3
ROLL	87	1	1.1	2	2.3	16	18.4	6	6.9	62	71.3	0	0.0	0	0.0
IL	46	0	0.0	0	0.0	7	15.2	1	2.2	38	82.6	0	0.0	0	0.0
LES	110	0	0.0	0	0.0	24	21.8	7	6.4	79	71.8	0	0.0	0	0.0
HESTER	13	0	0.0	1	7.7	0	0.0	0	0.0	11	84.6	0	0.0	1	7.7
DERICK	185	2	1.1	4	2.2	29	15.7	5	2.7	145	78.4	0	0.0	0	0.0
RETT	10	0	0.0	1	10.0	1	10.0	0	0.0	8	80.0	0	0.0	0	0.0
FORD	158	0	0.0	2	1.3	34	21.5	6	3.8	116	73.4	0	0.0	0	0.0
ARD	199	5	2.5	4	2.0	38	19.1	6	3.0	146	73.4	0	0.0	0	0.0
T	13	0	0.0	0	0.0	3	23.1	0	0.0	10	76.9	0	0.0	0	0.0
TGOMERY	463	8	1.7	48	10.4	143	30.9	42	9.1	222	47.9	0	0.0	0	0.0
NCE GEORGE'S	401	3	0.7	0	0.0	114	28.4	2	0.5	277	69.1	5	1.2	0	0.0
EN ANNE'S	22	0	0.0	0	0.0	3	13.6	1	4.5	18	81.8	0	0.0	0	0.0
MARY'S	78	1	1.3	0	0.0	15	19.2	0	0.0	62	79.5	0	0.0	0	0.0
RSET	17	0	0.0	0	0.0	5	29.4	0	0.0	12	70.6	0	0.0	0	0.0
BOT	15	0	0.0	0	0.0	3	20.0	1	6.7	11	73.3	0	0.0	0	0.0
HINGTON	40	0	0.0	1	2.5	8	20.0	6	15.0	24	60.0	1	2.5	0	0.0
OMICO	48	0	0.0	0	0.0	12	25.0	2	4.2	33	68.8	0	0.0	1	2.1
CESTER	20	0	0.0	0	0.0	7	35.0	3	15.0	10	50.0	0	0.0	0	0.0
TRANSFERS	378	6	1.6	31	8.2	142	37.6	48	12.7	150	39.7	1	0.3	0	0.0

Note: Transfers Between Units are Included in Individual Local Unit Totals, but Excluded from State Totals.

TABLE 47

TOTAL NEW CERTIFIED PROFESSIONAL STAFF AT ELEMENTARY SCHOOL LEVEL
BY PREPARATION
MARYLAND PUBLIC SCHOOLS: OCTOBER, 1986

LOCAL UNIT	TOTAL	DOCTOR'S DEGREE NUMBER	PCT.	MASTER'S DEGREE PLUS 30 HOURS NUMBER	PCT.	MASTER'S DEGREE NUMBER	PCT.	BACH.'S DEGREE PLUS 30 HOURS NUMBER	PCT.	BACHELOR'S DEGREE NUMBER	PCT.	2 - 3 YEARS COLLEGE NUMBER	PCT.	LESS THAN 2 YRS COLLEGE NUMBER	PCT.
TOTAL STATE	1,376	5	0.4	38	2.8	279	20.3	53	3.9	999	72.6	1	0.1	1	0.1
ALLEGANY	4	0	0.0	0	0.0	0	0.0	0	0.0	4	100.0	0	0.0	0	0.0
ANNE ARUNDEL	13	0	0.8	3	2.3	35	26.5	7	5.3	86	65.2	0	0.0	0	0.0
BALTIMORE CITY	1		0.7	5	3.4	27	18.5	8	5.5	105	71.9		0.0		0.0
BALTIMORE			1.1	13	7.1	52	28.6	14	7.7	101	55.5		0.0		0.0
CALVERT			0.0	0	0.0	3	20.0	1	6.7	11	73.3		0.0		0.0
CAROLINE	12	0	0.0	0	0.0	3	25.0	2	16.7	7	58.3	0	0.0	0	0.0
CARROLL	44	0	0.0		0.0	6	13.6	2	4.5	36	81.8	0	0.0	0	0.0
CECIL	21	0	0.0		0.0	5	23.8	0	0.0	16	76.2	0	0.0	0	0.0
CHARLES	56	0	0.0		0.0	12	21.4	5	8.9	39	69.6	0	0.0	0	0.0
DORCHESTER	8	0	0.0		0.0	0	0.0	0	0.0	7	87.5	0	0.0	1	12.5
FREDERICK	88	0	0.0	2	2.3	13	14.8	1	1.1	72	81.8	0	0.0	0	0.0
GARRETT	5	0	0.0	0	0.0	0	0.0	0	0.0	5	100.0	0	0.0	0	0.0
HARFORD	65	0	0.0		1.5	13	20.0		4.6	48	73.8	0	0.0	0	0.0
HOWARD	98	0	0.0		2.0	17	17.3		3.1	76	77.6	0	0.0	0	0.0
KENT	9	0	0.0		0.0	2	22.2		0.0	7	77.8	0	0.0	0	0.0
MONTGOMERY	297	5	1.7	25	8.4	84	28.3	20	6.7	163	54.9	0	0.0	0	0.0
PRINCE GEORGE'S	2	0	0.0	0	0.0	62	23.4	2	0.8	200	75.5		0.4		0.0
QUEEN ANNE'S			0.0	0	0.0	1	9.1	0	0.0	10	90.9		0.0		0.0
ST. MARY'S			0.0	0	0.0	6	13.3	0	0.0	39	86.7		0.0		0.0
SOMERSET			0.0	0	0.0	0	0.0	0	0.0	4	100.0		0.0		0.0
TALBOT	10	0	0.0	0	0.0	2	20.0	0	0.0	8	80.0	0	0.0	0	0.0
WASHINGTON	15	0	0.0	1	6.7	4	26.7	1		8		0	0.0	0	0.0
WICOMICO	29	0	0.0	0	0.0	5	17.2	1		2					
WORCESTER	11	0	0.0	0	0.0	1	9.1	2	1						
LEA TRANSFERS	196	4	2.0	14	7.1	74	37.8	19	9.7	85	43.4	0	0.0	0	0.0

TABLE
48

TOTAL NEW CERTIFIED PROFESSIONAL STAFF AT SECONDARY SCHOOL LEVEL
BY PREPARATION
MARYLAND PUBLIC SCHOOLS: OCTOBER, 1986

)CAL UNIT	TOTAL	DOCTOR'S DEGREE NUMBER	PCT.	MASTER'S DEGREE PLUS 30 HOURS NUMBER	PCT.	MASTER'S DEGREE NUMBER	PCT.	BACH.'S DEGREE PLUS 30 HOURS NUMBER	PCT.	BACHELOR'S DEGREE NUMBER	PCT.	2 - 3 YEARS COLLEGE NUMBER	PCT.	LESS THAN 2 YRS COLLEGE NUMBER	PCT.
L STATE	609	16	2.6	27	4.4	155	25.5	31	5.1	366	60.1	4	0.7	10	1.6
GANY	3	0	0.0	0	0.0	3	100.0	0	0.0	0	0.0	0	0.0	0	0.0
ARUNDEL	70	1	1.4	1	1.4	19	27.1	9	12.9	35	50.0	0	0.0	5	7.1
IMORE CITY	65	0	0.0	4	6.2	10	15.4	6	9.2	43	66.2	0	0.0	2	3.1
IMORE	66	1	1.5	12	18.2	24	36.4	2	3.0	27	40.9	0	0.0	0	0.0
VERT	10	0	0.0	0	0.0	3	30.0	0	0.0	6	60.0	0	0.0	1	10.0
LINE	10	1	10.0	0	0.0	0	0.0	1	10.0	7	70.0	0	0.0	1	10.0
ROLL	25	1	4.0	1	4.0	6	24.0	4	16.0	13	52.0	0	0.0	0	0.0
L	20	0	0.0	0	0.0	1	5.0	1	5.0	18	90.0	0	0.0	0	0.0
LES	25	0	0.0	0	0.0	7	28.0	1	4.0	17	68.0	0	0.0	0	0.0
HESTER	3	0	0.0	1	33.3	0	0.0	0	0.0	2	66.7	0	0.0	0	0.0
ERICK	54	2	3.7	1	1.9	12	22.2	3	5.6	36	66.7	0	0.0	0	0.0
ETT	4	0	0.0	1	25.0	1	25.0	0	0.0	2	50.0	0	0.0	0	0.0
ORD	62	0	0.0	1	1.6	11	17.7	1	1.6	49	79.0	0	0.0	0	0.0
RD	41	5	12.2	0	0.0	9	22.0	1	2.4	26	63.4	0	0.0	0	0.0
	3	0	0.0	0	0.0	1	33.3	0	0.0	2	66.7	0	0.0	0	0.0
GOMERY	133	3	2.3	18	13.5	47	35.3	19	14.3	46	34.6	0	0.0	0	0.0
CE GEORGE'S	64	3	4.7	0	0.0	20	31.3	0	0.0	37	57.8	4	6.3	0	0.0
N ANNE'S	4	0	0.0	0	0.0	0	0.0	0	0.0	4	100.0	0	0.0	0	0.0
MARY'S	18	0	0.0	0	0.0	5	27.8	0	0.0	13	72.2	0	0.0	0	0.0
RSET	8	0	0.0	0	0.0	3	37.5	0	0.0	5	62.5	0	0.0	0	0.0
OT	2	0	0.0	0	0.0	1	50.0	0	0.0	1	50.0	0	0.0	0	0.0
INGTON	14	0	0.0	0	0.0	1	7.1	3	21.4	9	64.3	1	7.1	0	0.0
MICO	15	0	0.0	0	0.0	6	40.0	0	0.0	8	53.3	0	0.0	1	6.7
ESTER	3	0	0.0	0	0.0	2	66.7	1	33.3	0	0.0	0	0.0	0	0.0
TRANSFERS	113	1	0.9	13	11.5	37	32.7	21	18.6	40	35.4	1	0.9	0	0.0

Note: Transfers Between Units are Included in Individual Local Unit Totals, but Excluded from State Totals.

TABLE 49

TOTAL NEW CERTIFIED PROFESSIONAL STAFF AT MIDDLE AND COMBINED SCHOOL LEVEL
BY PREPARATION
MARYLAND PUBLIC SCHOOLS: OCTOBER, 1986

LOCAL UNIT	TOTAL	DOCTOR'S DEGREE		MASTER'S DEGREE PLUS 30 HOURS		MASTER'S DEGREE		BACH.'S DEGREE PLUS 30 HOURS		BACHELOR'S DEGREE		2 - 3 YEARS COLLEGE		LESS THAN 2 YRS COLLEGE	
		NUMBER	PCT.	NUMBER	PCT.	NUMBER	PCT.	NUMBER	PCT.	NUMBER	PCT.	NUMBER	PCT.	NUMBER	PCT.
TOTAL STATE	435	2	0.5	13	3.0	122	28.0	21	4.8	277	63.7	0	0.0	0	0.0
ALLEGANY	5	0	0.0	0	0.0	1	20.0	0	0.0	4	80.0	0	0.0	0	0.0
ANNE ARUNDEL	32	1	3.1	0	0.0	9	28.1	2	6.3	20	62.5	0	0.0	0	0.0
BALTIMORE CITY	41	1	2.4	2	4.9	10	24.4	4	9.8	24	58.5		0.0		0.0
BALTIMORE	71	0	0.0		8.5	32	45.1	7	9.9	26	36.6		0.0		0.0
CALVERT	8	0	0.0		0.0	5	62.5	1	12.5	2	·25.0		0.0		0.0
CAROLINE	1	0	0.0	0	0.0	0	0.0	1	100.0			0	0.0	0	0.0
CARROLL	18	0	0.0		5.6	4	22.2		0.0	13	72.2	0	0.0		0.0
CECIL	5	0	0.0		0.0	1	20.0	.		4	80.0	0	0.0		0.0
CHARLES	29	0	0.0		0.0	5	17.2	.		23	79.3	0	0.0		0.0
DORCHESTER	2	0	0.0		0.0	0	0.0	.		2	100.0	0	0.0		0.0
FREDERICK	43	0	0.0	1	2.3	4	9.3	1	2.3	37	86.0	0	0.0	0	0.0
GARRETT	1	0	0.0	0	0.0	0	0.0	0	0.0	1	100.0	0	0.0	0	0.0
HARFORD	31	0	0.0		0.0	10	32.3		6.5	19	61.3	0	0.0	0	0.0
HOWARD	60	0	0.0		3.3	12	20.0		3.3	44	73.3	0	0.0	0	0.0
KENT	1	0	0.0		3.0	0	0.0		0.0	1	100.0	0	0.0	0	0.0
MONTGOMERY	33	0	0.0	5	15.2	12	36.4	3	9.1	13	39.4	0	0.0	0	0.0
PRINCE GEORGE'S	79			0	0.0	32	44.4			40	60.6				
QUEEN ANNE'S			0.0	0	0.0	2	28.6	1	14.3		.1		0.0		
ST MARY'S	1		6.7	0	0.0	4	26.7	0	0.0	1	.7		0.0		
SOMERSET			.0	0	0.0	2	40.0	0	0.0		.0		0.0		
TALBOT	3	0	0.0	0	0.0	0	0.0	1	33.3	2	66.7		0.0		0.0
WASHINGTON	11	0	0.0	0	0.0	3	27.3	2	18.2						
WICOMICO	4	0	0.0	0	0.0	1	25.0	1	25.0	.		.		.	
WORCESTER	6	0	0.0	0	0.0	4	66.7	0	0.0	.		.		.	
LEA TRANSFERS	69	1	1.4	4	5.8	31	44.9	8	11.6	25	36.2	0	0.0	0	0.0

rom State Totals.

TABLE
50

TOTAL CERTIFIED PROFESSIONAL STAFF AT SCHOOL LEVEL
BY YEARS OF EXPERIENCE
MARYLAND PUBLIC SCHOOLS: OCTOBER, 1986

LOCAL UNIT	TOTAL	1-5 YEARS NUMBER	PCT.	6-10 YEARS NUMBER	PCT.	11-15 YEARS NUMBER	PCT.	16-20 YEARS NUMBER	PCT	21-25 YEARS NUMBER	PCT.	26-30 YEARS NUMBER	PCT.	30+ YEARS NUMBER	PCT.
OTAL STATE	44,559	6,478	14.5	7,575	17.0	10,672	24.0	9,746	21.9	5,720	12.8	3,030	6 8	1,338	3.0
LLEGANY	726	70	9.6	116	16.0	164	22.6	161	22.2	114	15.7	75	10.3	26	3.6
NNE ARUNDEL	4,159	504	12.1	806	19.4	1,034	24.9	959	23.1	522	12.6	240	5.8	94	2.3
ALTIMORE CITY	6,705	802	12.0	949	14.2	1,671	24.9	1,427	21.3	952	14.2	500	7.5	404	6.0
ALTIMORE	5,938	792	13.3	832	14.0	1,360	22.9	1,383	23.3	870	14.7	552	9.3	149	2.5
ALVERT	503	64	12.7	109	21.7	131	26.0	107	21.3	63	12.5	20	4.0	9	1.8
AROLINE	297	67	22.6	65	21.9	71	23.9	38	12.8	28	9.4	19	6 4	9	3.0
ARROLL	1,230	195	15.9	275	22.4	329	26.7	231	18.8	125	10.2	54	4.4	21	1.7
ECIL	796	106	13.3	174	21.9	219	27.5	170	21.4	76	9.5	38	4.8	13	1 6
HARLES	1,048	232	22.1	254	24.2	263	25.1	176	16.8	77	7.3	30	2.9	16	1 5
ORCHESTER	330	41	12.4	66	20.0	83	25.2	72	21.8	39	11.8	22	6.7	7	2 1
REDERICK	1,563	350	22.4	316	20.2	380	24.3	285	18.2	143	9.1	63	4.0	26	1 7
ARRETT	292	35	12.0	67	22.9	82	28.1	54	18.5	35	12.0	15	5.1	4	1.4
ARFORD	1,812	248	13.7	305	16.8	467	25.8	450	24.8	208	11.5	94	5.2	40	2.2
OWARD	1,763	501	28.4	384	21.8	435	24.7	264	15.0	100	5.7	58	3.3	21	1.2
ENT	172	33	19.2	31	18.0	37	21.5	37	21.5	16	9.3	13	7.6	5	2.9
ONTGOMERY	6,868	908	13.2	1,171	17.1	1,499	21.8	1,570	22.9	897	13.1	552	8.0	271	3.9
RINCE GEORGE'S	6,454	885	13.7	904	14.0	1,449	22.5	1,618	25.1	1,039	16.1	432	6.7	127	2.0
UEEN ANNE'S	298	56	18.8	65	21.8	79	26.5	46	15.4	34	11.4	14	4.7	4	1.3
T. MARY'S	805	223	27.7	197	24.5	197	24.5	114	14.2	50	6.2	24	3.0	0	0.0
OMERSET	234	51	21.8	40	17.1	51	21.8	40	17.1	26	11.1	16	6.8	10	4.3
ALBOT	262	43	16.4	58	22.1	74	28.2	51	19.5	18	6.9	9	3.4	9	3.4
ASHINGTON	1,166	123	10.5	189	16.2	293	25.1	265	22.7	152	13.0	97	8.3	47	4.0
ICOMICO	742	90	12.1	137	18.5	178	24.0	152	20.5	92	12.4	69	9.3	24	3.2
ORCESTER	396	59	14.9	65	16.4	126	31.8	76	19.2	44	11.1	24	6.1	2	0.5

TABLE 51

TOTAL CERTIFIED PROFESSIONAL STAFF AT ELEMENTARY SCHOOL LEVEL
BY YEARS OF EXPERIENCE
MARYLAND PUBLIC SCHOOLS: OCTOBER, 1986

LOCAL UNIT	TOTAL	1-5 YEARS NUMBER	PCT.	6-10 YEARS NUMBER	PCT.	11-15 YEARS NUMBER	PCT.	16-20 YEARS NUMBER	PCT.	21-25 YEARS NUMBER	PCT.	26-30 YEARS NUMBER	PCT.	30+ YEARS NUMBER	PCT.
TOTAL STATE	20,085	3,435	17.1	3,456	17.2	4,730	23.5	4,116	20.5	2,399	11.9	1,288	6.4	661	3.3
ALLEGANY	265	21	7.9	46	17.4	65	24.5	64	24.5	35	13.2	21	7.9	13	4.9
ANNE ARUNDEL	1,931	274	14.2	398	20.6	466	24.1	386	20.0	205	10.6	114	7.9	88	4.9
BALTIMOR CITY	3,164	453	14.3	4	3.4		23.8	3		2		2			
BALTIMOR	2,384	422	17.7	3	6.1		21.7	5		3				2	
CALVERT	225	30	13.3		2.2		25.3								
CAROLINE	151	33	21.9	30	19.9	43	28.5	20	13.2	13	8.6	8	5.3	4	2.6
CARROLL	506	94	18.6	108	21.5	138	27.3	66	13.0	48				7	
CECIL	363	57	15.7		3.7		28.9		3						
CHARLES	423	98	23.2	1	3.9		26.5		1						
DORCHESTER	138	22	15.9		8.8		27.5		4						
FREDERICK	726	157	21.6	170	23.4	182	25.1	117	16.1	58	7.7	28	3.8	16	2.2
GARRETT	143	16	11.2	38	26.6	48	33.6	20			1			2	
HARFORD	789	112	14.2	1	5.5	2	26.7	1				3		2	
HOWARD	724	249	34.4	1	1.0	2	24.0					2		1	
KENT	64	19	29.7		0.3		18.8								
MONTGOMERY	3,285	524	16.0	590	18.0	712	21.7	720	21.9	367	11.2	241	7.3	131	4.0
PRINCE GEORGE'S	3,096	524	16.9	408	13.1	650	21.0	789	24.5	504	16.0	208			
QUEEN AN 'S	111	26	23.4		8.9		27.9								
ST. MARY 'S	389	126	32.4		3.4		24.2			2		1			
SO ERSET	62	11	17.7		9.7		17.7						1		
TALBOT	98	25	25.5	25	25.5	26	26.5	16	16.3			2	2.0	3	3.1
WASHINGTON	513	57	11.1	29	15.6	188	27.7	128		6	1.0	34	2.0	28	3.1
WICOMICO	385	53	13.8		8.2		24.4				1	5		3	
WORCESTER	150	32	21.3		9.3		32.7					0			

TABLE
52

TOTAL CERTIFIED PROFESSIONAL STAFF AT SECONDARY SCHOOL LEVEL
BY YEARS OF EXPERIENCE
MARYLAND PUBLIC SCHOOLS: OCTOBER, 1986

LOCAL UNIT	TOTAL	1-5 YEARS NUMBER	PCT.	6-10 YEARS NUMBER	PCT.	11-15 YEARS NUMBER	PCT.	16-20 YEARS NUMBER	PCT.	21-25 YEARS NUMBER	PCT.	26-30 YEARS NUMBER	PCT.	30+ YEARS NUMBER	PCT.
OTAL STATE	16,151	1,834	11.4	2,452	15.2	3,833	23.7	3,878	24.0	2,435	15.1	1,228	7.6	491	3.0
LLEGANY	243	24	9.9	41	16.9	53	21.8	49	20.2	41	16.9	29	11.9	6	2.5
NNE ARUNDEL	1,564	152	9.7	258	16.5	401	25.6	404	25.8	224	14.3	94	6.0	31	2.0
ALTIMORE CITY	2,524	225	8.9	338	13.4	620	24.6	590	23.4	410	16.2	199	7.9	142	5.6
ALTIMORE	2,063	185	9.0	206	10.0	474	23.0	543	26.3	379	18.4	222	10.8	54	2.6
ALVERT	146	19	13.0	33	22.6	35	24.0	29	19.9	26	17.8	2	1.4	2	1.4
AROLINE	94	26	27.7	20	21.3	14	14.9	12	12.8	8	8.5	9	9.6	5	5.3
ARROLL	407	59	14.5	92	22.6	109	26.8	75	18.4	45	11.1	21	5.2	6	1.5
ECIL	304	38	12.5	60	19.7	83	27.3	68	22.4	31	10.2	17	5.6	7	2.3
HARLES	359	78	21.7	82	22.8	87	24.2	63	17.5	31	8.6	12	3.3	6	1.7
ORCHESTER	113	8	7.1	26	23.0	22	19.5	29	25.7	21	18.6	5	4.4	2	1.8
REDERICK	488	103	21.1	85	17.4	108	22.1	109	22.3	54	11.1	23	4.7	6	1.2
ARRETT	84	13	15.5	17	20.2	17	20.2	13	15.5	14	16.7	9	10.7	1	1.2
ARFORD	633	95	15.0	106	16.7	150	23.7	156	24.6	85	13.4	31	4.9	10	1.6
OWARD	575	127	22.1	110	19.1	156	27.1	112	19.5	45	7.8	19	3.3	6	1.0
ENT	54	8	14.8	11	20.4	10	18.5	16	29.6	5	9.3	3	5.6	1	1.9
ONTGOMERY	3,158	309	9.8	463	14.7	692	21.9	766	24.3	498	15.8	296	9.4	134	4.2
RINCE GEORGE'S	2,067	178	8.6	269	13.0	479	23.2	577	27.9	383	18.5	141	6.8	40	1.9
UEEN ANNE'S	96	15	15.6	25	26.0	22	22.9	15	15.6	12	12.5	6	6.3	1	1.0
T. MARY'S	235	59	25.1	56	23.8	56	23.8	37	15.7	19	8.1	8	3.4	0	0.0
OMERSET	91	18	19.8	19	20.9	21	23.1	21	23.1	6	6.6	3	3.3	3	3.3
ALBOT	89	11	12.4	18	20.2	25	28.1	18	20.2	7	7.9	6	6.7	4	4.5
ASHINGTON	363	35	9.6	58	15.4	87	24.0	78	21.5	49	13.5	41	11.3	17	4.7
ICOMICO	263	32	12.2	40	15.2	66	25.1	63	24.0	31	11.8	25	9.5	6	2.3
ORCESTER	138	17	12.3	21	15.2	46	33.3	35	25.4	11	8.0	7	5.1	1	0.7

TABLE 53

TOTAL CERTIFIED PROFESSIONAL STAFF AT MIDDLE AND COMBINED SCHOOL LEVEL
BY YEARS OF EXPERIENCE
MARYLAND PUBLIC SCHOOLS: OCTOBER, 1986

LOCAL UNIT	TOTAL	1-5 YEARS NUMBER	PCT.	6-10 YEARS NUMBER	PCT.	11-15 YEARS NUMBER	PCT.	16-20 YEARS NUMBER	PCT.	21-25 YEAR NUMBER	PCT.	26-30 YEARS NUMBER	PCT.	30+ YEARS NUMBER	PCT.
TOTAL STATE	8,323	1,209	14.5	1,667	20.0	2,109	25.3	1,752	21.1	886	10.6	514	6.2	186	2.2
ALLEGANY	218	25	11.5	29	13.3	46	21.1	48	22.0	38	17.4	25	11.5	7	3.2
ANNE ARUNDE			12.2	151	22.7	168	25.3	157	23.6	67	10.1	35	5.3	8	1.2
BALTIMORE CITY				187	18.4	297	29.2	203	20.0	117	11.5	57	5.6	32	3.1
BALTIMORE	1.	1	12.4	241	16.2	369	24.7	328	22.0	184	12.3	133	8.9	51	3.4
CALVERT			11.4	26	19.7	39	29.5	32	24.2	14	10.6	5	3.8	1	0.8
CAROLINE	52	8	15.4	15	28.8	14	26.9	6	11.5	7	13.5	2	3.8	0	0.0
CARROLL	317	42	13.2	74	23.3	82	25.9	64	20.2	30	9.5	17	5.4	0	0.0
CECIL	129	11	8.5	28	21.7	31	24.0	43	33.3	10	7.8	5			
CHARLES	266	56	21.1	71	26.7	64	24.1	45	16.9	18	6.8	6	2.8		
DORCHESTER	79	11	13.9	14	17.7	23	29.1	19	24.1	5	6.3	6			
FREDERICK	349	90	25.8	61	17.5	90	25.8	59	16.9	33	9.5	12	3.4	4	
GARRETT	65	6	9.2	22	33.8	17	26.2	15	23.1	3	4.6	2	3.1	0	
HARFORD	390	41	10.5	77	19.7	106	27.2	98	25.1	35	9.0	24	6.2		
HOWARD	464	125	26.9	122	26.3	105	22.6	68	14.7	22	4.7	19	4.1		
KENT	54	6	11.1	7	13.0	15	27.8	12	22.2	6	11.1	5	9.3		
MONTGOMERY	425	75	17.6	118	27.8	95	22.4	84	19.8	32	7.5	15	3.5	6	1.4
PR.NCE GEORGE'S	91	183	14.2	230	17.8	320	24.8	294	22.8	154	11.9	85	6.6	25	1.9
QUEEN ANNE'S	91	15	16.5	19	20.9	26	28.6	16	17.6	8	8.8	5	5.5	2	2.2
ST. MARY'S	181	38	21.0	50	27.6	47	26.0	26	14.4	14	.7	6	3.3	0	0.0
SO ERSET	81	22	27.2	15	18.5	19	23.5	10	12.3	7	8.6	4	4.9	4	4.9
TALBOT	75	7	9.3	15	20.0	23	30.7	17	22.7	10	13.3	1	1.3	2	2.7
WASHINGTON	290	31	10.7	53	18.3	64	22.1	66	22.8	41	14.1	25	8.6	10	.4
WICOMICO	94	5	5.3	27	28.7	18	19.1	19	20.2	13	13.8	10	10.6	2	.1
WORCESTER	108	10	9.3	15	13.9	31	28.7	23	21.3	18	16.7	10	9.3	1	.9

TABLE
54

TOTAL NEW CERTIFIED PROFESSIONAL STAFF AT SCHOOL LEVEL
BY YEARS OF EXPERIENCE
MARYLAND PUBLIC SCHOOLS: OCTOBER, 1986

OCAL UNIT	TOTAL	1-5 YEARS NUMBER	PCT.	6-10 YEARS NUMBER	PCT.	11-15 YEARS NUMBER	PCT.	16-20 YEARS NUMBER	PCT.	21-25 YEARS NUMBER	PCT.	26-30 YEARS NUMBER	PCT.	30+ YEARS NUMBER	PCT.
AL STATE	2,420	1,864	77.0	348	14.4	151	6.2	47	1.9	7	0.3	2	0.1	1	0.0
EGANY	12	8	66.7	3	25.0	1	8.3	0	0.0	0	0.0	0	0.0	0	0.0
E ARUNDEL	234	152	65.0	60	25.6	17	7.3	4	1.7	0	0.4		0.0		0.0
TIMORE CITY	252	207	82.1	31	12.3	11	4.4	3	1.2		0.0		0.0		0.0
TIMORE	319	319	100.0	0	0.0	0	0.0	0	0.0		6.1		0.0		0.0
VERT	33	10	30.3	13	39.4	6	18.2	2	6.1						
OLINE	23	13	56.5	7	30.4	1	4.3	2	8.7	0	0.0	0	0.0	0	0.0
ROLL	87	64	73.6	13	14.9	9	10.3	1	1.1	0	0.0	0	0.0	0	0.0
IL	46	32	69.6	10	21.7	3	6.5		0.0		0.0	0	0.0	1	2.2
RLES	110	75	68.2	24	21.8	8	7.3		2.7		0.0	0	0.0	0	0.0
CHESTER	13	8	61.5	3	23.1	2	15.4		0.0		0.0	0	0.0	0	0.0
DERICK	185	155	83.8	16	8.6	13	7.0	1	0.5	0	0.0	0	0.0	0	0.0
RETT	10	9	90.0	1	10.0	0	0.0	0	0.0	0	0.0	0	0.0	0	0.0
FORD	158	113	71.5	23	14.6	13	11.4	3	1.9	0	0.0	1	0.6	0	0.0
ARD	199	170	85.4	20	10.1	5	2.5	3	1.5	1	0.5	0	0.0	0	0.0
T	13	9	69.2	3	23.1	0	0.0	1	7.7	1	0.0	0	0.0	0	0.0
TG MERD	463	263	56.8	118	25.5	54	11.7	22	4.8	4	0.9	1	0.2	1	0.2
NCE G RGE'S	4	284	70.8	79	19.7	30	7.5	5	1.2	0	0.5	0	0.2	0	0.0
EN AN 'S	17	17	77.3	2	9.1	1	4.5	2	9.1		0.0		0.0		0.0
M Y'S	60	60	76.9	9	11.5	6	7.7	3	3.8		0.0		0.0		0.0
ER& T	13	13	76.5	2	11.8	0	0.0	2	11.8		0.0		0.0		0.0
BOT	15	11	73.3	3	20.0	0	0.0	1	6.7	0	0.0	0	0.0	0	0.0
HINGTON	40	27	67.5		20.0		0.0		0.0		0.0		0.0		0.0
OMICO	48	34	70.8		.		.		.1		.		.		.
CESTER	20	8	40.0		.	3	.	1	.0		.		.		.
TRANSFERS	378	197	52.1	108	28.6	51	13.5	16	4.2	4	1.1	1	0.3	1	0.3

Note: Transfers Between Units are Included in Individual Local Unit Totals, but Excluded from State Totals.

TABLE
55

TOTAL NEW CERTIFIED PROFESSIONAL STAFF AT ELEMENTARY SCHOOL LEVEL
BY YEARS OF EXPERIENCE
MARYLAND PUBLIC SCHOOLS: OCTOBER, 1986

LOCAL UNIT	TOTAL	1-5 YEARS NUMBER	PCT.	6-10 YEARS NUMBER	PCT.	11-15 YEARS NUMBER	PCT.	16-20 YEARS NUMBER	PCT.	21-25 YEARS NUMBER	PCT.	26-30 YEARS NUMBER	PCT.	30+ YEARS NUMBER	PCT.
TOTAL STATE	1,376	1,075	78.1	194	14.1	88	6.4	14	1.0	4	0.3	1	0.1	0	0.0
ALLEGANY	4	4	100.0	0	0.0	0	0.0	0	0.0	0	0.0	0	0.0	0	0.0
ANNE ARUNDEL	132	87	65.9	32	24.2	10	7.6	2	1.5	1	0.8	0	0.0	0	0.0
BALTIMORE CITY	146	117	80.1	21	14.4	8	5.5		0.0		0.0		0.0		0.0
BALTIMORE	182	182	100.0	0	0.0	0	0.0		0.0		0.0		0.0		0.0
CALVERT	15	7	46.7	5	33.3	3	20.0		0.0		0.0		0.0		0.0
CAROLINE	12	8	66.7	2	16.7	1	8.3	1	8.3	0	0.0	0	0.0	0	0.0
CARROLL	44	35	79.5	8	18.2	1	2.3		0.0		0.0		0.0		0.0
CECIL	21	14	66.7	5	23.8	2	9.5		0.0		0.0		0.0		0.0
CHARLES	56	34	60.7	13	23.2	8	14.3		1.8		0.0		0.0		0.0
DORCHESTER	8	4	50.0	3	37.5	1	12.5		0.0		0.0		0.0		0.0
FREDERICK	88	71	80.7	13	14.8	4	4.5	0	0.0	0	0.0	0	0.0	0	0.0
GARRETT	5	5	100.0	0	0.0	0	0.0	0	0.0	0	0.0	0	0.0	0	0.0
HARFORD	65	49	75.4	7	10.8	8	12.3	0	0.0	0	0.0	1	1.5		0.0
HOWARD	98	87	88.8	8	8.2	1	1.0	1	1.0	1	1.0	0	0.0		0.0
KENT	9	6	66.7	2	22.2	0	0.0	1	11.1	0	0.0	0	0.0		
MONTGOMERY	297	178	59.9	70	23.6	36	12.1	9	3.0	2	0.7	1	0.3	1	0.3
PRINCE GEORGE'S	265	194	73.2	48	18.1	19	7.2	2	0.8	2	0.8	0	0.0	0	0.0
QUEEN ANNE'S	11	10	90.9	1	9.1	0	0.0		0.0		0.0		0.0		0.0
ST. MARY'S	45	38	84.4	4	8.9	2	4.4	1	2.2		0.0		0.0		
SOMERSET	4	4	100.0	0	0.0	0	0.0	0	0.0	0	0.0	0	0.0		
TALBOT	10	8	80.0	1	10.0	0	0.0	1	10.0	0	0.0	0	0.0	0	0.0
WASHINGTON	24	12	80.0		19.3		0.0	0	0.0	0	0.0	0	0.0	0	0.0
WICOMICO		20	89.0					1							
WORCESTER		7	63.8					0							
LEA TRANSFERS	196	106	54.1	56	28.6	24	12.2	6	3.1	2	1.0	1	0.5	1	0.5

TABLE
56

·TOTAL NEW CERTIFIED PROFESSIONAL STAFF AT SECONDARY SCHOOL LEVEL
BY YEARS OF EXPERIENCE
MARYLAND PUBLIC SCHOOLS: OCTOBER, 1986

LOCAL UNIT	TOTAL	1-5 YEARS NUMBER	PCT.	6-10 YEARS NUMBER	PCT.	11-15 YEARS NUMBER	PCT.	16-20 YEARS NUMBER	PCT.	21-25 YEARS NUMBER	PCT.	26-30 YEARS NUMBER	PCT.	30+ YEARS NUMBER	PCT.
OTAL STATE	609	449	73.7	93	15.3	39	6.4	23	3.8	3	0.5	1	0.2	1	0.2
LLEGANY	3	1	33.3	1	33.3	1	33.3	0	0.0	0	0.0	0	0.0	0	0.0
NNE ARUNDEL	70	43	61.4	21	30.0	5	7.1	1	1.4	0	0.0	0	0.0	0	0.0
ALTIMORE CITY	65	54	83.1	7	10.8	2	3.1	2	3.1	0	0.0		0.0		0.0
ALTIMORE	66	66	100.0	0	0.0	0	0.0	0	0.0	0	0.0		0.0		0.0
ALVERT	10	2	20.0	6	60.0	0	0.0	1	10.0	1	10.0		0.0		0.0
AROLINE	10	5	50.0	4	40.0	0	0.0	1	10.0	0	0.0	0	0.0	0	0.0
ARROLL	25	16	64.0	4	16.0	4	16.0	1	4.0	0	0.0		0.0	0	0.0
ECIL	20	14	70.0	4	20.0	1	5.0	0	0.0		0.0		0.0	1	5.0
HARLES	25	19	76.0	6	24.0	0	0.0	0	0.0		0.0		0.0	0	0.0
ORCHESTER	3	2	66.7	0	0.0	1	33.3	0	0.0		0.0		0.0	0	0.0
REDERICK	54	44	81.5	2	3.7	7	13.0	1	1.9	0	0.0	0	0.0	0	0.0
ARRETT	4	3	75.0	1	25.0	0	0.0	0	0.0		0.0		0.0		0.0
ARFORD	62	47	75.8	9	14.5	4	6.5		3.2		0.0		0.0		0.0
OWARD	41	33	80.5	4	9.8	2	4.9		4.9		0.0		0.0		0.0
ENT	3	2	66.7	1	33.3	0	0.0	0	0.0		0.0		0.0		0.0
ON G MERD	133	68	51.1	36	27.1	17	12.8	10	7.5	2	1.5	0	0.0	0	0.0
R NCB GE RGE'S	64	1	64.1	17	26.6	3	4.7	2	3.1	0	0.0		1.6		
U "N ANN 'S		3	75.0	1	25.0	0	0.0	0	0.0		0.0		0.0		
T. MARY'S	1	11	61.1	4	22.2	2	11.1	1	5.6		.		0.0		
OMERSET		6	75.0	0	0.0	0	0.0	2	25.0		.		0.0		
ALBOT	2	1	50.0	1	50.0	0	0.0	0	0.0	0	0.0	0	0.0	0	0.0
ASHINGTON	14	9			10.0	2	.1		10.0		0.0		0.0		0.0
ICOMICO	15	12	.		.		.3		.	3	.		.		.
ORCESTER	3	0	.		.		.7		.		.		.		.
EA TRANSFERS	113	53	46.9	39	34.5	15	13.3	5	4.4	1	0.9	0	0.0	0	0.0

Note: Transfers Between Units are Included in Individual Local Unit Totals, but Excluded from State Totals

TABLE 57

TOTAL NEW CERTIFIED PROFESSIONAL STAFF AT MIDDLE AND COMBINED SCHOOL LEVEL
BY YEARS OF EXPERIENCE
MARYLAND PUBLIC SCHOOLS: OCTOBER, 1986

LOCAL UNIT	TOTAL	1-5 YEARS NUMBER	PCT.	6-10 YEARS NUMBER	PCT.	11-15 YEARS NUMBER	PCT.	16-20 YEARS NUMBER	PCT.	21-25 YEARS NUMBER	PCT.	26-30 YEARS NUMBER	PCT.	30+ YEARS NUMBER	PCT.
TOTAL STATE	435	340	78.2	61	14.0	24	5.5	10	2.3	0	0.0	0	0.0	0	0.0
ALLEGANY	5	3	60.0	2	40.0	0	0.0	0	0.0	0	0.0				0.0
ANNE ARUNDEL	32	22	68.8	7	21.9	2	6.3	1	3.1	0	0.0	0	0.0	0	0.0
BALTIMORE CITY	41	36	87.8	3	7.3	1	2.4	1	2.4	0	0.0	0	0.0	0	0.0
BALTIMORE	71	71	100.0	0	0.0	0	0.0	0	0.0	0	0.0				0.0
CALVERT	8	1	12.5	2	25.0	3	37.5	1	12.5	1	12.5				0.0
CAROLINE	1	0	0.0	1	100.0	0	0.0	0	0.0	0	0.0	0	0.0	0	0.0
CARROLL	18	13	72.2	1	5.6	4	22.2	0	0.0	0	0.0	0	0.0	0	0.0
CECIL	5	4	80.0	1	20.0	0	0.0	0	0.0		0.0		0.0		
CHARLES	29	22	75.9	5	17.2	0	0.0	2	6.9		0.0		0.0		
DORCHESTER	2	2	100.0	0	0.0	0	0.0		0.0		0.0				
FREDERICK	43	40	93.0	1	2.3	2	4.7	0	0.0	0	0.0	0	0.0	0	0.0
GARRETT	1	1	100.0	0	0.0	0	0.0	0	0.0	0	0.0	0	0.0	0	0.0
HARFORD	31	17	54.8	7	22.6	6	19.4		3.2		0.0				0.0
HOWARD	60	50	83.3	8	13.3	2	3.3		0.0		0.0				0.0
KENT	1	1	100.0	0	0.0	0	0.0		0.0						0.0
MONTGOMERY	33	17	51.5	12	36.4	1	3.0	3	9.1	0	0.0	0	0.0	0	0.0
PRINCE GEORGE'S	72	49	68.1	14	19.4	8	11.1	1	1.4	0	0.0	0	0.0	0	0.0
QUEEN ANNE'S	7	4	57.1	0	0.0	1	14.3	2	28.6				0.0		
ST. MARY'S	15	11	73.3	1	6.7	2	13.3	1	6.7				0.0		
SOMERSET	5	3	60.0	2	40.0	0	0.0	0	0.0				0.0		
TALBOT	3	2	66.7	1	33.3	0	0.0	0	0.0	0	0.0	0	0.0	0	0.0
WASHINGTON	11	6	54.5	4	36.4	1	9.1	0	0.0	0	0.0	0	0.0	0	0.0
WICOMICO	4	2	50.0	1	25.0			2	.0						
WORCESTER	6	1	16.7	1	16.7			3	.3	3	.				
LEA TRANSFERS	69	38	55.1	13	18.8	12	17.4	5	7.2	1	1.4	0	0.0	0	0.0

TABLE
58

TOTAL CERTIFIED PROFESSIONAL STAFF AT SCHOOL LEVEL
BY TYPE OF CERTIFICATE
MARYLAND PUBLIC SCHOOLS: OCTOBER, 1986

AL UNIT	TOTAL	PROFESSIONAL TOTAL NUMBER	PCT.	ADVANCED	STANDARD	PROVISIONAL TOTAL NUMBER	PCT.	DEGREE	NON-DEGREE	INITIAL
STATE	44,342	43,362	97.8	35,993	7,369	980	2.2	916	63	1
ANY	721	716	99.3	645	70	5	0.7	5	0	0
ARUNDEL	4,151	4,134	99.6	3,496	638	17	0.4	12	5	0
MORE CITY	6,688	6,418	96.0	5,417	1,001	270	4.0	252	18	0
MORE	5,920	5,875	99.2	5,310	565	45	0.8	39	5	1
RT	501	492	98.2	396	95	9	1.8	8	1	0
INE	296	288	97.3	194	94	8	2.7	6	2	0
LL	1,228	1,211	98.6	930	281	17	1.4	16	1	0
	783	775	99.0	595	180	8	1.0	8	0	0
ES	1,045	1,003	96.0	736	267	42	4.0	41	1	0
ESTER	329	327	99.4	279	48	2	0.6	1	1	0
RICK	1,554	1,479	95.2	1,106	373	75	4.8	73	2	0
TT	284	271	95.4	212	59	13	4.6	11	2	0
RD	1,809	1,763	97.5	1,465	298	46	2.5	45	1	0
D	1,755	1,737	99.0	1,234	503	18	1.0	16	2	0
	170	167	98.2	121	46	3	1.8	2	1	0
OMERY	6,807	6,721	98.7	5,496	1,225	86	1.3	84	2	0
E GEORGE'S	6,448	6,177	95.8	5,325	852	271	4.2	258	13	0
ANNE'S	297	297	100.0	227	70	0	0.0	0	0	0
ARY'S	773	755	97.7	538	217	18	2.3	17	1	0
SET	234	223	95.3	166	57	11	4.7	11	0	0
T	261	260	99.6	204	56	1	0.4	1	0	0
NGTON	1,158	1,153	99.6	982	171	5	0.4	5	0	0
ICO	735	726	98.8	599	127	9	1.2	5	4	0
STER	395	394	99.7	319	75	1	0.3	0	1	0

TABLE
59

| LOCAL UNIT | TOTAL | PROFESSIONAL | | | PROVISIONAL | | | | INITIAL |
		TOTAL NUMBER	PCT.	ADVANCED	STANDARD	TOTAL NUMBER	PCT.	DEGREE	NON-DEGREE	
TOTAL STATE	19,970	19,531	97.8	15,860	3,671	439	2.2	438	0	1
ALLEGANY	265	264	99.6	239	25	1	0.4	1	0	0
ANNE ARUNDEL	1,925	1,921	99.8	1,602	319	4	0.2	4	0	0
BALTIMORE CITY	3,154	3,039	96.4	2,503	538	115	3.6	115	0	0
BALTIMORE	2,378	2,361	99.3	2,073	288	17	0.7	16	0	1
CALVERT	224	223	99.6	181	42	1	0.4	1	0	0
CAROLINE	150	146	97.3	101	45	4	2.7	4	0	0
CARROLL	505	498	98.6	384	114	7	1.4	7	0	0
CECIL	358	356	99.4	266	90	2	0.6	2	0	0
CHARLES	423	405	95.7	298	107	18	4.3	18	0	0
DORCHESTER	137	137	100.0	112	25	0	0.0	0	0	0
FREDERICK	721	691	95.8	526	165	30	4.2	30	0	0
GARRETT	139	134	96.4	105	29	5	3.6	5	0	0
HARFORD	788	776	98.5	654	122	12	1.5	12	0	0
HOWARD	722	716	99.2	477	239	6	0.8	6	0	0
KENT	64	62	96.9	38	24	2	3.1	2	0	0
MONTGOMERY	3,242	3,203	98.8	2,534	669	39	1.2	39	0	0
PRINCE GEORGE'S	3,091	2,932	94.9	2,456	476	159	5.1	159	0	0
QUEEN ANNE'S	110	110	100.0	86	24	0	0.0	0	0	0
ST. MARY'S	370	358	96.8	248	110	12	3.2	12	0	0
SOMERSET	62	61	98.4	49	12	1	1.6	1	0	0
TALBOT	98	97	99.0	69	28	1	1.0	1	0	0
WASHINGTON	512	512	100.0	441	71	0	0.0	0	0	0
WICOMICO	382	379	99.2	308	71	3	0.8	3	0	0
WORCESTER	150	150	100.0	110	40	0	0.0	0	0	0

L STATE	16,084	15,701	97.6	13,424	2,277	383	2.4	320	63	0
GANY	241	239	99.2	215	24	2	0.8	2	0	0
ARUNDEL	1,563	1,551	99.2	1,349	202	12	0.8	7	5	0
IMORE CITY	2,522	2,408	95.5	2,103	305	114	4.5	86	18	0
IMORE	2,056	2,037	99.1	1,879	158	19	0.9	14	5	0
ERT	145	140	96.6	107	33	5	3.4	4	1	0
LINE	94	91	96.8	58	33	3	3.2	1	2	0
OLL	406	398	98.0	304	94	8	2.0	7	1	0
L	299	294	98.3	227	67	5	1.7	5	0	0
LES	357	345	96.6	253	92	12	3.4	11	1	0
HESTER	113	111	98.2	100	11	2	1.8	1	1	0
ERICK	485	457	94.2	344	113	28	5.8	26	2	0
ETT	80	73	91.3	56	17	7	8.8	5	2	0
ORD	631	607	96.2	492	115	24	3.8	23	1	0
RD	574	505	98.4	423	142	9	1.6	7	2	0
	53	52	98.1	38	14	1	1.9	0	1	0
GOMERY	3,140	3,100	98.7	2,663	437	40	1.3	38	2	0
CE GEORGE'S	2,067	1,994	96.5	1,616	178	73	3.5	60	13	0
N ANNE'S	96	96	100.0	68	28	0	0.0	0	0	0
MARY'S	228	224	98.2	165	59	4	1.8	3	1	0
RSET	91	86	94.5	64	22	5	5.5	5	0	0
OT	88	88	100.0	73	15	0	0.0	0	0	0
INGTON	358	355	99.2	301	54	3	0.8	3	0	0
MICO	259	253	97.7	210	43	6	2.3	2	4	0
ESTER	138	137	99.3	116	21	1	0.7	0	1	0

TABLE 61

TOTAL CERTIFIED PROFESSIONAL STAFF AT MIDDLE AND COMBINED SCHOOL LEVEL
BY TYPE OF CERTIFICATE
MARYLAND PUBLIC SCHOOLS: OCTOBER, 1986

LOCAL UNIT	TOTAL	PROFESSIONAL				PROVISIONAL				INITIAL
		TOTAL NUMBER	PCT.	ADVANCED	STANDARD	TOTAL NUMBER	PCT.	DEGREE	NON-DEGREE	
TOTAL STATE	8,288	8,130	98.1	6,709	1,421	158	1.9	158	0	0
ALLEGANY	215	213	99.1	192	21	2	0.9	2	0	0
ANNE ARUNDEL	663	662	99.8	545	117	1	0.2	1	0	0
BALTIMORE CITY	1,012	971	95.9	811	160	41	4.1	41	0	0
BALTIMORE	1,486	1,477	99.4	1,358	119	9	0.6	9	0	0
CALVERT	132	129	97.7	108	21	3	2.3	3	0	0
CAROLINE	52	51	98.1	35	16	1	1.9	1	0	0
CARROLL	317	315	98.4	242	73	2	0.6	2	0	0
CECIL	126	125	99.2	102	23	1	0.8	1	0	0
CHARLES	265	253	95.5	185	68	12	4.5	12	0	0
DORCHESTER	79	79	100.0	67	12	0	0.0	0	0	0
FREDERICK	348	331	95.1	236	95	17	4.9	17	0	0
GARRETT	85	84	98.5	51	13	1	1.5	1	0	0
HARFORD	390	380	97.4	319	61	10	2.6	10	0	0
HOWARD	459	456	99.3	334	122	3	0.7	3	0	0
KENT	53	53	100.0	45	8	0	0.0	0	0	0
MONTGOMERY	425	418	98.4	299	119	7	1.6	7	0	0
PRINCE GEORGE'S	1,290	1,251	97.0	1,053	198	39	3.0	39	0	0
QUEEN ANNE'S	91	91	100.0	73	18	0	0.0	0	0	0
ST. MARY'S	175	173	98.9	125	48	2	1.1	2	0	0
SOMERSET	81	76	93.8	53	23	5	6.2	5	0	0
TALBOT	75	75	100.0	62	13	0	0.0	0	0	0
WASHINGTON	288	286	99.3	240	46	2	0.7	2	0	0
WICOMICO	94	94	100.0	81	13	0	0.0	0	0	0
WORCESTER	107	107	100.0	93	14	0	0.0	0	0	0

TABLE
62

TOTAL NEW CERTIFIED PROFESSIONAL STAFF AT SCHOOL LEVEL
BY TYPE OF CERTIFICATE
MARYLAND PUBLIC SCHOOLS: OCTOBER, 1986

L UNIT	TOTAL	PROFESSIONAL				PROVISIONAL				INITIAL
		TOTAL NUMBER	PCT.	ADVANCED	STANDARD	TOTAL NUMBER	PCT.	DEGREE	NON-DEGREE	
STATE	2,260	1,714	75.8	419	1,295	546	24.2	531	15	0
NY	12	10	83.3	3	7	2	16.7	2	0	0
RUNDEL	227	214	94.3	69	145	13	5.7	9	4	0
ORE CITY	245	143	58.4	32	111	102	41.6	101	1	0
ORE	306	280	91.5	143	137	26	8.5	25	1	0
T	32	28	87.5	10	18	4	12.5	3	1	0
NE	22	17	77.3	5	12	5	22.7	3	2	0
L	85	76	89.4	16	60	9	10.6	9	0	0
S	33	27	81.8	4	23	6	18.2	6	0	0
STER	108	72	66.7	16	56	36	33.3	36	0	0
	13	13	100.0	2	11	0	0.0	0	0	0
ICK	178	112	63.6	18	94	64	36.4	64	0	0
T	10	7	70.0	1	6	3	30.0	3	0	0
D	155	117	75.5	34	83	38	24.5	37	1	0
	193	180	93.3	39	141	13	6.7	13	0	0
	12	11	91.7	4	7	1	8.3	1	0	0
MERY	409	357	87.3	132	225	52	12.7	52	0	0
GEORGE'S	395	225	57.0	45	180	170	43.0	166	4	0
ANNE'S	21	21	100.0	5	16	0	0.0	0	0	0
RY'S	48	36	75.0	11	25	12	25.0	12	0	0
ET	17	13	76.5	4	9	4	23.5	4	0	0
	14	13	92.9	3	10	1	7.1	1	0	0
GTON	34	30	88.2	8	22	4	11.8	4	0	0
CO	43	38	88.4	15	23	5	11.6	4	1	0
TER	19	19	100.0	10	9	0	0.0	0	0	0
ANSFERS	369	345	93.5	210	135	24	6.5	24	0	0

Note: Transfers Between Units are Included in Individual Local Unit Totals, but Excluded from State Totals.

TABLE
63

TOTAL NEW CERTIFIED PROFESSIONAL STAFF AT ELEMENTARY SCHOOL LEVEL
BY TYPE OF CERTIFICATE
MARYLAND PUBLIC SCHOOLS: OCTOBER, 1986

LOCAL UNIT	TOTAL	PROFESSIONAL TOTAL NUMBER	PCT.	ADVANCED	STANDARD	PROVISIONAL TOTAL NUMBER	PCT.	DEGREE	NON-DEGREE	INITIAL
TOTAL STATE	1,290	1,028	79.7	231	797	262	20.3	262	0	0
ALLEGANY	4	4	100.0	0	4	0	0.0	0	0	0
ANNE ARUNDEL	127	124	97.6	37	87	3	2.4	3	0	0
BALTIMORE CITY	142	94	66.2	19	75	48	33.8	48	0	0
BALTIMORE	177	165	93.2	71	94	12	6.8	12	0	0
CALVERT	15	15	100.0	4	11	0	0.0	0	0	0
CAROLINE	11	9	81.8	3	6	2	18.2	2	0	0
CARROLL	43	40	93.0	7	33	3	7.0	3	0	0
CECIL	18	15	93.8	3	12	1	6.3	1	0	0
CHARLES	56	41	73.2	13	28	15	26.8	15	0	0
DORCHESTER	8	8	100.0	1	7	0	0.0	0	0	0
FREDERICK	83	57	68.7	12	45	26	31.3	26	0	0
GARRETT	5	3	60.0	0	3	2	40.0	2	0	0
HARFORD	64	54	84.4	18	36	10	15.6	10	0	0
HOWARD	97	92	94.8	16	76	5	5.2	5	0	0
KENT	9	8	88.9	3	5	1	11.1	1	0	0
MONTGOMERY	261	234	89.7	81	153	27	10.3	27	0	0
PRINCE GEORGE'S	260	153	58.8	30	123	107	41.2	107	0	0
QUEEN ANNE'S	10	10	100.0	2	8	0	0.0	0	0	0
ST. MARY'S	28	18	64.3	3	15	10	35.7	10	0	0
SOMERSET	4	4	100.0	0	4	0	0.0	0	0	0
TALBOT	10	9	90.0	3	6	1	10.0	1	0	0
WASHINGTON	14	14	100.0	4	10	0	0.0	0	0	0
WICOMICO	26	24	92.3	8	16	2	7.7	2	0	0
WORCESTER	11	11	100.0	3	8	0	0.0	0	0	0
LEA TRANSFERS	191	178	93.2	110	68	13	6.8	13	0	0

TABLE
64

TOTAL NEW CERTIFIED PROFESSIONAL STAFF AT SECONDARY SCHOOL LEVEL
BY TYPE OF CERTIFICATE
MARYLAND PUBLIC SCHOOLS: OCTOBER, 1986

LOCAL UNIT	TOTAL	PROFESSIONAL TOTAL NUMBER	PCT.	ADVANCED	STANDARD	PROVISIONAL TOTAL NUMBER	PCT.	DEGREE	NON-DEGREE	INITIAL
TOTAL STATE	559	376	67.3	102	274	183	32.7	168	15	0
ALLEGANY	3	2	66.7	2	0	1	33.3	1	0	0
ANNE ARUNDEL	69	60	87.0	23	37	9	13.0	5	4	0
BALTIMORE CITY	64	30	46.9	5	25	34	53.1	33	1	0
BALTIMORE	61	53	86.9	31	22	8	13.1	7	1	0
CALVERT	9	7	77.8	0	7	2	22.2	1	1	0
CAROLINE	10	7	70.0	2	5	3	30.0	1	2	0
CARROLL	24	19	79.2	7	12	5	20.8	5	0	0
CECIL	15	10	66.7	0	10	5	33.3	5	0	0
CHARLES	24	14	58.3	2	12	10	41.7	10	0	0
DORCHESTER	3	3	100.0	1	2	0	0.0	0	0	0
FREDERICK	51	26	51.0	4	22	25	49.0	25	0	0
GARRETT	4	3	75.0	1	2	1	25.0	1	0	0
HARFORD	60	39	65.0	8	31	21	35.0	20	1	0
HOWARD	40	35	87.5	9	26	5	12.5	5	0	0
KENT	2	2	100.0	1	1	0	0.0	0	0	0
MONTGOMERY	115	94	81.7	41	53	21	18.3	21	0	0
PRINCE GEORGE'S	84	29	45.3	7	22	35	54.7	31	4	0
QUEEN ANNE'S	4	4	100.0	0	4	0	0.0	0	0	0
ST. MARY'S	11	10	90.9	5	5	1	9.1	1	0	0
SOMERSET	8	5	62.5	3	2	3	37.5	3	0	0
TALBOT	1	1	100.0	0	1	0	0.0	0	0	0
WASHINGTON	10	8	80.0	2	6	2	20.0	2	0	0
WICOMICO	13	10	76.9	5	5	3	23.1	2	1	0
WORCESTER	3	3	100.0	3	0	0	0.0	0	0	0
LEA TRANSFERS	109	98	89.9	60	38	11	10.1	11	0	0

Note: Transfers Between Units are Included in Individual Local Unit Totals, but Excluded from State Totals.

TABLE 65

TOTAL NEW CERTIFIED PROFESSIONAL STAFF AT MIDDLE AND COMBINED SCHOOL LEVEL
BY TYPE OF CERTIFICATE
MARYLAND PUBLIC SCHOOLS: OCTOBER, 1986

LOCAL UNIT	TOTAL	PROFESSIONAL TOTAL NUMBER	PCT.	ADVANCED	STANDARD	PROVISIONAL TOTAL NUMBER	PCT.	DEGREE	NON-DEGREE	INITIAL
TOTAL STATE	411	310	75.4	86	224	101	24.6	101	0	0
ALLEGANY	5	4	80.0	1	3	1	20.0	1	0	0
ANNE ARUNDEL	31	30	96.8	9	21	1	3.2	1	0	0
BALTIMORE CITY	39	19	48.7	8	11	20	51.3	20	0	0
BALTIMORE	68	62	91.2	41	21	6	8.8	6	0	0
CALVERT	8	6	75.0	6	0	2	25.0	2	0	0
CAROLINE	1	1	100.0	0	1	0	0.0	0	0	0
CARROLL	18	17	94.4	2	15	1	5.6	1	0	0
CECIL	2	2	100.0	1	1	0	0.0	0	0	0
CHARLES	28	17	60.7	1	16	11	39.3	11	0	0
DORCHESTER	2	2	100.0	0	2	0	0.0	0	0	0
FREDERICK	42	29	69.0	2	27	13	31.0	13	0	0
GARRETT	1	1	100.0	0	1	0	0.0	0	0	0
HARFORD	31	24	77.4	8	16	7	22.6	7	0	0
HOWARD	56	53	94.6	14	39	3	5.4	3	0	0
KENT	1	1	100.0	0	1	0	0.0	0	0	0
MONTGOMERY	33	29	87.9	10	19	4	12.1	4	0	0
PRINCE GEORGE'S	71	43	60.6	8	35	28	39.4	28	0	0
QUEEN ANNE'S	7	7	100.0	3	4	0	0.0	0	0	0
ST MARY'S	9	8	88.9	3	5	1	11.1	1	0	0
SOMERSET	5	4	80.0	1	3	1	20.0	1	0	0
TALBOT	3	3	100.0	0	3	0	0.0	0	0	0
WASHINGTON	10	8	80.0	2	6	2	20.0	2	0	0
WICOMICO	4	4	100.0	2	2	0	0.0	0	0	0
WORCESTER	5	5	100.0	4	1	0	0.0	0	0	0
LEA TRANSFERS	69	69	100.0	40	29	0	0.0	0	0	0

TABLE

66

GED Testing by Test Center: State of Maryland: July 1986 - June 1987

Test Center	Total Tested	Passed	Incomplete Testing	Failed
Total State	12,207*	6,828	756	4,623
Baltimore Metropolitan Area				
Baltimore City	2,395	937	107	1,351
Bel Air	434	303	16	115
Catonsville	856	522	41	293
Dundalk	840	550	15	275
Parkville	823	495	33	295
Severn	628	424	27	177
Westminster	292	203	3	86
Northwest				
Cumberland	202	142	3	57
Frederick	230	167	2	61
Hagerstown	141	98	0	43
McHenry	39	31	0	8
Washington National Capital Area				
Lanham	144	86	2	56
Riverdale	274	166	10	98
Rockville	758	486	56	216
Largo	869	497	19	353
Southern Maryland				
Leonardtown	136	96	3	37
Waldorf	202	133	0	69
Eastern Shore				
Easton	243	141	18	84
Salisbury	203	126	5	72
North East	203	137	3	63
Special Testing				
Correctional Institutions	1,479	809	64	606
Handicapped Testing	107	86	1	20
Job corps	700	184	328	188
Office - MSDE	9	9	0	0

*Excludes 266 out-of-state diplomas issued.
NOTE: The GED test is used to appraise the educational development of adults who have not completed their formal
       high school education. Upon successful completion of the test, an adult is awarded a Maryland High
       School Diploma.

TABLE
67

Participation in Adult and Community Education Programs: 1986-87

Local Unit	Adult Basic Education*		Adult General Education	Adult Vocational Education		External High School Diploma+	School Community Centers	Multi-Service Community Centers	School Volunteers
	Local Education Agencies	Community Colleges		Local Education Agencies	Community Colleges				
Total State	‡26,961	2,007	84,825	9,434	11,542	706	647,427	48,220	148,862
Allegany	541	0	737	0	403	0	4,985	3,908	3,317
Anne Arundel	1,413	0	876	302	0	153	7,092	0	21,448
Baltimore City	2,452	0	1,579	126	584	80	9,247	3,150	40,576
Baltimore	2,495	0	12,130	4,168	4,572	65	22,099	5,667	13,135
Calvert	111	0	1,213	0	0	0	2,807	5,332	2,046
Caroline	241	0	0	0	0	0	8,603	0	132
Carroll	408	0	1,594	0	0	0	2,408	1,901	3,762
Cecil	0	193	0	0	360	0	24,552	0	1,484
Charles	419	0	1,162	0	686	136	2,268	5,254	2,528
Dorchester	254	0	860	0	0	0	5,378	9,507	4,051
Frederick	308	0	2,543	634	343	0	2,745	0	3,950
Garrett	0	213	0	0	577	0	27,450	0	981
Harford	0	886	0	0	0	0	3,654	0	2,819
Howard	0	715	0	0	275	0	7,647	0	9,571
Kent	183	0	1,123	0	0	0	1,430	0	642
Montgomery	13,403	0	51,101	2,169	0	0	156,866	0	26,338
Prince George's	3,220	0	4,450	2,035	0	0	249,420	0	5,792
Queen Anne's	77	0	1,473	0	624	0	918	4,284	616
St. Mary's	197	0	1,882	0	0	0	12,793	3,259	0
Somerset	98	0	386	0	0	94	7,820	5,958	196
Talbot	95	0	203	0	0	0	5,750	0	0
Washington	234	0	331	0	1,318	178	73,196	0	2,005
Wicomico	448	0	930	0	634	0	5,118	0	2,582
Worcester	219	0	252	0	0	0	3,181	0	891
Corrections Ed.	145	0	0	0	1,166	0	0	0	0

NOTE: Data between programs are not mutually exclusive.
*The Adult Basic Education program is designed to raise the literacy level of persons 16 years of age and older who lack the minimum competencies in mathematics, speaking, reading, and/or writing English.
+Graduates only
‡829 Adult Basic Education students served in community-based programs are included in Total.

Health Occupa- tions	Consumer & Home making Education	Occupa- tional Home Economics	Business and Office	Diver- sified Occupa- tions	Technical	Trades and Industry	Occupa- tional Support Services	Indus- trial Arts Education/
1,304	71,542	2,757	43,015	6,508	146	14,097	7,913	71,080
24	2,082	20	1,201	117	22	302	244	2,651
143	15,343	37	5,822	575	0	1,109	288	7,491
224	5,945	636	4,548	0	124	2,829	1,566	7,409
92	9,542	178	4,151	1,520	0	1,750	806	10,622
53	1,139	32	530	26	0	220	238	800
14	867	0	453	11	0	112	200	524
12	1,840	45	1,726	0	0	673	205	2,429
31	1,301	28	1,111	141	0	361	268	1,559
27	1,619	42	1,786	144	0	340	170	1,742
36	652	37	467	0	0	220	38	541
42	2,246	0	1,048	238	0	790	349	1,362
30	464	59	236	0	0	341	271	542
62	2,158	32	2,401	222	0	400	137	3,909
75	2,026	29	1,799	0	0	442	320	2,299
44	209	0	113	0	0	176	13	212
103	8,157	343	4,805	1,608	0	1,100	1,272	10,154
154	9,088	915	5,261	1,559	0	1,390	916	9,936
22	674	42	359	0	0	251	77	564
6	869	32	1,146	74	0	260	226	955
22	141	25	410	59	0	62	73	168
13	496	68	340	15	0	81	50	443
42	2,550	43	1,982	199	0	453	88	2,705
21	1,546	89	734	0	0	283	36	1,599
12	588	25	586	0	0	152	62	464

rial Arts.
te, 1,649; Allegany, 637; Anne Arundel, 726; Baltimore, 93; Cecil, 162; Montgomery, 23; Somerset, 8.

TABLE
69

VOCATIONAL REHABILITATION SERVICES RENDERED: STATE OF MARYLAND: 1986-87*

	Applications	Evaluations	Closed After Evaluation	Surveyed Under Advisement	Job Preparation	Service Completed	Rehabilit- ations	Closed- Other Reasons	Total Cases
e	4,104	327	9,189	999	4,540	2,449	3,859	1,730	27,197
	2	14	237	5	212	162	99	33	764
el	259	20	608	101	346	211	291	125	1,961
City	1,605	99	3,749	377	1,009	702	1,156	514	9,211
	531	66	1,195	201	476	267	469	323	3,528
	17	2	42	24	29	15	27	15	171
	21	0	47	4	45	14	30	13	174
	95	2	149	10	103	37	90	19	505
	28	0	104	7	54	52	67	37	349
	44	3	79	42	38	13	53	39	311
	22	5	54	3	21	15	40	9	169
	190	11	196	5	314	145	133	23	1,017
	1	5	44	0	73	17	47	6	193
	159	12	264	23	123	71	111	23	786
	70	6	188	4	135	50	122	61	636
	12	0	27	1	12	9	13	6	80
	252	26	691	73	408	121	297	131	1,999
rge's	385	33	863	61	631	277	398	193	2,841
's	10	0	60	0	30	12	26	8	146
	21	8	123	12	61	37	70	17	349
	18	1	32	0	23	16	31	7	128
	14	0	38	6	31	21	44	2	156
	125	6	174	6	236	109	152	90	898
	72	2	186	8	54	53	58	27	460
	16	0	39	7	24	10	35	9	140
	135	6	0	19	52	13	0	0	225

esents the distribution of clients served during various stages of thier rehabilitation as of September 30, 1987.
 undertermined.

TABLE
70
CHARACTERISTICS OF CLIENTS SERVED BY VOCATIONAL REHABILITATION: STATE OF MARYLAND: 1986-87

CHARACTERISTIC	TOTAL CLIENTS SERVED	REHABILITATED*		CHARACTERISTIC	TOTAL CLIENTS SERVED	REHABILITATED*	
		SEVERELY DISABLED	OTHER			SEVERELY DISABLED	OTHER
TOTAL CASES	29,277	2,400	1,459				
Age				**Dependents**			
Under 20	1,690	25	27	0	20,641	1,597	850
20-34	13,568	1,524	211	1	4,579	466	266
35-44	6,592	291	458	2 or 3	3,164	261	259
45-64	5,845	252	598	4 or more	893	76	84
65 and over	1,582	308	165				
Education-Grades Completed				**Primary Source of Support at Acceptance**			
None/Unknown	3,720	16	3	Current Earnings	2,482	281	386
1-7	1,424	215	82	Family or Friends	6,930	671	466
8	1,399	150	86	Private Rehabilitation Agency	22	6	1
9-11	6,083	465	308				
12	10,874	892	699	Public Assistance (some Federal)	4,514	532	118
13-15	1,997	173	110	Public Assistance (no Federal)	1,833	124	80
16 and over	961	122	51				
Special Education	2,819	367	120	Public Institutions (tax supported)	84	8	3
Race				Workmen's Compensation	837	49	80
White	15,048	1,541	833	Social Security Disability Benefits	1,463	252	3
Black	10,071	818	607				
Indian	29	5	1	Other Disability Benefits	770	108	86
Other	263	36	18	Non-Disability benefits	446	75	57
Not Reported	3,866	0	0	Other	830	115	58
Sex				Not Reported	9,066	179	121
Male	16,008	1,247	718				
Female	13,269	1,153	741				

*Clients who were rehabilitated into employment during the year.

TABLE
71

NUMBER OF VOCATIONAL REHABILITATION REFERRALS BY REPORTING AGENCY: STATE OF MARYLAND: 1986-87

TYPE OF REFERRAL	TOTAL CLIENTS SERVED	REHABILITATED*	
		SEVERELY DISABLED	OTHER
TOTAL	29,277	2,400	1,459
Educational Institutions	2,933	247	123
Hospitals and Sanitariums	2,306	257	95
Health Organizations and Agencies	2,048	196	78
Welfare Agencies	1,224	53	42
Public Organizations and Agencies (not specifically educational, health, or welfare)	5,794	248	189
Private Organizations and Agencies (not specifically educational, health, or welfare)	1,375	152	71
Individuals	13,597	1,247	861

*Clients who were rehabilitated into employment during the year.

TABLE
72

Rehabilitations by Nature and Severity of Disability: 1987

Primary Disability	Number of Rehabilitations	Number of Severely Disabled	Percent Severely Disabled
Total Rehabilitations	3,859	2,400	62%
Blind and Visual Impairments	262	180	69
Deaf and Hearing Impairments	759	519	68
Orthopedic Impairments	1,029	674	66
Mental Impairments	412	293	71
Alcoholism	115	26	23
Drug Addiction	45	29	64
Mental Retardation	364	271	74
Specific Development Disorders	247	102	41
Epilepsy	95	89	94
Heart & Circulatory Disorders	68	47	69
Respiratory Diseases	9	4	44
Digestive System Disorders	227	26	12
Speech Disorders	26	14	54
Others Not Classified	201	126	63

TABLE
73

Financial Statement

Expenditures and Encumbrances of the Maryland State Department of Education
Headquarters and Vocational Rehabilitation: 1986-87

Object of Expenditure	Office of the Superintendent & Deputy Superintendent	Office of Administration & Finance	Office of Management Information Systems	Division of Instruction	Division of Compensatory, Urban & Supplementary Programs	Division of Special Education & Support Services	Division of Vocational-Technical Education	Correctional Education
Salaries, Wages & Benefits	$1,946,510	$3,638,422	$1,346,509	$2,197,829	$1,186,763	$1,704,862	$1,943,144	$5,087,755
Technical & Special Fees	157,880	72,825	4,758	58,529	43,373	117,212	18,942	454,075
Communications	59,890	110,461	33,695	80,153	39,144	53,032	70,789	19,877
Travel	94,217	65,804	9,768	97,969	51,583	43,879	68,830	29,027
Food	0	0	0	0	0	0	0	0
Fuel & Utilities	27,250	78,961	24,000	40,336	22,855	32,189	33,857	7,155
Vehicle Operation & Maintenance	32,774	72,830	16,180	31,069	23,047	16,696	47,350	5,111
Contractual Services	708,855	448,190	354,163	641,010	69,591	210,045	92,953	262,855
Supplies & Materials	22,948	51,995	48,340	35,297	14,362	20,137	27,452	273,635
Replacement Equipment	3,766	984	. 490	957	543	2,427	904	98
Additional Equipment	20,250	8,592	129,380	25,135	4,271	4,693	2,082	130,931
Grants, Subsidies & Contributions	138,638	(239,931)	0	525,750	312,994	19,071	0	0
Fixed Charges	80,345	22,462	10,198	13,472	8,157	13,411	14,873	39,039
Land	189	0		0	0	0	0	0
TOTAL EXPENDITURE/ENCUMBRANCES	$3,293,511	$4,331,593	$1,977,482	$3,747,506	$1,776,683	$2,237,654	$2,321,175	$6,309,559

Object of Expenditure	Division of Instructional Technology	Division of Library Development & Services	Division of Certification & Accreditation	Division of Vocational Rehabilitation	Vocational Rehabilitation Field Operations	Maryland Rehabilitation Center	Disability Determination Services
Salaries, Wages & Benefits	$978,016	$1,230,129	$1,697,631	$1,221,162	$7,973,547	$5,586,020	$5,933,002
Technical & Special Fees	69,664	52,765	293,425	122,583	44,357	146,739	4,318,961
Communications	45,111	34,741	75,380	40,380	231,026	95,036	345,454
Travel	48,795	40,775	36,957	29,544	118,033	6,077	76,341
Food	0	0	0	0	0	0	0
Fuel & Utilities	0	17,518	33,729	19,637	6,649	383,908	47,080
Vehicle Operation & Maintenance	(603)	15,592	19,637	15,492	41,135	9,316	0
Contractual Services	367,212	131,468	322,118	62,990	47,147	759,486	397,976
Supplies & Materials	48,429	79,388	35,154	21,827	32,790	268,466	73,678
Replacement Equipment	4,511	436	404	1,248	5,608	35,521	8,063
Additional Equipment	183,729	10,211	9,916	170,448	58,370	70,128	16,614
Grants, Subsidies & Contributions	144,617	700	246,090	1,388,265	6,450,809	96,890	584
Fixed Charges	5,031	106,926	11,724	26,323	536,088	21,354	254,453
Land	0	0	0	0	0	10,298	0
TOTAL EXPENDITURE/ENCUMBRANCES	$1,894,513	$1,720,650	$2,782,166	$3,119,899	$15,545,559	$7,489,240	$11,472,206

SOURCE: ACCTG 17 Report

TABLE
74

Statement of Appropriations: Maryland State Department of Education Aid to Education: 1986-87

Program	Appropriations*				Expenditures and Encumbrances			Balance Available
	Total	General	Federal	Special	Total	Expenditures	Encumbrances	
Total Aid Programs	$1,565,891,356	$1,374,205,212	$175,874,487	$15,811,657	$1,551,952,774	$1,529,944,727	$22,008,046	$13,938,583
State Share of Current Expense	553,273,633	553,273,633	0	0	553,185,337	552,366,649	818,688	88,296
Compensatory Education	44,358,395	44,358,395	0	0	44,358,395	44,358,395	0	0
Local Employees Fringe Benefits	372,630,727	357,622,551	0	15,008,176	366,840,236	366,840,236	0	5,790,491
Children at Risk	80,000	80,000	0	0	79,999	22,000	57,999	1
Handicapped Children	93,530,260	93,530,260	0	0	92,837,280	86,495,812	6,341,468	692,980
Educating Handicapped Children	27,990,718	0	27,990,718	0	26,730,598	24,866,183	1,864,415	1,260,120
Gifted and Talented	1,491,708	688,227	0	803,481	1,456,799	1,419,895	36,904	34,909
Environmental Education	265,050	265,050	0	0	264,750	169,552	95,198	300
Disruptive Youth	615,818	615,818	0	0	614,825	528,441	86,384	993
Educationally Deprived	64,907,537	0	64,907,537	0	64,746,075	59,152,753	5,593,322	161,462
Innovative Programs	15,178,053	6,853,460	8,324,592	0	15,152,522	12,449,694	2,702,828	25,530
Adult Continuing Education	2,789,535	1,042,448	1,747,087	0	2,726,361	2,497,023	229,339	63,174
Transition for Refugee Children	906,227	0	906,227	0	903,984	684,717	219,267	2,244
Vocational Education	13,404,314	0	13,404,314	0	12,873,603	11,581,871	1,291,732	530,711
Job Training & Partnership	1,199,895	0	1,199,895	0	1,130,312	1,095,864	34,448	69,584
Food Service	61,876,040	6,566,851	55,309,189	0	56,992,503	56,992,503	0	4,883,537
Public Libraries	14,301,274	12,216,348	2,084,926	0	14,226,755	13,783,993	442,762	74,520
State Library Network	4,144,146	4,144,146	0	0	4,144,146	4,144,146	0	0
State Publications Depository	55,494	55,494	0	0	55,494	55,494	0	0
Transportation	113,379,689	113,379,689	0	0	113,379,689	113,379,689	0	0
School Construction	175,626,395	175,626,395	0	0	175,368,284	174,059,700	1,308,584	258,111
School Community Centers	1,611,168	1,611,168	0	0	1,609,549	1,439,390	170,159	1,619
Extended Elementary	2,275,279	2,275,279	0	0	2,275,279	1,560,729	714,550	0

*Includes adjustments and carryover appropriations

SOURCE: State Aid Summary Report, AID01

TABLE

75

Local Revenue Appropriations as a Percent of Total Local Revenue: Maryland Public Schools: 1986-87

Local Unit	Total Local Revenue*	Local Appropriations				Percent of Revenue Appropriated to Schools			
		All School Purposes	Current Expenses	School Construction	Debt Service	All School Purposes	Current Expenses	Construction	Debt Service
Total State	$3,490,972,323	$1,733,316,742	$1,559,354,659	$131,917,624	$42,044,351	49.65%	44.67%	3.78%	1.20%
Allegany	34,660,314	15,384,314	15,250,000	134,314	0	44.39	44.00	0.39	0.00
Anne Arundel	312,325,896	168,100,775	143,538,540	18,452,025	6,110,210	53.82	45.96	5.91	1.96
Baltimore City	531,104,843	143,432,500	126,388,283	0	17,044,217	27.01	23.80	0.00	3.21
Baltimore	519,746,499	266,844,311	257,704,484	4,968,440	4,171,387	51.34	49.58	0.96	0.80
Calvert	32,110,782	19,649,734	18,976,102	484,382	189,250	61.19	59.10	1.51	0.59
Caroline	9,980,300	5,288,820	5,174,998	113,822	0	52.99	51.85	1.14	0.00
Carroll	61,335,713	33,895,603	32,002,065	1,293,358	600,180	55.26	52.18	2.11	0.98
Cecil	32,431,562	18,599,158	17,194,011	952,926	452,221	57.35	53.02	2.94	1.39
Charles	53,691,126	29,975,093	27,800,000	2,175,093	0	55.83	51.78	4.05	0.00
Dorchester	14,911,948	7,448,894	7,099,988	168,240	180,666	49.95	47.61	1.13	1.21
Frederick	80,853,576	47,332,670	43,737,341	1,855,768	1,739,561	58.54	54.09	2.30	2.15
Garrett	12,809,899	6,152,499	6,152,499	0	0	48.03	48.03	0.00	0.00
Harford	91,378,900	46,461,487	44,094,834	962,272	1,404,381	50.84	48.25	1.05	1.54
Howard	139,421,461	92,509,951	78,538,628	10,264,208	3,707,115	66.35	56.33	7.36	2.66
Kent	9,015,665	5,097,344	4,956,294	0	141,050	56.54	54.97	0.00	1.56
Montgomery+	841,999,425	487,358,627	398,053,260	89,305,367	0	57.88	47.27	10.61	0.00
Prince George's	511,749,082	232,241,806	227,674,256	0	4,567,550	45.38	44.49	0.00	0.89
Queen Anne's	16,566,629	10,289,330	10,205,850	0	83,480	62.11	61.60	0.00	0.50
St. Mary's	29,484,718	18,216,290	17,773,736	442,554	0	61.78	60.28	1.50	0.00
Somerset	6,560,400	3,278,127	3,278,127	0	0	49.97	49.97	0.00	0.00
Talbot	15,064,808	8,813,363	8,688,663	0	124,700	58.50	57.68	0.00	0.83
Washington	52,158,797	32,261,600	30,615,521	343,296	1,302,783	61.85	58.70	0.66	2.50
Wicomico	35,418,768	17,276,902	17,276,902	0	0	48.78	48.78	0.00	0.00
Worcester	46,191,212	17,407,544	17,180,277	1,559	225,600	37.69	37.19	0.00	0.49

*Figures, from State Department of Fiscal Services, include county and municipal revenues form taxes, fines, forteitures, licenses, and permits.
+Montgomery County appropriation for food service is not included.

TABLE 76

REVENUE FROM ALL SOURCES: MARYLAND PUBLIC SCHOOLS: 1986 - 87

	TOTAL REVENUE & NONREVENUE	STATE	FEDERAL	LOCAL APPROPRIATION	LOCAL OTHER+	NONREVENUE#	STATE	FED.	LOCAL	NON-REVENUE
			REVENUE				PERCENT FROM EACH SOURCE			
TOTAL STATE	$3,241,663,250	$1,241,509,674	$164,245,512	$1,733,429,354	$83,835,466	$18,643,244	38.3	5.1	56.0	0.6
ALLEGANY	43,731,744	23,331,340	3,386,797	15,384,314	1,601,605	27,688	53.4	7.7	38.9	@
ANNE ARUNDEL	301,791,373	111,880,859	13,561,604	168,100,775	7,519,136	728,999	37.1	4.5	58.2	0.2
BALTIMORE CITY	453,400,560	247,213,991	51,094,039	143,432,500	6,600,270	5,059,760	54.5	11.3	33.1	1.1
BALTIMORE	420,580,616	131,011,772	12,170,073	266,956,923	9,440,504	1,001,344	31.2	2.9	65.7	0.2
CALVERT	35,372,910	12,800,147	1,772,308	19,649,734	1,035,344	115,377	36.2	5.0	58.5	0.3
CAROLINE	16,526,397	9,331,848	1,291,515	5,288,820	448,947	165,267	56.5	7.8	34.7	1.0
CARROLL	76,960,578	37,740,301	2,868,835	33,895,603	2,336,194	119,545	49.0	3.7	47.1	0.2
CECIL	45,594,038	23,319,045	2,310,391	18,589,158	1,292,790	72,654	51.1	5.1	43.6	0.2
CHARLES	74,083,512	37,451,086	3,772,353	29,975,093	2,883,009	1,971	50.6	5.1	44.3	.0
DORCHESTER	20,385,689	10,218,247	1,953,104	7,448,894	755,293	10,151	50.1	9.6	40.3	@
FREDERICK	99,321,123	43,936,156	4,039,089	47,332,670	3,705,547	307,661	44.2	4.1	51.4	0.3
GARRETT	22,194,143	13,313,595	1,680,475	6,152,499	926,665	120,909	60.0	7.6	31.9	0.5
HARFORD	109,731,884	53,028,472	6,162,726	46,461,487	3,747,132	332,067	48.3	5.6	45.8	0.3
HOWARD	142,533,958	41,560,385	3,208,443	92,509,951	5,154,277	100,902	29.2	2.3	68.5	@
KENT	10,897,958	4,684,728	674,263	5,097,344	431,372	10,251	43.0	6.2	50.8	@
MONTGOMERY	649,037,096	135,802,156	13,173,897	487,358,627	12,411,428	290,988	20.9	2.0	77.1	@
PRINCE GEORGES	479,792,882	199,195,660	23,995,910	232,241,806	16,199,684	8,159,822	41.5	5.0	51.8	1.7
QUEEN ANNE'S	21,114,180	8,646,392	1,483,000	10,289,330	691,073	4,385	41.0	7.0	52.0	@
ST. MARY'S	47,049,776	23,204,725	4,060,760	18,216,290	1,427,722	140,279	49.3	8.6	41.8	0.3
SOMERSET	12,636,461	7,264,853	1,432,249	3,278,127	332,619	328,613	57.5	11.3	28.6	2.6
TALBOT	14,838,551	4,596,087	884,217	8,813,363	544,134	750	31.0	6.0	63.0	.0
WASHINGTON	74,079,937	33,366,994	5,202,050	32,261,600	1,945,517	1,303,776	45.0	7.0	46.2	1.8
WICOMICO	43,509,557	21,847,495	2,485,064	17,276,902	1,793,673	106,423	50.2	5.7	43.9	0.2
WORCESTER	26,498,327	6,763,340	1,582,250	17,407,544	611,531	133,662	25.5	6.0	68.0	0.5

*INCLUDES REVENUE FROM THE FOLLOWING FUNDS: CURRENT EXPENSE, SCHOOL CONSTRUCTION, DEBT SERVICE, AND FOOD SERVICE.
+INCLUDES THE FOLLOWING: TUITION, TRANSPORTATION FEES, TRANSFERS FROM SCHOOL UNITS IN OTHER STATES, AND OTHER MISCELLANEOUS REVENUES
#INCLUDES THE SALE OF PROPERTY, NET INSURANCE PROCEEDS, AND OTHER MISCELLANEOUS SOURCES WHICH MAY INCUR FUTURE OBLIGATIONS.
@LESS THAN 0.1 PERCENT.

TABLE

77

Revenue from All Sources for Current Expenses*: Maryland Public Schools: 1986 - 87
(Includes Teachers' Retirement and Social Security Paid Direct by State)

L UNIT	TOTAL REVENUE & NONREVENUE	STATE	FEDERAL	LOCAL APPROPRIATION	LOCAL OTHER+	NONREVENUE#	STATE	FED.	LOCAL	NON-REV.
			------- REVENUE -------				PERCENT FROM EACH SOURCE			
L STATE	$2,916,431,595	$1,179,081,515	$153,124,523	$1,559,467,271	$22,323,529	$2,434,757	40.4	5.2	54.4	@
GANY	41,847,341	22,940,412	3,081,610	15,250,000	566,109	9,210	54.8	7.3	37.9	@
ARUNDEL	266,240,239	108,142,792	12,924,115	143,538,540	1,634,792	0	40.6	4.8	54.6	
IMORE CITY	413,877,266	236,676,817	49,575,031	126,388,283	1,237,135	0	57.1	11.9	31.0	
IMORE	393,110,580	123,279,931	10,860,768	257,817,096	614,935	537,850	31.3	2.7	65.9	0.1
ERT	33,603,534	12,517,461	1,618,849	18,976,102	387,439	103,683	37.2	4.8	57.7	0.3
LINE	15,692,137	9,196,343	1,179,978	5,174,998	14,389	126,429	58.6	7.5	33.1	0.8
OLL	69,351,432	34,473,826	2,460,494	32,002,065	337,425	77,622	49.7	3.5	46.7	0.1
L	42,895,338	23,294,045	2,079,753	17,194,011	259,189	68,340	54.3	4.8	40.8	0.1
LES	64,594,401	32,224,772	3,386,849	27,800,000	1,181,296	1,484	49.8	5.2	45.0	@
HESTER	19,284,251	10,011,579	1,856,849	7,099,988	305,684	10,151	51.9	9.6	38.5	@
ERICK	90,178,031	41,789,011	3,381,709	43,737,341	984,517	285,453	46.3	3.7	49.7	0.3
ETT	19,316,747	11,165,238	1,680,475	6,152,499	201,056	117,479	57.8	8.6	33.0	0.6
ORD	101,625,637	50,937,123	5,578,411	44,094,834	1,015,269	0	50.1	5.4	44.5	
RD	124,153,963	40,416,645	2,763,342	78,538,628	2,334,446	100,902	32.5	2.2	65.3	@
	10,455,100	4,684,728	625,034	4,956,294	183,917	5,127	44.8	5.9	49.3	@
GOMERY	535,242,061	121,704,130	12,656,578	398,053,260	2,825,249	2,844	22.7	2.3	75.0	@
CE GEORGE'S	448,355,915	192,745,619	21,397,648	227,674,256	6,406,265	132,127	42.9	4.7	52.4	@
N ANNE'S	20,513,311	8,646,392	1,393,050	10,205,850	264,802	3,217	42.1	6.7	51.2	@
MARY'S	44,575,785	22,393,299	3,885,791	17,773,736	382,680	140,279	50.2	8.7	40.8	0.3
RSET	12,401,444	7,264,853	1,432,249	3,278,127	106,216	319,999	58.5	11.5	27.5	2.5
OT	14,223,305	4,596,087	770,476	8,688,663	167,329	750	32.3	5.4	62.3	@
INGTON	68,433,622	32,827,636	4,625,031	30,615,521	136,294	229,140	47.9	6.7	45.1	0.3
MICO	42,006,479	21,644,245	2,328,183	17,278,902	728,140	29,009	51.5	5.5	43.0	@
ESTER	24,453,676	5,508,531	1,582,250	17,180,277	48,956	133,662	22.5	6.4	70.6	0.5

ludes revenue for purchase of replacement and additional equipment for current expense purposes, and federal and state revenue
food service operations; excludes value of U.S.D.A. commodities.
cludes tuition, transportation fees, transfer of funds from school units in other states, and miscellaneous other revenues.
ludes the sale of property, net insurance proceeds, and other miscellaneous sources which may incur future obligations.
s than 0.1 percent.

TABLE 78

Revenue from All Sources for Current Expenses*: Maryland Public Schools: 1986 - 87
(Excludes Teachers' Retirement and Social Security Paid Direct by State)

LOCAL UNIT	TOTAL REVENUE & NONREVENUE	REVENUE STATE	FEDERAL	LOCAL APPROPRIATION	LOCAL OTHER+	PERCENT FROM EACH SOURCE NONREVENUE#	STATE	FED.	LOCAL	NON-REV.
TOTAL STATE	$2,553,357,844	$816,007,764	$153,124,523	$1,559,467,271	$22,323,529	$2,434,757	31.9	5.9	82.2	@
ALLEGANY	36,652,551	17,745,622	3,081,610	15,250,000	566,109	9,210	48.4	8.4	43.2	@
ANNE ARUNDEL	232,449,201	74,351,754	12,924,115	143,538,540	1,634,792	0	31.9	5.5	62.8	@
BALTIMORE CITY	365,794,923	188,594,474	49,575,031	126,388,283	1,237,135	0	51.5	13.5	35.0	
BALTIMORE	340,086,277	70,255,628	10,860,768	257,817,096	614,935	537,850	20.6	3.1	76.2	0.1
CALVERT	29,530,895	8,444,822	1,618,849	18,976,102	387,439	103,683	28.5	5.4	65.8	0.3
CAROLINE	13,815,920	7,320,126	1,179,978	5,174,998	14,389	126,429	52.9	8.5	37.7	0.9
CARROLL	60,539,902	25,662,296	2,460,494	32,002,065	337,425	77,622	42.3	4.0	53.6	0.1
CECIL	37,595,641	17,994,348	2,079,753	17,194,011	259,189	68,340	47.8	5.5	46.6	0.1
CHARLES	57,253,922	24,884,293	3,386,849	27,600,000	1,181,296	1,484	43.4	5.9	50.7	@
DORCHESTER	17,027,537	7,754,865	1,856,849	7,099,988	305,684	10,151	45.5	10.9	43.6	@
FREDERICK	79,004,601	30,615,581	3,381,709	43,737,341	984,517	285,453	38.7	4.2	56.8	0.3
GARRETT	17,083,363	8,931,854	1,680,475	6,152,499	201,056	117,479	52.2	9.8	37.4	0.6
HARFORD	88,786,099	38,097,585	5,578,411	44,094,834	1,015,269	0	42.9	6.2	50.9	
HOWARD	109,669,335	25,932,017	2,763,342	78,538,628	2,334,446	100,902	23.6	2.5	73.9	@
KENT	9,280,990	3,510,618	625,034	4,956,294	183,917	5,127	37.8	6.7	55.5	@
MONTGOMERY	467,680,233	54,142,302	12,656,578	398,053,260	2,825,249	2,844	11.5	2.7	85.8	@
PRINCE GEORGE'S	392,877,875	137,067,579	21,397,848	227,674,256	6,406,265	132,127	34.9	5.4	59.7	@
QUEEN ANNE'S	18,079,613	6,212,694	1,393,050	10,205,850	264,802	3,217	34.3	7.7	58.0	@
ST. MARY'S	39,419,945	17,237,459	3,885,791	17,773,736	382,680	140,279	43.7	9.8	46.2	0.3
SOMERSET	10,946,858	5,810,267	1,432,249	3,278,127	106,216	319,999	53.0	13.0	31.1	2.9
TALBOT	12,397,265	2,770,047	770,476	8,688,663	167,329	750	22.3	6.2	71.5	@
WASHINGTON	59,780,715	24,174,729	4,625,031	30,615,521	136,294	229,140	40.4	7.7	51.6	0.3
WICOMICO	36,462,230	16,099,996	2,328,183	17,276,902	728,140	29,009	44.1	6.3	49.6	@
WORCESTER	21,341,953	2,396,808	1,582,250	17,180,277	48,956	133,662	11.2	7.4	80.8	0.6

*Includes revenue for purchase of replacement and additional equipment for current expense purposes, and federal and state revenue for food service operations; excludes value of U.S.D.A. commodities.
+Includes tuition, transportation fees, transfers of funds from school units in other states, and miscellaneous other revenues.
#Includes the sale of property, net insurance proceeds, and other miscellaneous sources which may incur future obligations.
@Less than 0.1 percent.

TABLE
79

Revenue from All Sources for School Construction: Maryland Public Schools: 1986 - 87

UNIT	TOTAL REVENUE & NONREVENUE	STATE	FEDERAL	LOCAL APPROPRIATION	LOCAL OTHER	NONREVENUE*	STATE	FED.	LOCAL	NON-REV.
STATE	$193,348,119	$44,400,591	$0	$131,917,732	$454,915	$16,574,881	22.9		68.6	8.5
NY	363,602	214,608	0	134,314	7,477	7,203	59.0		39.1	1.9
RUNDEL	21,852,648	2,840,210	0	18,452,025	127,724	432,689	12.9		85.2	1.9
ORE CITY	13,671,054	7,167,277	0	0	0	6,503,777	52.4			47.5
ORE	8,595,459	3,456,688	0	4,968,440	0	170,331	40.2		57.9	1.9
T	776,250	282,686	0	484,382	0	9,182	36.4		62.5	1.1
NE	128,047	0	0	113,822	0	14,225			88.9	11.1
L	4,559,833	3,266,475	0	1,293,358	0	0	71.6		28.4	
	982,240	25,000	0	952,928	0	4,314	2.5		97.1	0.4
S	6,625,426	4,443,214	0	2,175,093	7,119	0	67.0		33.0	
STER	168,240	0	0	168,240	0	0			100.0	
ICK	3,416,271	1,538,295	0	1,855,768	0	22,208	45.0		54.4	0.6
T	2,160,169	2,148,357	0	0	11,812	0	99.4		0.8	
D	2,720,703	1,426,364	0	962,272	0	332,087	52.4		35.4	12.2
	11,529,623	1,041,740	0	10,264,208	223,675	0	9.0		91.0	
	5,124	0	0	0	0	5,124				100.0
MERY	100,837,367	11,532,000	0	89,305,367	0	0	11.4		88.6	
GEORGE'S	10,966,276	2,938,581	0	0	0	8,027,695	26.7			73.2
ANNE'S	68,325	0	0	0	68,325	0			100.0	
RY'S	1,262,763	811,426	0	442,554	8,783	0	64.2		35.8	
ET	0	0	0	0	0	0				
	0	0	0	0	0	0				
GTON	1,329,728	12,861	0	343,296	0	973,571	0.9		25.9	73.2
CO	72,495	0	0	0	0	72,495				100.0
TER	1,256,476	1,254,809	0	1,667	0	0	99.8		0.2	

des net insurance recovery, sale of bonds, sale of property & equipment, and interest earnings.

TABLE 80

Revenue from All Sources for Debt Service:* Maryland Public Schools: 1986 - '87

LOCAL UNIT	TOTAL REVENUE & NONREVENUE	STATE	FEDERAL	LOCAL APPROPRIATION	LOCAL OTHER	NONREVENUE	STATE	FED.	LOCAL	NON-REV.
TOTAL STATE	$60,551,005	$18,027,568	$0	$42,044,351	$1,950,533	$1,471,447	29.7		67.9	2.4
ALLEGANY	176,320	176,320		0	0	0	100.0			
ANNE ARUNDEL	7,008,067	897,857		6,110,210	0	0	12.8		87.2	
BALTIMORE CITY	20,414,114	3,369,897		17,044,217	1,471,447	1,471,447	16.5		76.3	7.2
BALTIMORE	8,446,540	4,275,153	0	4,171,387	0	0	50.6		49.4	
CALVERT	189,250	0	0	189,250	0	0			100.0	
CAROLINE	135,505	135,505		0	0	0	100.0			
CARROLL	800,180	0	0	800,180	0	0			100.0	
CECIL	452,221	0	0	452,221	0	0			100.0	
CHARLES	783,100	783,100	0	0	0	0	100.0			
DORCHESTER	387,334	206,668	0	180,666	0	0	53.3		46.7	
FREDERICK	2,348,411	608,850		1,739,561	0	0	25.9		74.1	
GARRETT	0	0	0	0	0	0				
HARFORD	2,069,366	664,985	0	1,404,381	0	0	32.1		87.9	
HOWARD	3,809,115	102,000	0	3,707,115	0	0	2.6		97.4	
KENT	141,050	0	0	141,050	0	0			100.0	
MONTGOMERY	2,5 8,08	2,566,026		0	2,058	0	99.9		0.1	
PRINCE GEORGE'S	8,5 6,03	3,511,460		4,567,550	477,028	0	41.0		59.0	
QUEEN ANNE'S	83,48	0		83,480	0	0			100.0	
ST. MARY'S	4	0	0	0	0	0				
SOMERSET	0	0	0	0	0	0				
TALBOT	1 4,7	0	0	124,700	0	0			100.0	
WASHINGTON	1,8 9,2	528,497	0	1,302,783	0	0	28.7		71.3	
WICOMICO	203,200	203,250	0	0	0	0	100.0			
WORCESTER	2 5,6 0	0	0	225,600	0	0			100.0	

*Includes revenue for payment of both principal and interest.

TABLE
81

Revenue from all Sources for Food Services: Maryland Public Schools: 1986 - 87

-------------------- R E V E N U E --------------------

UNIT	TOTAL REVENUE & NONREVENUE	STATE	FEDERAL*	CHILDRENS PAYMENTS	LOCAL OTHER FOOD SALES	OTHER	NONREVENUE+	% FROM EACH SOURCE STATE	FED	LOCAL	NON-REV.
STATE	$115,975,935	$8,643,301	$49,121,092	$42,632,977	$14,699,166	$1,774,346	$1,105,053	5.7	42.3	51.1	0.9
NY	2,741,922	222,610	1,480,018	661,024	137,448	229,547	11,275	8.1	53.9	37.6	0.4
RUNDEL	8,816,558	286,986	2,475,642	3,489,076	2,136,280	131,264	296,310	3.2	28.0	65.5	3.3
ORE CITY	22,020,871	2,466,901	15,634,852	1,189,268	2,702,420	0	27,430	11.2	71.0	17.7	0.1
ORE	13,122,000	396,858	3,606,410	5,220,613	3,590,902	14,054	293,163	3.0	27.4	67.4	2.2
T	1,132,843	38,967	443,459	489,195	158,710	0	2,512	3.4	39.1	57.3	0.2
NE	995,617	63,718	472,728	434,558	0	0	24,613	6.3	47.4	43.9	2.4
L	2,944,019	40,570	862,757	1,369,484	629,285	0	41,923	1.3	29.3	68.0	1.4
S	1,875,404	88,420	753,383	569,534	448,575	15,492	0	4.7	40.1	55.2	@
STER	2,878,784	107,607	1,076,096	1,188,198	427,948	78,448	487	3.7	37.3	59.0	@
	1,075,746	85,413	540,724	443,782	0	5,827	0	7.9	50.2	41.9	
ICK	4,411,244	137,428	1,552,786	2,083,608	445,818	181,604	0	3.1	35.2	61.7	
T	1,311,637	94,221	500,189	432,059	35,712	246,026	3,430	7.1	38.1	54.6	0.2
D	4,535,451	180,920	1,622,668	2,718,926	0	12,937	0	3.9	35.7	60.4	
	3,589,197	47,925	945,116	2,542,774	0	53,382	0	1.3	26.3	72.4	
	467,138	25,492	194,191	141,099	102,445	3,911	0	5.4	41.5	53.1	
MERY	14,188,698	675,856	3,640,577	8,332,154	1,166,113	85,854	288,144	4.7	25.6	67.7	2.0
GEORGE'S	19,124,072	1,083,024	8,724,657	7,027,117	1,958,254	331,020	0	5.6	45.6	48.8	
ANNE'S	718,480	39,314	320,052	331,183	26,763	0	1,168	5.4	44.5	50.0	0.1
RY'S	1,944,689	115,604	792,826	892,579	141,881	1,799	0	5.9	40.7	53.4	
ET	759,981	75,670	449,294	226,403	0	0	8,614	9.9	59.1	29.9	1.1
	701,953	27,313	297,835	212,846	149,533	14,428	0	3.8	42.4	53.8	
GTON	3,673,869	175,743	1,587,838	1,777,127	0	32,096	101,065	4.7	43.2	49.4	2.7
CO	1,924,964	99,911	754,601	587,414	441,079	37,040	4,919	5.1	39.2	55.5	0.2
TER	1,020,798	66,830	391,393	262,956	0	299,619	0	6.5	38.3	55.2	

des value of U.S.D.A. commodities.
des sale of equipment, net insurance recovery, and other miscellaneous revenues.
than 0.1 percent.

TABLE 82

Revenue from the State of Maryland for Public School Purposes: 1986 - 87
. . . . .CURRENT EXPENSE FUND. . . . .

LOCAL UNIT	TOTAL STATE FUNDS	STATE SHARE OF CURRENT EXPENSES	COMPEN-SATORY EDUCATION	HANDICAPPED CHILDREN	GIFTED & TALENTED	ENVIRON-MENTAL EDUCATION	DISRUPTIVE YOUTH	INNO-VATIVE PROGRAMS	ADULT CONTINUING EDUCATION
TOTAL STATE	$1,241,493,581	$554,582,687	$42,320,543	$83,901,696	$14,307	$85,214	$402,982	$207,507	$836,712
ALLEGANY	23,323,921	12,569,130	964,976	1,027,051	0	5,000	0	1,218	17,426
ANNE ARUNDEL	111,980,859	53,351,917	1,908,016	7,189,052	1,746	0	1,125	3,441	16,625
BALTIMORE CITY	247,213,991	126,269,564	25,404,067	23,585,572	0	3,455	193,097	0	111,073
BALTIMORE	131,005,772	46,852,530	1,835,357	7,029,507	0	10,760	19,569	0	98,600
CALVERT	12,800,147	5,480,809	299,619	497,126	1,939	8,140	20,000	0	32,836
CAROLINE	9,331,848	5,336,346	62,068	464,963	0	0	21,000	0	0
CARROLL	37,740,301	19,430,454	442,443	1,551,062	0	0	20,000	0	24,699
CECIL	23,318,123	13,540,956	669,264	1,096,497	5,962	0	0	0	0
CHARLES	37,449,980	17,021,488	845,037	1,852,430	581	532	23,273	6,168	117,198
DORCHESTER	10,218,247	5,009,695	480,488	444,749	0	15,750	19,898	1,912	30,109
FREDERICK	43,936,156	24,230,439	152,587	1,590,484	0	5,881	15,000	32,858	13,320
GARRETT	13,312,949	5,964,210	536,614	474,817	0	0	0	30,858	0
HARFORD	53,028,472	29,266,561	275,902	2,689,158	0	5,000	0	0	0
HOWARD	41,560,385	17,859,858	92,244	2,859,727	0	3,082	14,945	0	0
KENT	4,684,728	2,034,721	133,557	333,627	2,862	0	0	1,486	13,767
MONTGOMERY	135,802,156	28,131,096	973,980	9,895,221	1,217	3,863	6,377	13,647	78,240
PRINCE GEORGE'S	199,195,660	91,860,206	3,673,054	16,159,028	0	5,200	9,495	0	27,433
QUEEN ANNE'S	8,646,392	4,042,607	194,060	320,514	0	0	7,800	0	32,556
ST. MARY'S	23,204,725	11,480,163	751,124	1,518,255	0	6,866	0	49,588	20,619
SOMERSET	7,264,853	3,811,059	368,876	301,596	0	5,000	13,826	30,858	92,491
TALBOT	4,596,087	1,392,149	113,998	322,445	0	0	0	0	6,206
WASHINGTON	33,366,994	17,666,903	1,188,557	1,541,705	0	6,685	15,936	0	81,900
WICOMICO	21,847,495	11,664,082	818,592	940,014	0	0	1,641	3,500	11,233
WORCESTER	6,763,340	315,744	136,063	217,096	0	0	0	31,973	10,381

TABLE

82

Revenue from the State of Maryland for Public School Purposes: 1986 - 87

— — — — — — — — — — — — — — — — — — CURRENT EXPENSE FUND (continued)— — — — — — — — —

OCAL UNIT	VOCATIONAL CENTERS	TRANSPOR- TATION	DRIVER EDUCATION	SCHOOL COMMUNITY CENTERS	EXTENDED ELEMENTARY	OTHER *	TEACHERS' RETIREMENT#	SOCIAL SECURITY#
AL STATE	$0	$113,319,614	$1,822,691	$1,226,741	$2,200,579	$8,011,574	$272,480,897	$90,592,854
EGANY	0	2,842,303	40,155	39,311	0	9,023	3,866,674	1,328,116
E ARUNDEL	0	11,076,815	304,555	0	208,224	3,252	25,064,423	8,726,615
TIMORE CITY	0	9,453,303	0	73,036	837,768	196,638	36,692,969	11,389,374
TIMORE	0	13,629,401	222,380	150,585	110,584	3,000	39,765,297	13,259,006
VERT	0	1,862,098	38,220	32,307	128,000	4,781	3,055,840	1,016,799
OLINE	0	1,325,125	10,945	29,261	0	6,700	1,408,902	487,315
ROLL	0	3,979,434	113,650	48,944	0	11,040	6,561,950	2,249,580
IL	0	2,371,906	59,410	29,261	124,550	7,200	3,931,623	1,368,074
RLES	0	4,499,542	96,090	55,580	161,000	96,661	5,441,022	1,899,457
CHESTER	0	1,360,511	4,590-	48,061	132,500	130,369	1,694,124	562,590
DERICK	0	4,194,145	107,075	89,254	0	47,110	8,353,808	2,819,624
RETT	0	1,645,708	31,655	28,082	96,021	29,868	1,684,379	549,005
FORD	0	5,578,654	0	43,390	58,000	0	9,503,624	3,335,914
ARD	0	4,957,734	54,075	36,445	0	5,982	10,815,950	3,668,678
T	0	927,041	6,825	29,261	0	1,979	867,372	306,738
TGOMERY	0	12,210,502	304,345	134,677	93,587	1,094,022	51,299,058	16,262,772
NCE GEORGE'S	0	17,623,390	225,770	182,512	0	6,238,467	41,737,096	13,940,944
EN ANNE'S	0	1,485,241	25,795	46,061	0	18,746	1,810,060	623,638
MARY'S	0	3,046,323	33,765	1,759	202,765	10,628	3,860,582	1,295,258
ERSET	0	1,048,180	14,029	25,160	0	23,522	1,105,825	348,761
BOT	0	867,713	4,212	38,011	0	0	1,292,742	533,298
HINGTON	0	3,282,422	78,780	29,261	47,580	59,257	6,403,076	2,249,831
OMICO	0	2,500,939	27,005	29,261	0	3,818	3,941,889	1,602,380
CESTER	0	1,551,184	28,545	29,261	0	9,731	2,322,816	789,107

UPPLEMENTARY INFORMATION FOLLOWING TABLE 7 FOR DESCRIPTION OF PROGRAM.
DIRECT BY STATE.

TABLE
82

Revenue from the State of Maryland for Public School Purposes: 1986 - 87

| LOCAL UNIT NAME | FOOD SERVICE FUND | | SCHOOL CONSTRUCTION FUND | | DEBT SERVICE FUND | |
	FOOD SERVICE AID	OTHER	CONSTRUCTION AID	OTHER	CONSTRUCTION AID	OTHER
TOTAL STATE	$6,273,227	$370,074	$44,265,916	$134,029	$18,027,568	$0
ALLEGANY	222,610	0	214,608	0	176,320	0
ANNE ARUNDEL	286,986	0	2,840,210	0	897,857	0
BALTIMORE CITY	2,204,434	262,467	7,167,277	0	3,369,897	0
BALTIMORE	396,858	0	3,456,688	0	4,275,153	0
CALVERT	38,967	0	282,686	0	0	0
CAROLINE	63,718	0	0	0	135,505	0
CARROLL	40,570	0	3,286,475	0	0	0
CECIL	88,420	0	25,000	0	0	0
CHARLES	0	107,607	4,443,214	0	783,100	0
DORCHESTER	85,413	0	0	0	206,668	0
FREDERICK	137,428	0	1,538,295	0	608,850	0
GARRETT	94,221	0	2,013,682	134,029	0	0
HARFORD	180,920	0	1,428,364	0	664,985	0
HOWARD	47,925	0	1,041,740	0	102,000	0
KENT	25,492	0	0	0	0	0
MONTGOMERY	675,856	0	11,532,000	0	2,566,026	0
PRINCE GEORGE'S	1,083,024	0	2,938,581	0	3,511,460	0
QUEEN ANNE'S	39,314	0	0	0	0	0
ST. MARY'S	115,604	0	811,426	0	0	0
SOMERSET	75,670	0	0	0	0	0
TALBOT	27,313	0	0	0	0	0
WASHINGTON	175,743	0	12,861	0	526,497	0
WICOMICO	99,811	0	0	0	203,250	0
WORCESTER	66,830	0	1,254,809	0	0	0

TABLE
82

Revenue from the State of Maryland for Maryland Public Schools: 1986-87 (cont.)

ription of "Other State" as shown on preceding page.

ett	Antitrust	$ 494	Prince George's	MRA	$ 75,003
	Career Guidance	1,000	(cont.)	Personnel Assignment	54,001
	Certification and	2,500		Principal Staff Development	3,052
	Accreditation			Psychological Skills Develop	1,195
	Education of the Handicapped	375		Retiree Outreach	17,151
	Maryland Educational			RICA	547,315
	Technology	25,000		Space Ambassadors	1,845
	Physical Education Inservice	300		Valley View	499
				Miscellaneous	1,361
			Queen Anne's	Career Education	3,504
rd	Curriculum Development	3,300		Inservice	5,931
	Environment Education	2,682		METN	2,000
				Pupil Services	5,312
				Special Programs	2,000
	Career Guidance	1,016	St. Mary's	Apprenticeship	2,604
	Instruction	963		Training	8,024
			Somerset	Miscellaneous	23,522
gomery	Child Abuse	6,927	Washington	Gifted and Talented	1,506
	Instruction	1,988		Improvement Project	20,203
	Noyes Children Center	25,319		Pupil Services	17,983
	RICA	1,059,791		Miscellaneous	19,566
ce George's	Apprenticeship	16,838	Wicomico	Electrical Apprentice	3,818
	Bowie State College	13,048			
	Foreign Language Institute	2,000	Worcester	Miscellaneous	9,731
	Higher Education	4,525			
	Home Economics	634			
	Magnet Schools	5,500,000			

TABLE
82

Revenue from the State of Maryland for Maryland Public Schools: 1986-87 (cont.)

Description of "Other State" as shown on preceding page.

Local Unit	Funding Purpose	Amount	Local Unit	Funding Purpose	Amount
Allegany	Pupil Services	$ 1,869	Charles	Doncaster Youth Center	$ 5,437
	Miscellaneous	7,154	(cont.)	Industrial Arts	478
Anne Arundel	Miscellaneous	3,252		Inservice	2,771
				Maryland Professional Academy	125
Baltimore City	Block Grant	53,431		MRA	26,088
	Maryland Assessment Center	21,756		Parent Resources	4,750
	Project Smart	960		Pre-Release	4,000
	Walter P. Carter	111,961		Psychological Skills Development	532
	Miscellaneous	8,530		Pupil Services	5,408
				Miscellaneous	25,575
Baltimore	Pupil Services	3,000	Dorchester	Assessment Center	12,676
Calvert	Miscellaneous	4,761		Certification & Accreditation	1,898
				Library Theater	2,000
Caroline	Music	5,000		Pupil Services	261
	Miscellaneous	1,700		Project Basic	30,858
				Project Help	61,400
Carroll	Miscellaneous	11,040		Regional Center	16,460
				Thinking Skills	1,896
Cecil	Positive Youth Development	7,200		Teacher Effectiveness	443
				Miscellaneous	756
Charles	Certification & Accreditation	1,296	Frederick	Robert Cavanaugh Project	40,614
	Charles Co Education Center	19,500		Thinking Skills	3,700
	Curriculum/Staff Development	700		Miscellaneous	2,796

TABLE
83

Revenue from the Federal Government for Maryland Public Schools: 1986 - 87

Local Unit	Total Federal Funds	Adult Education Act	Bilingual Education Programs	Education Consolidation and Improvement Act Migrant Programs	Handicapped	Other	Chapter II- Block Grant	Education of the Handicapped Act
Total State	$164,248,851	$1,244,183	$ 315,104	$ 308,365	$ 557,220	$ 56,035,284	$ 6,532,092	$166,565,021
Allegany	3,386,806	36,350	-	-	8,436	1,047,268	123,300	472,278
Anne Arundel	13,561,612	86,700	-	-				248,842
Baltimore City	51,061,098	263,289	-	-		2	1,	6
Baltimore	12,173,193	152,230	-	-				9
Calvert	1,772,314	31,179	-	-				8
Caroline	1,291,518	-	-	-		321, 11	43,437	247, 57
Carroll	2,888,946	42,960	-	-	16,713	572, 39	163,987	851, 51
Cecil	2,310,395	-	-	-	24,396	657, 53	98,680	381, 04
Charles	3,772,404	30,700	-	-	15,945	1,103,403	187,000	772,072
Dorchester	1,953,084	35,297	-	123,998	4,591	561,877	71,708	317,596
Frederick	4,039,101	46,496	-	-	16,958	812,644	202,920	830,522
Garrett	1,677,866	-	-	-				807
Harford	6,162,717	-	-	-	32,837	1,	2	72
Howard	3,208,451	-	-	-	14,070		2	65
Kent	674,267	19,700	-	-				15
Montgomery	12,9 0,210	147,016	14 ,019	-	92,479	2,699,822	834,712	2,970,985
Prince George's	23,9 5,823	179,000	155,349	-	11 ,663	5,808,888		2,889,888
Queen Anne's	1,4 3,003	37,037	-	71,703				1
St. Mary's	4,0 0,763	25,541	-	-	1	1,	1	7
Somerset	1,482,255	13,348	-	77,031				3
Talbot	884,218	-	-	-		235,0	47,195	151,010
Washington	5,167,173	48,547	-	-	29,330	1,486,5	166,985	798,529
Wicomico	2,475,069	30,563	-	-	15,326	966,966	101,465	401,504
Worcester	1,582,259	18,250	19,736	35,835	1,459	510,480	53,860	241,786

TABLE
83

Revenue from the Federal Government for Maryland Public Schools: 1986 -87

Local Unit	Education for Economic Security	Emergency Immigration	Food Service Programs School Lunch & Child Nutrition	Food Service Programs Value of U.S.D.A. Commodities	Headstart	Impact Aid
Total State	$ 938,887	$ 3,595,398	$ 266,000,721	$ 11,120,989	$ 1,277,723	$ 12,183,608
Allegany	2,347	-	1,174,831	305,187		-
Anne Arundel	16,035	-	1,839,153	637,489	-	4,330,897
Baltimore City	4,207	27,638	14,115,844	1,519,008		229,924
Baltimore	-	68,57?	2,297,105	1,309,305		283,489
Calvert	1,529	-	290,000	153,459		102,586
Caroline	1,904	-	361,191	111,537	-	
Carroll	5,872	-	454,318	408,441	85,288	
Cecil	1,339	-	522,745	230,638	-	
Charles	3,901	-	690,592	385,504		
Dorchester	1,712	-	444,468	96,255		
Frederick	7,777	-	895,406	657,380		245,352
Garrett	1,799	-	500,189	-		
Harford	6,211	-	1,038,353	584,315		1,770,762
Howard	4,559	-	500,015	445,101		305,806
Kent	678	-	144,962	49,229		
Montgomery	35,181	204,882	3,123,258	517,319	-	531,848
Prince George's	25,643	212,526	6,126,395	2,598,262	913,873	2,529,484
Queen Anne's	740	-	230,102	89,950	-	
St. Mary's	-	-	617,857	174,969		1,068,389
Somerset	1,587	-	449,294	-		
Talbot	-	-	184,094	113,741		
Washington	4,875	-	1,???,???	???,???	278,564	309,789
Wicomico	3,887	-		56,	-	-
Worcester	2,698	-		-		
Worcester						

TABLE
83

Revenue from the Federal Government for Maryland Public Schools: 1986 - 87

1 Unit	Indian Education	Job Training Partnership Act	Math and Science Education	Maternal and Child Health	Refugee Assistance	ROTC	Vocational Education	Other Miscellaneous
1 State	$ 143,247	$ 2,547,707	$ 373,504	$ 5,511	$ 233,555	$ 415,227	$ 7,994,360	$ 253,992
gany	-	52,006	5,285	-	8,285	-	159,517	-
Arundel	-	42,926	10,799	-	4,350	-	442,286	2,311
imore City	88,995	381,440	52,901	-	9,017	-	1,421,885	32,941
imore	-	148,164	67,786	2,078	-	-	758,661	-
ert	-	11,700	3,233	-	-	-	117,286	-
line	-	111,829	-	-	-	-	88,152	5,000
oll	-	8,453	9,755	-	3,487	-	147,681	37,390
l	-	62,026	16,982	-	-	-	166,478	-
les	8,154	156,298	6,937	929	-	-	201,450	65,839
hester	-	144,815	7,660	1,413	4,132	-	125,100	39
erick	-	13,355	8,192	1,093	3,469	-	265,939	32,898
ett	-	85,701	2,199	-	-	-	113,698	2,617
ord	-	32,313	15,763	-	7,128	-	163,833	-
ord	-	7,088	12,023	-	2,800	-	271,713	-
rd	-	47,274	1,946	-	-	-	63,128	-
gomery	8,310	168,133	73,563	-	102,451	-	1,640,572	183,713
ce George's	37,784	326,329	46,515	-	81,090	415,227	842,296	39,754
n Anne's	-	118,476	3,230	-	-	-	151,829	45,000
Mary's	-	135,641	6,328	-	1,273	-	220,310	26,000
rset	-	9,723	2,400	-	-	-	117,383	-
ot	-	100,887	-	-	932	-	51,464	-
ington	-	52,816	15,884	-	4,602	-	293,114	34,892
mico	-	114,201	6,123	-	-	-	80,455	10,003
ester	-	216,313	-	-	559	-	90,170	-

TABLE
84

Expenditures for All Purposes: Maryland Public Schools: 1986-87

Local Unit	Total Expenditures	Interest on Debt	Capital Outlay	Gross Food Service	Transfers To Maryland LEAs* Instruc- tion+	Transfers To Maryland LEAs* Special Education	Transfers Outside Maryland School Systems
Total State	$3,125,898,793	$24,256,723	$142,979,860	$114,385,479	$917,055	$10,082,220	$20,547,586
Allegany	44,209,977	16,320	1,068,185	2,823,268	4,928	-	35,044
Anne Arundel	280,443,800	2,470,067	12,317,534	7,975,766	72,325	-	1,905,586
Baltimore City	435,488,042	8,004,684	10,382,913	21,909,900	237,102	8,509,699	215
Baltimore	413,653,318	2,221,165	9,693,185	12,741,838	-	84,941	3,885,797
Calvert	35,146,379	39,250	1,033,648	1,140,286	-	25,733	126,419
Caroline	16,543,401	15,505	469,197	1,033,474	-	-	252,578
Carroll	76,225,701	123,787	5,224,140	2,998,263	-	31,55²	287,239
Cecil	44,918,849	189,039	1,007,361		26,88³	-	177,766
Charles	73,169,190	133,100	8,032,818		21,60	71,16⁴	215,374
Dorchester	19,905,108	126,116	258,554		-	65,57	4,649
Frederick	97,977,223	1,016,011	5,332,309	4,473,986	178,109	-	131,216
Garrett	22,083,565	-	2,875,151	1,251,910	196,619	2,08⁵	45,427
Harford	108,160,691	498,065	04,630	4,407,942	-	-	541,671
Howard	140,188,038	1,811,695	I 65,949	3,942,058	27,330	764,682	761,930
Kent	10,602,894	1 , 0	32,148	465,873	-	-	15,000
Montgomery	600,543,383	7,235,436	51,295,991	14,742,261	-	48,466	7,063,556
Prince George's	468,526,936	1,833,020	10,755,162	19,492,299	34,960	85,798	4,673,824
Queen Anne's	21,272,674	53,415	331,685	890,887	110,877	-	2,500
St. Mary's	46,973,899	-	1,633,710	1,819,567	3,108	21,572	95,220
Somerset	12,404,919	-	89,516	466,863	-	-	-
Talbot	14,927,638	24,700	105,609	693,454	-	2,356	134,279
Washington	72,445,222	399,458	1,941,709	3,410,984	-	325,232	-
Wicomico	43,705,936	3,250	1,546,415	1,414,269	3,207	4,811	185,268
Worcester	26,382,010	25,600	2,082,341	659,333	-	20,556	7,010

*Includes instructional transfers which ar not shown on Table 2
+Duplicated with expenditures reported by he receiving LEA

TABLE
84

Expenditures for All Purposes: Maryland Public Schools: 1986-87

| Local Unit | Total Current Expenses | Current Expenses | | | | |
		Adminis- tration	Instruc- tion	Special Education	Student Personnel Services	Health Services
Total State	$2,812,729,890	$ 123,571,513	$1,392,015,421	$222,642,012	$ 13,693,882	$5,607,884
Allegany	40,262,232	1,504,651	20,285,334	2,385,908	176,243	4,887
Anne Arundel	255,702,522	9,975,091	132,359,388	17,631,383	1,711,898	-
Baltimore City	388,443,529	17,668,736	177,177,194	47,541,549	2,146,663	893
Baltimore	385,026,392	13,754,750	198,653,257	27,548,065	2,075,654	1,519,574
Calvert	32,781,043	1,574,938	16,285,409	2,337,106	225,820	9,373
Caroline	14,772,647	685,684	7,606,982	884,475	55,318	2,077
Carroll	67,677,989	2,667,902	35,359,425	4,310,469	261,382	333,900
Cecil	41,840,548	1,716,275	21,332,981	2,731,193	169,274	62,555
Charles	61,802,381	2,469,784	29,616,635	5,140,000	391,567	3,646
Dorchester	18,453,947	903,063	9,257,336	1,148,607	88,547	26,525
Frederick	86,845,592	4,337,056	44,860,396	4,746,050	212,273	40,189
Garrett	18,112,373	674,730	8,888,118	.	109,320	1,127
Harford	98,608,383	2,927,722	52,971,69	. :	418,451	528,900
Howard	120,208,404	6,587,066	59,230,10	. :	397,176	646,814
Kent	9,978,823	517,737	4,617,64	. :	19,455	124
Montgomery	520,157,673	28,684,302	255,994,900	41,858,385	1,402,185	33,311
Prince George'	431,651,873	16,877,612	206,375,006	34,222,988	2,838,649	1,801,540
Queen Anne's	19,883,310	823,847	9,931,580	1,450,493	122,595	99,898
St. Mary's	43,400,722	2,058,990	20,489,105	3,772,718	228,521	24,627
Somerset	11,848,540	727,178	5,672,850	801,967	43,829	54,293
Talbot	13,987,240	704,778	7,285,193	926,247	76,867	23,273
Washington	66,307,879	3,238,632	33,973,717	3,871,493	246,444	
Wicomico	40,5 8, 8	1,516,298	21,298,070	2,393,981	157,45	187,
Worcester	23,5 7, 0	974,701	12,485,104	1,481,678	18,18	102,

TABLE
84

Expenditures for All Purposes: Maryland Public Schools: 1986-87

Local Unit	Student Transpor- tation	Operation of Plant	Maintenance of Plant	Fixed Charges Local Share	State Share	Community Services
Total State	$137,631,147	$238,384,165	$ 88,389,043	$ 221,930,460	$ 363,073,751	$ 5,790,612
Allegany	2,740,732	3,585,965	828,767	3,412,362	5,194,790	142,583
Anne Arundel	13,396,573	21,206,792	8,134,405	17,449,819	33,791,038	46,035
Baltimore City	12,869,187	39,528,615	12,035,053	31,341,697	48,082,343	50,599
Baltimore	13,010,298	34,077,263	12,397,074	28,761,981	53,024,303	204,193
Calvert	2,206,063	2,474,778	803,802	2,869,257	4,072,639	121,858
Caroline	1,265,142	1,184,374	334,875	877,523	1,876,217	154,318
Carroll	4,724,035	4,881,829	1,960,892	4,212,312	8,811,530	
Cecil	2,427,738	3,503,756	1,484,122	2,825,247	5,299,697	
Charles	4,402,191	5,559,771	1,823,409	4,227,918	7,340,479	8
Dorchester	1,299,113	1,536,093	512,970	1,393,492	2,256,714	
Frederick	5,134,273	8,087,961	2,717,824	5,357,864	11,173,430	178,276
Garrett	1,611,088	1,340,044	528,840	1,415,026	2,233,384	35,881
Harford	5,913,224	8,592,566	2,959,815	7,062,714	12,839,538	50,538
Howard	6,613,418	9,739,972	4,363,175	8,569,405	14,484,628	1,455,814
Kent	926,945	808,899	483,629	659,603	1,174,110	53,289
Montgomery	24,394,474	34,891,896	14,879,168	49,936,906	67,561,828	520,328
Prince George'	21,081,829	39,403,077	15,870,868	36,560,697	55,678,040	841,567
Queen Anne's	1,568,729	1,256,441	591,161	1,538,023	2,433,698	66,844
St. Mary's	3,034,342	3,681,198	1,481,981	3,289,337	5,155,840	174,063
Somerset	1,057,845	871,973	274,538	793,398	1,454,586	96,083
Talbot	889,296	1,031,849	343,054	796,877	1,826,040	63,766
Washington	3,030,105	8,356,585	1,961,528	4,574,237	8,652,907	461,914
Wicomico	2,483,258	3,108,978	1,110,027	2,654,503	5,544,249	94,347
Worcester	1,551,249	1,672,500	508,066	1,549,282	3,111,723	32,143

TABLE
85

EXPENDITURES FOR INSTRUCTION: MARYLAND PUBLIC SCHOOLS: 1986-87

TOTAL INSTRUCTION*	SALARIES AND WAGES	CONTRACTED SERVICES	SUPPLIES AND MATERIALS				OTHER CHARGES
			TOTAL SUPPLIES AND MATERIALS	TEXTBOOKS	LIBRARY BOOKS	OTHER	
1,392,015,421	1,317,181,456	14,022,178	56,352,031	17,140,706	5,973,263	33,238,062	4,479,756
20,285,334	19,104,037	202,142	912,523	225,835	144,714	541,974	66,632
132,359,388	124,687,938	867,365	6,612,266	1,528,816	530,971	4,552,479	211,818
177,177,194	168,328,631	3,110,388	5,594,587	2,331,661	270,980	2,991,946	143,588
198,653,257	189,912,518	1,043,242	7,283,841	2,362,727	556,215	4,364,899	413,656
16,285,409	14,589,281	684,159	929,155	299,116	124,808	505,233	82,814
7,606,982	7,110,464	100,113	324,149	80,407	45,606	198,136	72,256
35,359,425	32,917,696	418,625	1,939,955	491,340	275,702	1,072,913	183,149
21,332,881	20,316,363	157,990	787,190	196,258	74,361	516,571	71,438
29,616,635	27,094,967	681,442	1,762,269	455,989	317,111	989,169	77,957
9,257,336	8,686,268	175,515	345,163	46,193	39,334	259,636	50,390
44,860,396	42,104,980	488,366	1,976,871	573,982	242,935	1,160,054	310,079
8,886,119	8,326,525	78,784	406,813	173,954	44,335	188,524	73,997
52,971,696	50,185,072	222,134	2,497,462	1,017,375	335,555	1,144,532	68,028
59,230,102	54,476,819	1,171,170	3,273,455	713,674	376,722	2,183,059	308,658
4,617,642	4,284,419	67,217	233,495	64,340	33,399	135,756	32,511
255,994,900	244,538,576	1,663,724	8,766,454	2,370,305	1,329,267	5,066,882	1,025,146
206,375,006	196,310,335	1,674,706	7,796,957	2,633,722	468,301	4,694,934	593,008
9,931,580	9,133,671	53,366	531,082	353,324	93,968	83,790	213,461
20,499,105	18,953,593	353,577	1,045,536	197,492	182,397	665,647	146,399
5,672,850	5,345,306	40,162	235,421	62,219	17,439	155,763	51,961
7,285,193	6,771,902	110,052	366,822	61,153	49,490	256,179	36,417
33,973,717	32,553,979	248,053	1,045,838	305,874	190,248	549,716	125,847
21,298,070	19,834,727	210,149	1,170,091	406,634	166,208	597,249	83,103
12,485,104	11,611,389	219,737	814,536	188,316	53,199	363,021	39,442

ITURES FOR COCURRICULAR ACTIVITIES, PREVIOUSLY REPORTED UNDER A SEPARATE CATEGORY. SEE TABLE 2-C FOR DETAILS

expenditures for summer school as follows: Baltimore City, $546; Cecil, $29,449; Dorchester, $19,138; ne's, $52,309.

TABLE 85

EXPENDITURES FOR INSTRUCTION: MARYLAND PUBLIC SCHOOLS: 1986-87

GRADES PREKINDERGARTEN - 12

LOCAL UNIT	TOTAL PREK - 12 INSTRUCTION*	SALARIES AND WAGES	CONTRACTED SERVICES	TOTAL SUPPLIES AND MATERIALS	TEXTBOOKS	LIBRARY BOOKS	OTHER	OTHER CHARGES
TOTAL STATE	$1,377,436,832	$1,305,394,799	$12,806,831	$55,178,520	$16,906,515	$5,973,235	$32,298,770	$4,056,682
ALLEGANY	20,230,458	19,058,734	201,723	907,432	225,835	144,713	536,884	62,569
ANNE ARUNDEL	131,218,350	123,601,420	867,083	6,539,608	1,495,348	530,968	4,513,294	210,239
BALTIMORE CITY	175,520,059	167,016,531	2,976,296	5,390,154	2,327,256	270,980	2,791,918	137,078
BALTIMORE	197,092,603	188,607,437	881,769	7,189,742	2,351,242	556,214	4,282,286	413,655
CALVERT	16,028,021	14,418,196	664,104	864,610	299,115	124,804	440,691	79,111
CAROLINE	7,512,280	7,048,881	109,112	324,141		45,603	198,132	39,146
CARROLL	34,742,938	32,454,362	829,668	1,298,754	48,858	279,701	1,024,235	170,413
CECIL	21,054,802	20,118,711		9,926		7,360	489,309	64,220
CHARLES	29,210,705	26,785,697	1,	9,548		31,111	959,021	49,514
DORCHESTER	9,144,954	8,624,317		0,192		3,331	254,809	32,657
FREDERICK	44,691,967	41,983,856	446,838	1,961,583	572,113	242,933	1,146,537	299,690
GARRETT	8,841,618		78	400,909	951	44,334	188,520	72,793
HARFORD	52,376,15	4,	135		1,1,375	335,555	1,047,973	66,028
HOWARD	58,343,11	5,	1,036		1,672	376,721	2,070,406	301,722
KENT	4,498,98		42		6,338	33,398	108,656	23,179
MONTGOMERY	254,035,130	242,891,481	1,505,302	8,618,691	2,270,403	1,329,265	5,019,023	1,019,656
PRINCE GEORGE'S	202,841,117	193,214,638	1,505,515	7,706,578	2,569,522	468,301	4,668,755	414,386
QUEEN ANNE'S	9,829,247	9,054,510	49,589	518,615	341,717	93,967	82,931	206,533
ST. MARY'S	20,182,897	18,754,366	315,676	998,408	196,147	182,397	619,864	114,447
SOMERSET	5,525,906	5,234,466	29,473	220,063	62,218	17,438	140,407	41,904
TALBOT	7,275,214	6,768,879	106,052	364,536	60,497	49,490	254,549	35,747
WASHINGTON	33,890,348	32,495,908	247,182	1,038,524	305,873	190,245	542,406	108,734
WICOMICO	21,073,547	19,668,181	184,057	1,155,835	406,633	166,207	582,995	65,474
WORCESTER	12,278,417	11,465,795	198,154	586,681	188,313	63,199	335,169	27,787

*EXCLUDES EXPENDITURES FOR COCURRICULAR ACTIVITIES, PREVIOUSLY REPORTED UNDER A SEPARATE CATEGORY. SEE TABLE 2-C FOR DETAILS

TABLE
85

EXPENDITURES FOR INSTRUCTION: MARYLAND PUBLIC SCHOOLS: 1986-87

ADULT EDUCATION

| NIT | TOTAL ADULT EDUCATION | SALARIES AND WAGES | CONTRACTED SERVICES | ----------------SUPPLIES AND MATERIALS ---------------- | | | | OTHER CHARGES |
				TOTAL SUPPLIES AND MATERIALS	TEXTBOOKS	LIBRARY BOOKS	OTHER	
TE	$7,617,588	$6,712,387	$256,238	$574,277	$232,835		$341,442	$74,686
	49,461	44,998	216	3,421			3,421	826
DEL	1,140,988	1,066,504	27	72,638	33,464		39,174	1,568
CITY	882,964	755,487	48,93	72,034	4,405		67,629	6,510
	1,379,168	1,305,075	1,41.	72,679	11,484		61,195	
	82,790	61,204	2,60.	15,283			15,283	3,703
	217,238	189,531	2,046	15,643	2,521		13,122	10,018
	181,252	156,505	7,917	12,081	2,573		9,508	4,749
R	48,167	42,812	142	4,964	140		4,824	249
	168,404	121,117	21,524	15,377	1,867		13,510	10,386
	52,982	38,478	3,970	9,621			9,621	913
Y	1,957,056	1,648,080	158,415	147,603	99,899		47,704	2,958
ORGE'S	989,172	903,755	5,044	78,844	64,199		14,645	1,529
E'S	41,908	30,200	100	10,282	10,282			726
S	72,726	56,145	11	16,007	1,345		14,662	563
	112,674	85,930	2,759	14,780			14,780	9,205
	5,978	3,023		2,285	656		1,629	670
N	83,351	58,063	869	7,309			7,309	17,110
	60,835	58,833		1,678			1,678	324
	91,074	86,647		1,748			1,748	2,679

TABLE 85

EXPENDITURES FOR COCURRICULAR ACTIVITIES: MARYLAND PUBLIC SCHOOLS: 1986-87

LOCAL UNIT	TOTAL COCURRICULAR ACTIVITIES	SALARIES AND WAGES	CONTRACTED SERVICES	SUPPLIES AND MATERIALS	OTHER CHARGES
TOTAL STATE	$5,996,466	$4,119,433	$949,898	$581,612	$345,523
ALLEGANY	5,402	300	200	1,667	3,235
ANNE ARUNDEL					
BALTIMORE CITY	773,622	556,610	84,613	132,399	
BALTIMORE	181,462		180,055	21,407	
CALVERT	176,586	109,878	17,452	49,256	
CAROLINE	94,688	61,580			33,108
CARROLL	399,232	273,796	87,170	35,554	2,712
CECIL	248,720	177,779	46,045	19,495	5,401
CHARLES	224,878	152,765	27,579	20,640	23,694
DORCHESTER	45,064		27,582		17,482
FREDERICK					
GARRETT	44,476	43,276			1,200
HARFORD	595,543	412,512	86,473	96,558	
HOWARD	888,961	632,267	135,117	112,647	6,930
KENT	65,651	18,857	20,908	17,471	8,415
MONTGOMERY	2,665			144	2,521
PRINCE GEORGE'S	1,682,606	1,345,179	155,840	4,532	177,055
QUEEN ANNE'S	8,711		3,376		5,268
ST. MARY'S	243,482	143,082	37,890	67	31,389
SOMERSET	33,686	24,909	7,929	31,121	848
TALBOT	4,000		4,000		
WASHINGTON					
WICOMICO	163,664	107,708	26,089	12,567	17,300
WORCESTER	115,567	58,935	21,580	26,087	8,965

TABLE
86

EXPENDITURES FOR STUDENT PERSONNEL AND HEALTH SERVICES: MARYLAND PUBLIC SCHOOLS: 1986-87

	STUDENT PERSONNEL SERVICES					HEALTH SERVICES				
T	TOTAL STUDENT PERSONNEL	SALARIES AND WAGES	CONTRACTED SERVICES	SUPPLIES AND MATERIALS	OTHER CHARGES	TOTAL HEALTH SERVICES	SERVICES AND WAGES	CONTRACTED SERVICES	SUPPLIES AND MATERIALS	OTHER CHARGES
TE	$13,693,882	$13,028,180	$308,313	$168,146	$189,243	$5,607,884	$5,281,794	$100,754	$194,258	$31,078
DEL CITY	176,243	160,342		6,978	8,923	4,887			4,887	
	1,711,998	1,639,740	20,676	2,975	48,607					
	2,146,663	2,077,426	52,979	16,258		893		893		
	2,075,654	2,053,536	270	2,129	19,719	1,519,574	1,463,793	25,213	29,818	750
	225,820	206,218	952	15,443	3,207	9,373	5,100	360	3,747	166
	55,318	48,562	1,264	2,197	3,295	2,077			2,077	
	261,382	237,429	3,238	3,072	17,643	333,900	314,887		17,027	1,986
	169,274	159,032	1,453	1,429	7,360	62,555	55,143	260	4,196	2,956
R	391,567	315,460	63,224	11,051	1,832	3,646			3,646	
	88,547	81,664	555	2,312	4,016	26,525	22,050	1,461	1,441	1,573
	212,273	207,464		1,570	3,239	40,189	30,350	268	9,117	454
	109,320	91,204		6,755	5,965	1,127		75	1,052	
	418,451	408,358	5,396	8,092	1,425	528,900	506,068		22,578	254
	397,176	316,560	576	17,881	10,835	646,814	583,399	10,639	43,372	9,404
	19,455	18,197	51,900	825	172	124			124	
Y	1,402,185	1,402,185		13,720	34,503	3,311	23,753	8,458	1,100	
ORGE'S	2,838,649	2,704,038	86,388	3,392	6,602	1,9 1,540	1,840,000	19,043	34,755	7,742
E'S	122,596	112,027	575	12,532	2,203	9,898	94,955	853	3,054	1,036
S	228,521	197,230	16,556	274	1,738	4,627	19,471	519	3,509	1,128
	43,829	41,747	70			84,293	47,860	3,012	1,504	1,917
	76,867	69,295		5,346	2,226	23,27		23,273		
N	246,447	217,772		26,494	2,181	27		274		
	157,458	149,715	1,270	5,999	474	187,54	177,019	6,334	3,781	415
	118,189	112,979	710	1,422	3,078	102,53	97,053	712	3,473	1,297

TABLE
87

EXPENDITURES FOR OPERATION OF PLANT: MARYLAND PUBLIC SCHOOLS: 1986-87

LOCAL UNIT	TOTAL OPERATION OF PLANT	SALARIES AND WAGES	CONTRACTED SERVICES	SUPPLIES AND MATERIALS	OTHER CHARGES
TOTAL STATE	$238,384,165	$128,379,368	$20,240,569	$7,316,550	$82,447,678
ALLEGANY	3,585,965	2,068,881	40,187	132,794	1,344,123
ANNE ARUNDEL	21,206,792	11,620,917	430,920	347,608	8,807,347
BALTIMORE CITY	39,529,615	20,328,652	16,696,753	2,504,210	
BALTIMORE	34,077,263	21,349,799	454,243	436,806	11,836,415
CALVERT	2,474,778	1,238,921	33,523	82,183	1,120,151
CAROLINE	1,184,374	541,886	34,564	52,656	555,268
CARROLL	4,881,829	2,291,317	68,731	165,400	2,356,381
CECIL	3,503,756	1,673,444	39,671	121,652	1,668,989
CHARLES	5,559,771	2,558,158	93,878	210,002	2,697,733
DORCHESTER	1,536,093	600,671	4,380	47,884	883,158
FREDERICK	8,087,961	3,965,087	175,388	341,352	3,606,134
GARRETT	1,340,044	585,126	78,868	42,280	633,770
HARFORD	8,592,566	3,493,980	38,326	407,372	4,652,888
HOWARD	9,739,972	4,572,635	467,875	243,726	4,455,736
KENT	808,899	321,323	2,300	37,314	447,962
MONTGOMERY	34,891,886	20,562,443	65,839	771,962	13,491,642
PRINCE GEORGE'S	39,403,077	22,304,054	566,137	740,000	15,792,886
QUEEN ANNE'S	1,258,441	496,673		61,376	698,392
ST. MARY'S	3,681,198	1,771,066	191,187	121,844	1,597,101
SOMERSET	871,973	325,149	15,541	26,380	504,803
TALBOT	1,031,849	464,823	24,412	29,630	512,984
WASHINGTON	6,356,585	3,170,647	584,216	220,640	2,381,082
WICOMICO	3,108,978	1,504,864	101,088	102,362	1,400,684
WORCESTER	1,672,500	568,872	32,562	69,117	1,001,949

TABLE
88

EXPENDITURES FOR MAINTENANCE OF PLANT: MARYLAND PUBLIC SCHOOLS: 1986-87

LOCAL UNITS	TOTAL MAINTENANCE OF PLANT	SALARIES AND WAGES	CONTRACTED SERVICES	SUPPLIES AND MATERIALS	OTHER CHARGES	EQUIPMENT REPLACE- MENT
TOTAL STATE	$88,389,043	$43,099,149	$19,122,705	$12,122,837	$687,718	$13,356,634
ALLEGANY	828,767	428,738	54,646	201,156	172	144,057
ANNE ARUNDEL	8,134,405	2,976,938	2,837,515	1,402,016	51,825	866,111
BALTIMORE CITY	12,035,053	4,564,171	3,766,763	645,045		3,059,074
BALTIMORE	12,397,074	5,561,121	3,576,880	1,725,244	53,516	1,587,345
CALVERT	803,802	599,546	29,625	161,952	1,368	11,311
CAROLINE	334,875	123,463	58,926	49,823	3,539	99,124
CARROLL	1,960,892	779,343	321,885	342,506	24,593	492,565
CECIL	1,484,122	768,023	172,629	305,926	2,956	234,588
CHARLES	1,823,409	886,573	327,466	289,613	6,262	313,495
DORCHESTER	512,970	173,549	204,957	90,628	6,182	37,654
FREDERICK	2,717,824	1,005,218	634,909	623,181	7,592	446,924
GARRETT	528,840	162,078	55,656	116,046	7,322	187,738
HARFORD	2,959,815	1,327,422	452,291	640,286	1,054	538,762
HOWARD	4,363,175	1,938,070	736,547	451,851	90,475	1,146,232
KENT	483,629	132,971	170,447	52,695	55	127,461
MONTGOMERY	14,879,168	10,290,652	532,820	1,373,155	447,786	2,234,755
PRINCE GEORGE'S	15,870,868	8,769,608	3,590,584	2,479,198	14,679	1,016,799
QUEEN ANNE'S	591,181	263,740	181,484	41,074	29,430	75,433
ST. MARY'S	1,481,981	712,548	232,735	428,369	3,501	104,828
SOMERSET	274,538	125,859	59,195	79,089	5,500	4,895
TALBOT	343,054	138,882	92,965	42,015	1,563	67,629
WASHINGTON	1,961,528	706,721	623,514	328,570	21,509	281,214
WICOMICO	1,110,027	477,050	255,346	169,220	13,730	194,681
WORCESTER	508,066	186,887	152,920	84,179	141	83,959

TABLE
89

* * * * * * * * * * * * * * GENERAL ADMINISTRATION * * * * * * * * * * * * * *

LOCAL UNIT	TOTAL ADMINIS-TRATION	TOTAL GENERAL ADMIN.	SALARIES AND WAGES	CONTRACTED SERVICES	SUPPLIES AND MATERIALS	OTHER CHARGES
TOTAL STATE	$123,571,514	$68,777,704	$52,936,519	$10,221,987	$3,345,063	$2,274,155
ALLEGANY	1,504,661	780,627	484,688	67,778	21,684	208,497
ANNE ARUNDEL	9,975,091	5,944,662	4,691,204	765,287	334,820	153,551
BALTIMORE CITY	17,668,738	11,267,702	8,956,018	1,875,950	392,586	43,148
BALTIMORE	13,754,750	8,672,204	5,530,264	423,297	470,348	248,295
CALVERT	1,574,938	701,944	481,946	89,973	64,326	65,699
CAROLINE	685,664	400,979	236,937	101,394	25,876	36,772
CARROLL	2,667,902	1,400,164	1,051,565	242,612	33,223	72,764
CECIL	1,716,275	815,491	638,710	84,562	48,896	43,323
CHARLES	2,469,784	1,226,551	891,338	258,823	20,598	55,792
DORCHESTER	903,063	400,890	277,983	73,056	19,261	30,590
FREDERICK	4,337,056	2,247,447	1,626,431	135,545	112,809	372,662
GARRETT	674,730	297,902	228,564	38,827	9,352	21,159
HARFORD	2,927,722	1,708,293	1,378,522	160,770	115,660	53,341
HOWARD	6,587,066	3,143,468	1,927,479	743,262	340,668	132,059
KENT	517,737	318,045	203,623	65,555	12,411	36,456
MONTGOMERY	28,684,302	18,525,889	14,808,410	2,680,375	772,331	264,773
PRINCE GEORGE'S	16,877,613	8,081,682	6,230,824	1,620,125	165,018	65,717
QUEEN ANNE'S	823,847	472,785	254,863	132,000	36,005	49,917
ST. MARY'S	2,058,990	938,343	530,574	221,817	80,617	105,335
SOMERSET	727,178	397,836	264,154	64,082	26,180	43,420
TALBOT	704,778	445,880	298,826	83,566	24,671	38,817
WASHINGTON	3,238,632	1,432,117	1,046,341	119,665	160,183	105,928
WICOMICO	1,518,298	733,299	592,157	90,540	37,709	12,893
WORCESTER	974,701	423,504	305,118	83,106	20,033	15,247

TABLE
89

EXPENDITURES FOR ADMINISTRATION: MARYLAND PUBLIC SCHOOLS: 1986-87

* * * * * * * * * * * * * SCHOOL INSTRUCTIONAL SUPPORT * * * * * * * * * * * * *

LOCAL UNIT	TOTAL INSTRUCT. SUPPORT *	SALARIES AND WAGES	CONTRACTED SERVICES	SUPPLIES AND MATERIALS	OTHER CHARGES
TOTAL STATE	$54,793,810	$49,301,765	$2,086,575	$1,625,937	$1,779,533
ALLEGANY	724,034	670,205	7,650	16,192	29,987
ANNE ARUNDEL	4,030,429	3,759,296	65,659	91,329	114,145
BALTIMORE CITY	6,401,034	5,902,323	337,271	150,831	10,609
BALTIMORE	7,082,546	6,402,228	297,381	239,597	143,340
CALVERT	872,994	869,929			3,065
CAROLINE	284,685	243,861	10,035	6,664	24,125
CARROLL	1,267,738	1,169,906	15,594	19,022	63,216
CECIL	900,784	836,885	5,708	22,057	36,134
CHARLES	1,243,233	1,046,150	100,588	52,289	44,206
DORCHESTER	502,173	376,729	31,525	33,301	60,618
FREDERICK	2,089,609	1,985,280	14,640	38,122	51,567
GARRETT	376,828	318,547	14,298	26,212	17,771
HARFORD	1,219,429	1,170,302	8,173	25,829	15,125
HOWARD	3,443,598	3,010,469	58,486	62,128	312,515
KENT	199,692	169,807	5,058	8,089	18,738
MONTGOMERY	10,158,413	9,220,077	332,751	348,509	257,076
PRINCE GEORGE'S	8,795,931	7,446,853	702,023	255,515	391,540
QUEEN ANNE'S	351,062	326,344		4,105	20,613
ST. MARY'S	1,120,647	992,347	23,675	52,002	52,623
SOMERSET	329,342	297,581	4,624	10,628	16,509
TALBOT	258,898	229,381	6,327	595	22,615
WASHINGTON	1,806,515	1,611,485	27,954	139,380	27,696
WICOMICO	782,999	735,499	9,801	14,849	22,850
WORCESTER	551,197	510,301	7,354	10,692	22,850

* DUE TO AN AMENDMENT TO TITLE 5, SECTION 5-101 OF THE EDUCATION ARTICLE, EFFECTIVE 1/1/82, EXPENDITURES FOR SCHOOL INSTRUCTIONAL SUPPORT SERVICES ARE CHARGEABLE TO ADMINISTRATION RATHER THAN INSTRUCTION. FOR HISTORICAL CONTINUITY OR COMPARATIVE STUDIES, THE AMOUNTS REPORTED ABOVE SHOULD BE SUBTRACTED FROM ADMINISTRATION AND INCLUDED WITH INSTRUCTIONAL EXPENDITURES ON TABLE 2.

TABLE
90

EXPENDITURES FOR STUDENT TRANSPORTATION: MARYLAND PUBLIC SCHOOLS: 1986-87

LOCAL UNITS	TOTAL STUDENT TRANSPOR- TATION	SALARIES AND WAGES	CONTRACTED SERVICES	SUPPLIES AND MATERIALS	OTHER CHARGES	VEHICLE REPLACE- MENT
TOTAL STATE	$137,631,147	$53,811,488	$65,108,749	$9,308,054	$4,778,301	$4,624,555
ALLEGANY	2,740,732	338,064	2,049,636	83,407	127,410	142,215
ANNE ARUNDEL	13,396,573	1,921,145	10,647,603	229,507	598,318	
BALTIMORE CITY	12,869,187	1,994,025	9,838,798	334,996	583,394	117,976
BALTIMORE	13,010,298	9,038,357	1,186,680	1,919,381	235,519	630,381
CALVERT	2,206,063	138,800	2,013,150	15,749	38,364	
CAROLINE	1,265,142	144,556	1,057,742	25,764	37,080	
CARROLL	4,724,035	375,921	4,161,376	35,506	83,828	67,404
CECIL	2,427,738	226,615	1,984,764	38,658	177,701	
CHARLES	4,402,191	217,975	4,039,919	14,515	129,450	332
DORCHESTER	1,299,113	142,565	1,085,180	26,972	41,732	2,664
FREDERICK	5,134,273	1,856,559	1,809,994	572,650	671,044	224,026
GARRETT	1,611,088	83,486	1,500,224	11,014	16,364	
HARFORD	5,913,224	830,782	4,552,771	207,686	189,485	132,500
HOWARD	6,613,418	279,570	6,057,560	17,234	259,054	
KENT	926,945	80,251	735,232	11,111	47,244	53,107
MONTGOMERY	24,394,474	16,500,385	1,229,043	2,665,689	1,085,415	2,933,942
PRINCE GEORGE'S	21,081,829	17,797,552	547,502	2,709,871	26,904	
QUEEN ANNE'S	1,568,729	146,380	1,281,289	27,230	49,700	64,130
ST. MARY'S	3,034,342	226,077	2,577,777	62,880	99,010	68,598
SOMERSET	1,057,845	64,272	888,200	1,913	105,460	
TALBOT	889,296	65,980	806,576	4,626	12,114	
WASHINGTON	3,030,105	1,131,423	1,407,859	285,174	18,369	187,280
WICOMICO	2,483,258	126,033	2,233,181	3,870	120,174	
WORCESTER	1,551,249	84,715	1,418,695	2,671	45,168	

EXPENDITURES FOR FIXED CHARGES BY OBJECT: MARYLAND PUBLIC SCHOOLS: 1986-87

TABLE
91

			PAID BY LOCAL BOARDS OF EDUCATION					PAID DIRECT BY STATE	
LOCAL UNIT	TOTAL FIXED CHARGES	TOTAL	RETIREMENT FUNDS	SOCIAL SECURITY	OTHER EMPLOYEE BENEFITS	OTHER INSURANCE & JUDGEMENTS	RENT & OTHER	TEACHER'S RETIREMENT SYSTEM	TEACHER'S SOCIAL SECURITY
AL STATE	$585,004,212	$221,930,461	$35,738,668	$43,247,243	$119,229,410	$18,434,795	$5,280,345	$272,480,897	$90,592,854
EGANY	8,607,152	3,412,362	600,004	573,584	1,778,640	442,137	17,997	3,866,674	1,328,116
E ARUNDEL	51,240,857	17,449,819	2,495,896	3,593,658	9,030,419	2,230,681	99,165	25,064,423	8,726,615
TIMORE CITY	79,424,040	31,341,697	5,669,376	6,896,716	17,519,922	1,187,580	68,103	36,692,969	11,389,374
TIMORE	81,786,264	28,761,961	1,554,652	5,471,893	20,000,476	1,042,023	692,817	39,765,297	13,259,006
VERT	6,741,896	2,669,257	382,771	504,231	1,864,998	-66,062	51,195	3,055,840	1,016,799
OLINE	2,753,740	877,523	161,471	182,188	391,192	126,329	16,343	1,408,902	467,315
ROLL	13,023,842	4,212,312	553,476	843,930	1,861,939	734,138	218,829	6,561,950	2,249,580
IL	8,124,944	2,825,247	184,474	562,201	1,756,270	322,302		3,931,623	1,368,074
RLES	11,568,397	4,227,918	697,864	792,401	2,177,339	560,297	17	5,441,022	1,899,457
CHESTER	3,650,206	1,393,492	250,572	256,698	752,468	133,673	81	1,694,124	562,590
DERICK	16,531,294	5,357,864	894,623	1,217,970	2,867,357	336,790	41,124	8,353,806	2,819,624
RETT	3,649,410	1,416,026	194,820	228,202	802,232	147,332	43,440	1,884,379	549,005
FORD	19,902,252	7,062,714	653,263	1,287,695	4,158,029	899,720	66,007	9,503,624	3,335,914
ARD	23,054,033	8,569,405	1,105,135	1,716,000	5,001,647	642,620	104,003	10,815,950	3,668,678
T	1,833,713	659,603	86,903	112,110	279,782	164,488	16,320	867,372	306,738
TGOMERY	117,498,734	49,936,906	10,630,960	8,661,940	26,914,086	2,930,202	799,718	51,299,056	16,262,772
GEORGE'S	92,238,737	36,560,897	7,488,185	7,307,325	14,387,480	4,583,319	2,794,408	41,737,096	13,940,944
EN ANNE'S	3,971,721	1,538,023	234,246	229,539	796,041	260,411	17,786	1,810,060	623,638
MARY'S	8,445,177	3,289,337	421,502	609,447	1,911,401	346,987		3,860,582	1,295,258
ERSET	2,247,984	793,398	212,000	172,793	224,243	166,092	18,270	1,105,825	348,761
BOT	2,622,917	796,877	86,054	156,307	419,077	117,136	18,303	1,292,742	533,298
HINGTON	13,227,144	4,574,237	673,873	1,100,737	2,461,704	306,315	31,608	6,403,076	2,249,831
OMICO	8,198,753	2,854,504	370,848	496,387	1,178,824	486,160	122,285	3,941,889	1,602,360
CESTER	4,661,005	1,549,282	135,720	273,291	895,844	202,001	42,426	2,322,616	789,107

TABLE 92

EXPENDITURES FROM FOOD SERVICE FUND FOR FOOD SERVICES: MARYLAND PUBLIC SCHOOLS: 1986-87

LOCAL UNIT	TOTAL FOOD SERVICE FUND	SALARIES AND WAGES	CONTRACTED SERVICES	SUPPLIES AND MATERIALS TOTAL	FOOD	VALUE OF DONATED COMMODITIES	OTHER	OTHER CHARGES	EQUIPMENT REPLACEMEN
TOTAL STATE	$114,385,479	$45,864,243	$2,117,475	$52,424,269	$37,061,365	$10,524,053	$4,838,851	$13,126,599	$852,893
ALLEGANY	2,823,268	1,134,651	90,921	1,348,487	964,423	305,187	76,877	230,195	21,014
ANNE ARUNDEL	7,975,766	2,737,759	210,976	3,914,005	2,894,073	637,489	382,443	948,133	164,893
BALTIMORE CITY	21,909,900	9,548,430	655,619	8,848,759	6,450,399	1,519,008	879,352	2,780,783	76,309
BALTIMORE	12,741,838	5,513,367	359,188	5,944,854	4,024,365	996,279	924,210	860,738	63,691
CALVERT	1,140,286	414,694	22,823	623,002	425,262	153,459	44,281	67,589	12,178
CAROLINE	1,033,474	384,297	12,703	505,047	353,321	111,537	40,189	100,041	31,296
CARROLL	2,880,994	1,025,426	5,208	1,426,147	938,142	408,441	79,564	361,126	63,087
CECIL	1,877,252	792,665	339	942,909	661,088	230,638	51,183	134,918	6,421
CHARLES	2,892,747	1,101,377	28,673	1,451,088	990,484	385,504	75,100	300,118	11,491
DORCHESTER	978,268	359,256	34,820	435,999	399,973		38,026	126,156	22,037
FREDERICK	4,473,986	1,542,269	227,439	2,209,150	1,323,490	657,380	228,280	465,966	29,162
GARRETT	1,251,910	506,261	18,826	523,970	341,251	153,799	28,920	181,943	20,910
HARFORD	4,407,942	1,796,169	26,898	2,052,205	1,351,815	584,315	116,075	530,853	1,817
HOWARD	3,942,058	1,658,569		1,734,547	1,734,547			548,942	
KENT	465,873	188,991	11,197	227,553	148,180	49,229	30,144	33,611	4,521
MONTGOMERY	14,742,261	6,614,243	167,046	5,771,596	4,538,352	651,743	581,501	2,140,295	49,081
PRINCE GEORGE'S	19,492,299	8,125,537	101,972	8,980,724	5,448,430	2,624,244	908,050	2,227,411	56,655
QUEEN ANNE'S	890,887	287,088	5,693	463,446	324,697	89,950	48,799	111,507	23,153
ST. MARY'S	1,819,567	604,967	9,774	971,820	690,238	198,932	82,650	150,788	82,218
SOMERSET	466,863		11,845	394,578	351,567		43,011	60,440	
TALBOT	693,454	201,745	12,676	411,634	404,205		7,429	67,399	.10
WASHINGTON	3,410,984	1,326,482	25,867	1,683,511	1,029,896	577,019	76,596	371,964	8.2
WICOMICO	1,414,269		54,521	1,020,994	812,819	156,881	51,294	244,922	9,82
WORCESTER	659,333		22,361	540,244	460,348	33,019	46,877	80,761	10,967

TABLE
93

EXPENDITURES FOR COMMUNITY SERVICES: MARYLAND PUBLIC SCHOOLS: 1986-87

LOCAL UNIT	TOTAL COMMUNITY SERVICE	SALARIES AND WAGES	CONTRACTED SERVICES	SUPPLIES AND MATERIALS	OTHER CHARGES	REPLACEMENT EQUIPMENT
TOTAL STATE	$5,790,612	$3,550,514	$1,260,871	$384,253	$573,848	$21,126
ALLEGANY	142,583	103,614	2,362	7,356	29,251	
ANNE ARUNDEL	46,035	271	78	45,686		
BALTIMORE CITY	50,599	46,136	2,465	1,883	115	
BALTIMORE	204,193	162,972		8,884	32,337	
CALVERT	121,858	112,839	666	1,486	6,867	
CAROLINE	154,313	84,855	61,286	6,246	1,926	
CARROLL	87,710	50,678		7,760	29,272	
CECIL						
CHARLES	826,981	183,406	610,253	9,071	21,597	2,654
DORCHESTER	31,487		828	466	30,193	
FREDERICK	178,276	85,769	5,760	78,358	1,512	6,877
GARRETT	35,881	26,324		3,719	5,838	
HARFORD	50,538	41,763		8,104	671	
HOWARD	1,455,814	605,257	353,364	148,046	339,475	9,672
KENT	53,289	36,470	9,688	5,510	1,621	
MONTGOMERY	520,328	469,519		10,569	40,240	
PRINCE GEORGE'S	841,567	696,713	125,164	9,521	10,169	
QUEEN ANNE'S	66,844	37,583	29,261			
ST. MARY'S	174,063	173,565			498	
SOMERSET	96,083	86,168	900	4,689	4,326	
TALBOT	63,766	23,618	34,952	3,240	1,956	
WASHINGTON	461,914	427,839	2,985	17,667	13,423	
WICOMICO	94,347	66,132	19,907	4,512	1,873	1,923
WORCESTER	32,143	29,023	952	1,480	688	

TABLE
94

EXPENDITURES FOR DEBT SERVICE: MARYLAND PUBLIC SCHOOLS: 1986-87

LOCAL UNIT	TOTAL	LONG TERM COUNTY BONDS		STATE LOANS	
		REDEMPTION	INTEREST	REDEMPTION	INTEREST
TOTAL STATE	$79,677,194	$40,804,409	$21,792,347	$14,616,062	$2,464,376
ALLEGANY	176,320	160,000	16,320		
ANNE ARUNDEL	7,008,067	3,774,106	2,336,104	783,894	133,963
BALTIMORE CITY	20,414,114	8,051,260	4,717,460	6,358,170	1,287,224
BALTIMORE	8,446,540	6,207,000	2,195,656	18,375	25,509
CALVERT	189,250	150,000	39,250		
CAROLINE	135,505	120,000	15,505		
CARROLL	600,180	476,393	123,787		
CECIL	452,221	263,182	189,039		
CHARLES	783,100			650,000	133,100
DORCHESTER	387,334	253,428	113,953	7,790	12,163
FREDERICK	2,348,411	1,332,400	1,016,011		
GARRETT					
HARFORD	2,069,368	1,583,511	485,902	7,790	12,163
HOWARD	3,809,115	1,991,430	1,817,685		
KENT	141,050	130,000	11,050		
MONTGOMERY	21,608,71	10,806,849	6,82,098	3,566,431	409,338
PRINCE GEORGE'S	8,641,59	3,595,028	1,436,919	3,213,547	397,501
QUEEN ANNE'S	83,486			30,065	53,415
ST. MARY'S					
SOMERSET					
TALBOT	124,700	100,000	24,700		
WASHINGTON	1,829,280	1,429,822	399,458		
WICOMICO	203,250	200,000	3,250		
WORCESTER	225,600	200,000	25,600		

TABLE
95

EXPENDITURES FOR SPECIAL EDUCATION: MARYLAND PUBLIC SCHOOLS: 1986-87

PROGRAMS   IN   LOCAL   UNIT   SCHOOLS

TOTAL*	SALARIES AND WAGES	CONTRACTED SERVICES	-----SUPPLIES AND MATERIALS -----			OTHER CHARGES	OUTGOING TRANSFERS	
			TOTAL	TEXTBOOKS	OTHER		OTHER MD LOCAL UNITS	OTHER
$222,642,012	$215,844,697	$2,697,759	$3,078,486	$510,648	$2,567,838	$1,021,070	$10,082,220	$20,541,368
2,385,908	2,310,575	29,173	30,134	402	29,732	16,026		35,044
17,631,383	17,263,401	70,641	227,497	27,969	199,528	69,844		1,905,586
47,541,549	45,935,251	1,002,680	588,542	129,688	458,854	15,076	8,509,699	215
27,548,065	27,196,741	59,224	245,079	87,603	157,476	47,021	84,941	3,885,797
2,337,106	2,244,870	12,650	60,255	38	60,217	19,331	25,733	126,419
884,475	846,675	13,373	19,781	266	19,515	4,646		250,226
4,310,469	4,055,267	96,219	110,859	12,661	98,198	48,124	31,552	287,239
2,731,193	2,578,309	98,984	39,147		39,147	14,753		177,766
5,140,000	4,811,547	196,781	87,15.	6,153	81,005	44,514	71,163	215,374
1,148,607	1,030,200	85,074	23,968	240	23,726	9,367	83,574	4,649
4,746,050	4,556,894	37,962	119,65	10,193	109,463	31,538		131,216
1,275,814	1,211,759	23,063	18,66	7,914	10,752	22,328	2,085	44,081
5,343,219	5,200,472	11,699	90,706	37,680	53,020	40,348		541,671
8,120,834	7,796,117	154,608	112,036	8,008	104,028	58,073	764,682	761,930
717,380	641,049	50,863	16,312	2,723	13,589	9,166		15,000
41,858,385	40,773,781	115,005	789,865	73,044	716,821	179,734	48,466	7,063,556
34,222,988	33,659,501	18,341	245,255	48,467	196,788	137,891	85,798	4,673,824
1,450,493	1,177,36	7,202	43,990	41,663	2,327	150,665		
3,772,718	3,459,98	19,819	87,247	13,759	73,488	32,254	21,572	95,220
801,967	732,618	30,232	6,636		6,636	26,781		
926,247	851,070	55,68	13,232	2,177	11,055	6,256	2,356	134,279
3,871,493	3,781,880	42,43	25,492		25,492	21,686	325,232	
2,393,981	2,309,421	35,90	42,344		42,344	6,307	4,811	185,268
1,481,678	1,420,565	17,13	34,637		34,637	9,343	0,556	7,010

ING TRANSFERS.

TABLE 96

. . . . S C H O O L   C O N S T R U C T I O N   F U N D . . . .

LOCAL UNIT	TOTAL CAPITAL OUTLAY	TOTAL CURRENT EXPENSE FUND	TOTAL SCHOOL CONSTRUCTION FUND	SITES AND SITE IMPROVEMENT	BUILDINGS & BUILDING ADDITIONS	REMODELING	EQUIPMENT AND OTHER	FOOD SERVICE FUND EQUIPMENT
TOTAL STATE	$142,979,860	$16,730,741	$125,506,185	$2,578,031	$73,640,439	$31,087,751	$18,199,964	$742,934
ALLEGANY	1,068,185	467,487	591,969	11,131			294,837	8,729
ANNE ARUNDEL	12,317,034	1,912,024	10,391,958	441,618	6,078,711	286,001	805,974	13,552
BALTIMORE CITY	10,382,013	14,095	10,367,960	397	8,221,539	3,065,855	430,938	
BALTIMORE	9,693,085	1,876,800	7,527,210	58,378	7,246,341	1,715,086	222,491	289,170
CALVERT	1,033,648	250,999	776,499		381,682		394,837	6,155
CAROLINE	49,197	287,512	181,685					
CARROLL	5,244,140	639,553	4,561,329		3,855,824	181,685	705,505	23,258
CECIL	1,047,361	146,291	860,948	229,528	559,398		221,537	122
CHARLES	8,042,818	1,197,735	6,827,975	168,383	6,374,879	50,485	284,713	7,108
DORCHESTER	258,554	89,692	168,240		168,240			622
FREDERICK	5,332,339	1,916,992	3,394,063	38,275	1,805,491		711,112	21,254
GARRETT	2,475,111	405,114	2,063,982			2,063,982		6,055
HARFORD	3,104,600	383,927	2,720,703	197,148	1,621,454	901,304	737	
HOWARD	12,665,909	1,338,591	11,301,045		1,185,217	9,554,287	561,571	26,313
KENT	132,148	131,822	326		227		99	
MONTGOMERY	51,295,911	2,006,025	49,096,309	936,774	30,573,546	8,876,509	8,709,480	193,657
PRINCE GEORGE'S	10,755,162	1,927,198	8,827,964		2,684,597	1,703,929	4,439,438	
QUEEN ANNE'S	331,685	172,016	159,669				19,427	
ST. MARY'S	1,633,710	281,886	1,351,824	140,242	1,351,824			
SOMERSET	89,516	89,516						
TALBOT	105,609	93,577						12,032
WASHINGTON	1,941,709	498,131	1,329,728	356,157		973,571		113,850
WICOMICO	1,546,415	199,183	1,330,361		48,411	876,042	405,909	16,871
WORCESTER	2,082,341	403,715	1,674,438		1,483,079		191,359	4,188

TABLE
97

Percent Distribution of Current Expenses: Maryland Public Schools: 1986 - 87

Local Unit	Student Transportation	Administration	INSTRUCTION Regular	Special Education	Student Personnel Services	Health Services	Operation of Plant	Maintenance of Plant	FIXED CHARGES Local Share	State Share	Community Services	Outgoing Transfers*	Current Capital Outlay
STATE AVERAGE	4.8%	4.3%	48.4%	7.7%	0.5%	0.2%	8.3%	3.1%	7.7%	12.6%	0.2%	1.1%	1.1%
ALLEGANY	6.7	3.7	49.6	5.8	0.4	+	8.8	2.0	6.3	12.7	0.3	0.1	1.5
ANNE ARUNDEL	5.1	3.9	50.8	6.8	0.7	+	8.1	3.1	6.7	13.0	+	0.8	1.1
BALTIMORE CITY	3.2	4.4	44.3	11.9	0.5	+	9.9	3.0	7.8	12.0	+	2.2	0.8
BALTIMORE	3.3	3.5	50.6	7.0	0.5	0.4	8.7	3.2	7.3	13.5	0.1	1.0	0.9
CALVERT	6.6	4.7	49.1	7.0	0.7	+	7.5	2.4	8.0	12.3	0.4	0.5	0.8
CAROLINE	8.2	4.4	49.2	5.7	0.4	+	7.7	2.2	5.7	12.1	0.2	1.8	2.5
CARROLL	6.8	3.9	51.1	6.2	0.4	0.5	7.1	2.8	6.1	12.7	0.2	0.5	1.6
CECIL	5.7	4.1	50.5	6.5	0.4	0.1	8.3	3.5	6.7	12.6	0.2	0.5	0.9
CHARLES	6.9	3.9	46.5	8.1	0.6	+	8.7	2.9	6.6	11.5	1.3	0.5	2.4
DORCHESTER	7.0	4.8	49.6	6.2	0.5	0.1	8.2	2.7	7.5	12.1	0.2	0.5	0.7
FREDERICK	5.7	4.8	50.1	5.3	0.2	+	9.0	3.0	6.0	12.5	0.2	0.3	2.6
GARRETT	8.5	3.6	46.9	6.7	0.6	+	7.1	2.8	7.5	11.8	0.2	1.3	3.1
HARFORD	5.9	2.9	52.4	5.3	0.4	0.5	8.5	2.9	7.0	12.7	0.1	0.5	0.9
HOWARD	5.3	5.3	47.7	6.5	0.3	0.5	7.8	3.5	6.9	11.7	1.2	1.3	2.0
KENT	9.0	5.0	44.8	7.0	0.2	+	7.8	4.7	6.4	11.4	0.8	0.4	2.5
MONTGOMERY	4.6	5.4	48.2	7.9	0.3	+	6.6	2.8	9.4	12.7	0.1	1.3	0.8
PRINCE GEORGE'S	4.8	3.8	47.0	7.9	0.6	0.4	9.0	3.6	8.3	12.7	0.2	1.1	0.7
QUEEN ANNE'S	7.7	4.1	49.1	7.2	0.6	0.5	6.2	2.9	7.6	12.0	0.3	0.6	1.2
ST. MARY'S	6.9	4.7	46.7	8.6	0.5	0.1	8.4	3.4	7.5	11.7	0.4	0.3	0.9
SOMERSET	8.8	6.2	47.5	6.7	0.4	0.5	7.3	2.3	6.6	12.2	0.8	+	0.9
TALBOT	6.2	4.9	51.1	6.5	0.5	0.2	7.2	2.4	5.6	12.8	0.4	1.0	1.1
WASHINGTON	4.5	4.8	50.4	5.7	0.4	+	9.4	2.9	6.8	12.8	0.7	0.5	1.2
WICOMICO	5.9	3.6	50.8	5.7	0.4	0.4	7.4	2.6	8.2	13.2	0.2	0.5	0.9
WORCESTER	6.4	4.0	51.4	6.1	0.5	0.4	6.9	2.4	6.4	12.8	0.1	0.1	2.4

Includes transfers made to other Maryland Local Units

Less than 0.1 percent

NE: Percentages may not equal 100% due to rounding

TABLE
98

Percent Distribution of Day School Current Expenses
Maryland Public Schools: 1986 - 87

Local Unit	Student Transpor- tation	Adminis- tration	INSTRUCTION Regular	Special Education	Student Personnel Services	Health Services	Operation of Plant	Main- tenance of Plant	Fixed Charges*
STATE AVERAGE	5.6	5.1	57.0	9.1	0.6	0.2	9.8	3.6	9.1
ALLEGANY	7.8	4.3	58.1	6.8	0.5	+	10.3	2.4	9.8
ANNE ARUNDEL	6.0	4.5	59.7	7.9	0.8	+	9.6	3.7	7.9
BALTIMORE CITY	3.8	5.2	52.1	14.0	0.6	+	11.6	3.5	9.2
BALTIMORE	3.9	4.1	59.9	8.3	0.6	0.5	10.3	3.7	8.7
CALVERT	7.7	5.5	57.0	8.2	0.8	+	8.7	2.8	9.3
CAROLINE	9.8	5.3	59.0	6.9	0.4	+	9.2	2.6	5.8
CARROLL	8.0	4.5	60.2	7.3	0.4	0.6	8.3	3.3	7.2
CECIL	6.7	4.7	58.8	7.5	0.5	0.2	9.7	4.1	7.8
CHARLES	8.2	4.6	55.2	9.6	0.7	+	10.4	3.4	7.9
DORCHESTER	8.0	5.6	57.3	7.1	0.5	0.2	9.5	3.2	8.6
FREDERICK	6.8	5.7	59.4	6.3	0.3	0.1	10.7	3.6	7.1
GARRETT	10.2	4.3	56.1	8.1	0.7	+	8.5	3.3	8.9
HARFORD	6.8	3.4	61.1	6.2	0.5	0.6	9.9	3.4	8.1
HOWARD	6.3	5.3	56.8	7.8	0.4	0.6	9.3	4.2	8.2
KENT	10.6	5.9	52.8	8.2	0.2	+	9.2	5.5	7.5
MONTGOMERY	5.4	6.3	56.6	9.3	0.3	+	7.7	3.3	11.0
PRINCE GEORGE'S	5.6	4.5	55.0	9.1	0.8	0.5	10.5	4.2	9.7
QUEEN ANNE'S	9.0	4.7	57.1	8.3	0.7	0.5	7.2	3.4	8.8
ST. MARY'S	8.0	5.4	53.8	9.9	0.6	0.1	9.7	3.9	8.6
SOMERSET	10.3	7.1	55.1	7.8	0.4	0.5	8.5	2.7	7.7
TALBOT	7.4	5.8	60.3	7.7	0.6	0.2	8.5	2.8	6.6
WASHINGTON	5.3	5.7	59.3	6.8	0.4	+	11.1	3.4	8.0
WICOMICO	7.1	4.3	61.0	6.9	0.5	0.5	8.9	3.2	7.6
WORCESTER	7.6	4.8	60.9	7.2	0.6	0.5	8.2	2.8	7.6

* Expenditures for State Share of Teachers' Retirement and Social Security are not included.

+ Less than 0.1 percent

NOTE: Percentages may not equal 100% due to rounding

TABLE
99

Cost Per Pupil Belonging for Current Expenses: Prek.-12: Maryland Public Schools: 1977-78 - 1986-87
(Excluding State Share of Teachers' Retirement and Social Security)

Local Unit	1977-78	1978-79	1979-80	1980-81	1981-82	1982-83	1983-84	1984-85	1985-86	1986-87
Total State	$1,694.23	$1,873.23	$2,077.32	$2,323.17	$2,568.71	$2,764.99	$2,949.91	$3,194.40	$3,465.92	$3,738.49
Allegany	1,516.83	1,718.97	1,920.57	2,122.12	2,378.89	2,464.07	2,480.09	2,708.95	2,914.52	3,122.76
Anne Arundel	1,534.47	1,708.33	1,903.83	2,138.50	2,344.99	2,617.12	2,765.25	3,049.78	3,304.70	3,576.57
Baltimore City	1,584.86	1,729.33	1,886.96	2,092.41	2,306.97	2,363.83	2,544.09	2,740.37	3,007.72	3,184.59
Baltimore	1,813.90	1,993.49	2,244.77	2,548.73	2,838.88	3,103.30	3,418.81	3,694.32	3,940.26	4,255.73
Calvert	1,705.38	1,863.84	2,085.90	2,380.73	2,610.93	2,757.80	2,968.80	3,138.49	3,377.99	3,486.77
Caroline	1,384.51	1,551.90	1,753.52	2,022.55	2,165.18	2,357.06	2,300.47	2,528.89	2,690.69	2,962.43
Carroll	1,297.71	1,423.08	1,631.89	1,847.35	2,051.37	2,206.64	2,453.92	2,666.20	2,823.88	3,097.10
Cecil	1,324.22	1,522.19	1,692.81	1,917.38	2,191.38	2,392.86	2,580.40	2,693.14	2,922.30	3,131.94
Charles	1,523.64	1,686.84	2,867.09	2,193.11	2,348.41	2,506.64	2,529.61	2,843.08	3,014.86	3,259.39
Dorchester	1,792.06	1,961.25	2,198.81	2,359.87	2,452.22	2,557.06	2,699.01	2,970.38	3,252.13	3,387.21
Frederick	1,421.67	1,577.56	1,793.94	2,044.66	2,257.75	2,479.55	2,565.37	2,838.46	2,959.46	3,179.51
Garrett	1,328.47	1,552.09	1,747.70	2,037.92	2,073.04	2,278.45	2,449.21	2,443.79	2,850.62	3,114.16
Harford	1,444.78	1,588.14	1,804.17	2,043.89	2,209.75	2,483.99	2,617.75	2,781.58	2,979.92	3,171.99
Howard	1,667.59	1,838.45	2,103.35	2,350.53	2,637.94	2,945.05	3,195.66	3,496.23	3,789.80	4,144.55
Kent	1,772.41	1,942.07	2,229.04	2,400.53	2,630.88	2,853.69	2,857.05	3,062.09	3,489.83	3,793.01
Montgomery	2,150.72	2,389.53	2,661.63	3,000.54	3,334.41	3,682.96	3,919.21	4,216.37	4,585.04	4,899.60
Prince George's	1,778.31	1,989.71	2,148.00	2,315.28	2,597.20	2,710.09	2,850.99	3,103.59	3,410.06	3,763.40
Queen Anne's	1,415.76	1,591.22	1,896.50	2,192.30	2,428.01	2,645.68	2,821.17	2,999.65	3,396.63	3,733.96
St. Mary's	1,499.33	1,682.25	1,842.94	2,227.14	2,336.45	2,632.09	2,706.45	2,821.70	3,206.19	3,430.50
Somerset	1,509.59	1,783.83	1,892.43	2,165.60	2,260.61	2,359.40	2,471.11	2,660.04	2,878.63	3,114.31
Talbot	1,668.40	1,866.88	2,030.97	2,244.10	2,509.16	2,751.10	2,949.59	3,111.14	3,300.06	3,349.85
Washington	1,517.65	1,665.10	1,891.78	2,116.89	2,300.27	2,449.41	2,684.24	2,938.87	3,131.73	3,413.99
Wicomico	1,452.54	1,602.24	1,815.44	2,047.12	2,243.19	2,374.99	2,526.12	2,753.77	2,914.48	3,123.54
Worcester	1,735.61	1,914.66	2,235.45	2,474.12	2,780.91	3,032.41	3,196.78	3,396.30	3,639.77	4,100.78

TABLE 100

Cost per Pupil Belonging* for Current Expenses+

Maryland Public Schools: 1986 - 87

| Local Unit | ALL COSTS INCLUDING TRANSPORTATION | | | | ALL COSTS EXCLU | | | |
	Total Including State Share of Teachers' Retirement and Social Security Cost	Rank	Total Excluding State Share of Teachers' Retirement and Social Security Cost	Rank	Total Including State Shar of Teachers' Retirement an Social Security Cost	Rank	Cost	Rank
TOTAL STATE	$4,299.77		$3,738.49		$4,094.15		$3,532.87	
ALLEGANY	3,591.75	20	3,122.76	20	3,357.15	20	2,888.16	20
ANNE ARUNDEL	4,126.27	8	3,576.57	8	3,908.34	8	3,358.64	8
BALTIMORE CITY	3,639.94	17	3,184.56	15	3,519.17	14	3,063.79	14
BALTIMORE	4,943.29	2	4,255.73	2	4,782.76	2	4,095.20	2
CALVERT	3,985.16	9	3,488.77	9	3,715.19	10	3,218.80	10
CAROLINE	3,396.75	24	2,962.43	24	3,103.88	24	2,669.56	24
CARROLL	3,568.15	21	3,097.10	23	3,319.21	21	2,848.17	21
CECIL	3,592.77	19	3,131.94	18	3,381.67	19	2,920.84	18
CHARLES	3,709.63	14	3,259.39	14	3,439.63	16	2,989.40	15
DORCHESTER	3,862.66	12	3,387.21	12	3,589.52	13	3,114.07	12
FREDERICK	3,655.38	15	3,179.51	16	3,446.26	15	2,970.38	16
GARRETT	3,558.42	22	3,114.16	22	3,237.95	22	2,793.69	22
HARFORD	3,648.30	16	3,171.99	17	3,432.20	17	2,958.89	17
HOWARD	4,726.70	4	4,144.55	3	4,460.90	3	3,878.75	3
KENT	4,315.83	6	3,793.01	5	3,926.72	7	3,403.89	7
MONTGOMERY	5,643.57	1	4,899.60	1	5,407.25	1	4,663.29	1
PRINCE GEORGE'S	4,324.98	5	3,763.40	6	4,112.34	5	3,550.77	5
QUEEN ANNE'S	4,262.23	7	3,733.96	7	3,935.63	6	3,407.36	6
ST. MARY'S	3,898.11	11	3,430.50	10	3,629.13	11	3,161.52	11
SOMERSET	3,557.28	23	3,114.31	21	3,233.84	23	2,790.87	23
TALBOT	3,859.43	13	3,349.85	13	3,611.26	12	3,101.68	13
WASHINGTON	3,934.99	10	3,413.99	11	3,763.82	9	3,242.83	9
WICOMICO	3,623.26	18	3,123.54	19	3,399.44	18	2,899.72	19
WORCESTER	4,730.35	3	4,100.78	4	4,416.50	4	3,786.93	4

* Half-time kindergarten pupils are expressed in full-time equivalents in arriving at per pupil costs.

+ Includes the following expenditures: Administration, Instruction, Student Personnel Services, Health Services, Student Transportation, Operation and Maintenance of Plant and Fixed Charges; excludes Adult Education, Food Service operations, Outgoing Transfers, Community Services, and equipment.

TABLE
101

Cost per Pupil Belonging* for Current Expenses+

Maryland Public Schools: 1986 - 87

Local Unit	Total Cost per Pupil Cost	R	Administration Cost	R	Instruction Cost	R	Special Education Cost	R	Student Personnel Services Cost	R	Health Services Cost	R	Student Transportation Cost	R	Operation of Plant Cost	R	Maintenance of Plant Cost	R	Fixed Charges Cost	R
TOTAL STATE	$3,738.49		$191.03		$2,140.19		$344.19		$ 21.17		$ 8.66		$205.62		$368.52		$115.99		$343.09	
ALLEGANY	3,122.76	20	135.84	22	1,826.92	19	215.40	21	15.91	14	0.44	17	234.59	15	323.74	13	61.81	23	308.07	8
ANNE ARUNDEL	3,576.57	8	162.27	16	2,134.61	6	286.82	11	27.85	2	0.00	23	217.93	17	344.98	8	118.23	7	283.86	13
BALTIMORE CITY	3,184.56	15	167.44	15	1,669.64	24	450.25	2	20.33	11	0.00	24	120.76	24	374.37	6	85.01	17	296.83	10
BALTIMORE	4,255.73	2	178.35	13	2,558.02	2	357.21	3	26.91	4	19.70	4	160.52	23	441.87	1	140.16	3	372.95	2
CALVERT	3,486.77	9	192.73	8	1,982.79	11	286.00	12	27.63	3	1.14	15	269.96	9	302.85	17	96.98	12	326.65	6
CAROLINE	2,962.43	24	158.72	17	1,760.92	22	204.74	22	12.80	22	0.48	15	292.86	6	274.16	20	54.57	24	203.13	24
CARROLL	3,097.10	23	142.62	20	1,878.64	16	230.43	19	13.97	20	17.85	7	248.93	12	260.97	24	78.49	20	225.18	22
CECIL	3,131.94	18	149.23	19	1,854.98	17	237.48	17	14.71	18	5.44	12	211.10	20	304.66	16	108.65	9	245.66	18
CHARLES	3,259.39	14	151.48	18	1,805.45	20	315.26	8	24.01	6	0.22	19	269.99	8	341.01	10	92.61	14	259.32	17
DORCHESTER	3,387.21	12	190.26	9	1,940.20	13	241.99	16	18.65	12	5.58	11	273.13	7	323.62	14	100.14	11	293.59	12
FREDERICK	3,179.51	16	184.71	11	1,903.41	15	202.13	23	9.04	23	1.71	14	209.12	21	344.46	9	96.71	13	228.19	21
GARRETT	3,114.16	22	134.22	23	1,787.61	21	253.78	14	21.74	8	0.22	20	320.47	4	266.56	23	67.85	22	281.68	14
HARFORD	3,171.99	17	107.92	24	1,952.72	12	196.97	24	15.42	16	19.49	5	213.09	18	316.75	15	89.24	15	260.35	16
HOWARD	4,144.55	3	264.74	2	2,380.50	4	326.38	6	15.96	13	25.99	1	265.79	11	391.45	3	129.29	5	344.41	4
KENT	3,793.01	5	230.55	3	2,032.63	9	319.46	7	8.66	7	0.05	21	389.11	1	360.20	7	158.60	1	293.72	11
MONTGOMERY	4,899.60	1	315.86	1	2,797.36	1	460.92	1	15.44	15	0.36	18	236.31	14	384.21	4	139.23	4	549.88	1
PRINCE GEORGE'S	3,763.40	6	170.23	14	2,071.55	7	345.17	4	28.63	1	19.17	6	212.63	19	397.42	2	149.82	2	368.75	3
QUEEN ANNE'S	3,733.96	7	178.83	12	2,146.84	5	314.85	9	26.61	5	21.68	2	326.59	2	272.73	21	111.94	8	333.85	5
ST. MARY'S	3,430.50	10	186.74	10	1,852.56	18	342.16	5	20.72	10	2.23	13	268.97	10	333.86	12	124.90	6	298.32	9
SOMERSET	3,114.31	21	225.06	4	1,699.93	23	245.20	15	13.40	21	16.60	9	323.43	3	266.60	22	82.44	19	242.59	19
TALBOT	3,349.85	13	196.67	6	2,031.37	10	258.48	13	21.45	9	6.49	10	248.17	13	287.95	18	76.86	21	222.38	23
WASHINGTON	3,413.99	11	195.00	7	2,040.54	8	233.10	18	14.83	17	0.01	22	171.16	22	382.73	5	101.17	10	275.41	15
WICOMICO	3,123.54	19	136.67	21	1,914.18	14	215.77	20	14.19	19	16.90	8	223.82	16	280.22	19	82.50	18	239.26	20
WORCESTER	4,100.78	4	197.21	5	2,507.61	3	299.78	10	23.91	7	20.74	3	313.85	5	338.38	11	85.80	16	313.47	7

Half-time kindergarten pupils are expressed in full-time equivalents in arriving at per pupil costs.

State share of Teachers' Retirement and Social Security are not included.

te : R = Rank

TABLE
102

Cost Per Pupil Belonging* for Materials of Instruction, Textbooks, and Library Books: Prek-12
Maryland Public Schools: 1984-85 - 1986-87

Local Unit	Total Supplies and Materials+			Textbooks			Library Books		
	1984-85	1985-86	1986-87	1984-85	1985-86	1986-87	1984-85	1985-86	1986-87
Total State	$ 76.40	$ 84.45	$ 90.99	$ 22.27	$ 25.09	$ 26.91	$ 6.80	$ 8.73	$ 9.30
Allegany	81.81	86.90	84.79	22.21	21.76	20.42	5.49	12.34	13.06
Anne Arundel	86.56	102.66	110.08	16.00	22.11	24.78	7.59	8.01	8.63
Baltimore City	54.98	63.68	57.91	20.27	23.78	23.19	2.95	3.38	2.56
Baltimore	74.86	81.27	96.68	25.18	27.36	31.62	2.61	6.35	7.21
Calvert	116.16	129.92	119.21	39.09	39.86	36.60	13.07	14.11	15.37
Caroline	59.60	78.41	79.62	25.98	41.80	18.67	11.66	7.90	10.55
Carroll	95.58	97.34	103.45	25.02	26.28	26.80	13.64	11.55	14.98
Cecil	86.10	80.64	71.85	30.11	21.45	17.06	10.69	11.75	6.46
Charles	62.12	79.96	112.69	16.93	21.69	28.18	7.16	10.35	19.54
Dorchester	74.14	73.66	76.72	6.62	10.31	9.75	6.26	10.10	8.28
Frederick	85.70	80.97	88.70	21.71	19.99	24.80	14.05	8.45	10.34
Garrett	57.30	69.63	84.64	21.72	28.57	36.17	3.93	7.30	8.81
Harford	87.42	93.22	95.40	34.40	32.80	38.89	14.19	14.26	12.52
Howard	125.04	129.39	136.06	31.02	30.20	29.00	14.66	21.76	15.22
Kent	91.92	105.78	106.96	29.70	29.46	29.86	11.48	12.52	14.87
Montgomery	87.43	95.11	103.60	21.24	23.99	25.80	7.74	13.89	14.92
Prince George's	59.23	70.47	80.32	20.66	26.16	26.40	2.30	3.72	4.72
Queen Anne's	88.26	91.16	122.60	24.56	83.60	83.50	14.90	0.00	20.39
St. Mary's	91.17	92.91	101.28	18.26	17.42	19.03	16.87	20.95	16.61
Somerset	81.29	77.57	69.42	23.88	20.54	19.02	5.27	5.57	5.33
Talbot	121.41	116.98	105.42	13.63	11.95	17.49	17.32	17.79	14.69
Washington	59.25	59.19	64.07	18.65	14.73	18.41	9.08	8.98	11.45
Wicomico	94.44	90.46	109.13	32.10	26.72	36.65	13.13	12.94	14.98
Worcester	128.32	140.02	130.99	20.99	29.80	38.10	11.61	11.06	12.84

*Half-time kindergarten pupils are expressed in full-time equivalents in arriving at per pupil costs.
+Includes textbooks, library books, and all other instructional supplies and materials.

TABLE
103

Cost per Pupil Belonging for Current Expenses, Capital Outlay, and Debt Service: Prek - 12*

Maryland Public Schools: 1986 - 87

Local Unit	Grand Total	CURRENT EXPENSE Total	Regular Programs	Transpor- tation	Teachers' Retirement and Social Security	Current Capital Outlay and Debt Service+
TOTAL STATE	$4,476.81	$4,299.77	$3,532.87	$ 205.62	$ 561.28	$ 177.04
ALLEGANY	3,675.72	3,591.75	2,888.16	234.59	468.99	83.97
ANNE ARUNDEL	4,285.46	4,126.27	3,358.64	217.93	549.70	159.19
BALTIMORE CITY	3,863.49	3,639.93	3,063.79	120.76	455.37	223.56
BALTIMORE	5,105.89	4,943.28	4,095.20	160.52	687.55	162.61
CALVERT	4,040.41	3,985.15	3,216.80	269.96	498.38	55.26
CAROLINE	3,517.62	3,396.75	2,669.56	292.86	434.32	120.87
CARROLL	3,664.35	3,568.14	2,848.17	248.93	471.04	96.21
CECIL	3,665.20	3,592.76	2,920.84	211.10	460.82	72.44
CHARLES	3,850.52	3,709.62	2,989.40	269.99	450.23	140.90
DORCHESTER	3,971.64	3,862.65	3,114.07	273.13	475.44	108.99
FREDERICK	3,865.91	3,655.38	2,978.38	209.12	475.87	210.53
GARRETT	3,676.35	3,558.42	2,793.69	320.47	444.26	117.93
HARFORD	3,750.48	3,645.30	2,958.89	213.09	473.31	115.18
HOWARD	4,980.03	4,726.69	3,878.75	265.79	582.14	253.34
KENT	4,517.74	4,315.83	3,403.89	389.11	522.82	201.91
MONTGOMERY	5,960.51	5,643.56	4,663.29	236.31	743.96	316.95
PRINCE GEORGE'S	4,441.82	4,324.97	3,550.77	212.63	561.57	116.85
QUEEN ANNE'S	4,347.98	4,262.23	3,407.36	326.59	528.27	85.75
ST. MARY'S	3,939.39	3,898.10	3,161.52	268.97	467.60	41.29
SOMERSET	3,591.26	3,559.04	2,790.87	323.43	444.73	32.22
TALBOT	3,939.21	3,859.43	3,101.68	248.17	509.58	79.78
WASHINGTON	4,103.32	3,934.98	3,242.83	171.16	520.99	168.34
WICOMICO	3,677.34	3,623.26	2,899.72	223.82	499.72	54.08
WORCESTER	4,894.30	4,730.35	3,786.93	313.85	629.57	163.95

+Half-time kindergarten pupils are expressed in full-time equivalents in arriving at per pupil costs.

+Current Capital Outlay are expenditures of current funds which result in the acquisition of new fixed assets or additions to existing fixed assets; Debt Service expenditures include both principal and interest payments.

TABLE
104

Basic State Aid for Current Expenses: Maryland Public School: 1986 -87

Local Unit	Total Pupils 9/30/85	Pupils X $1,651	Total Local Wealth* (Thousands)	Local Share	State Share Total	Per Pupil	Voc-Tec Set Aside	Tuition Bylaw	Total Current Expense Aid
Total State	638,867.6875	$1,054,770,552	$88,723,966	$507,456,726	$547,410,332	$ 856.84	$3,900,000	$ 61,704	$ 547,472,036
Allegany	11,177.7500	18,454,485	1,036,719	5,929,514	12,524,951	1,120.53	140,629	-	12,570,251
Anne Arundel	61,129.2500	100,924,392	8,326,864	47,625,501	53,298,891	871.90	404,521	45,300	53,298,891
Baltimore City	103,839.0000	171,438,189	8,791,437	50,282,625	121,155,564	1,166.76	788,901	-	121,155,564
Baltimore	77,177.2500	127,419,640	14,086,390	80,567,110	46,852,530	607.08	331,167	-	46,852,530
Calvert	7,700.0000	12,712,700	1,265,264	7,236,677	5,476,023	711.17	43,821	-	5,476,023
Caroline	4,134.0000	6,825,234	312,718	1,788,588	5,036,646	1,218.35	38,088	-	5,036,646
Carroll	18,788.1875	31,015,996	2,025,530	11,585,019	19,430,977	1,034.32	142,931	-	19,430,977
Cecil	11,585.5000	19,127,681	976,739	5,586,458	13,541,203	1,168.81	114,651	-	13,541,203
Charles	16,200.5000	26,747,026	1,700,417	9,725,537	17,021,488	1,050.68	146,383	-	17,021,488
Dorchester	4,619.0000	7,625,969	457,431	2,616,274	5,009,695	1,084.58	57,494	-	5,009,695
Frederick	22,811.5000	37,661,787	2,436,555	13,935,875	23,725,912	1,040.09	172,711	-	23,725,912
Garrett	5,073.2500	8,375,936	421,667	2,411,726	5,964,210	1,175.62	42,878	-	5,964,210
Harford	26,431.2500	43,637,994	2,681,410	15,336,322	28,301,672	1,070.77	170,528	-	28,301,672
Howard	24,095.2500	39,781,258	3,868,541	22,126,123	17,655,135	732.32	111,379	765	17,655,135
Kent	2,283.5000	3,770,059	303,731	1,737,189	2,032,869	890.4	20,167	-	2,033,634
Montgomery	88,249.0000	145,699,099	20,564,390	117,618,028	28,081,071	318.20	159,451	-	28,081,071
Prince George's	99,589.5000	164,422,285	12,872,253	72,478,948	91,943,316	923.22	578,080	1,145	91,944,461
Queen Anne's	4,502.5000	7,433,628	592,735	3,390,150	4,043,477	898.05	39,875	-	4,043,477
St. Mary's	10,462.0000	17,272,762	1,011,217	5,783,653	11,489,109	1,098.18	126,878	-	11,489,109
Somerset	3,123.5000	5,156,899	235,307	1,345,839	3,811,059	1,220.12	40,078	-	3,811,059
Talbot	3,527.0000	5,823,077	774,705	4,430,928	1,392,149	394.71	14,038	-	1,392,149[2]
Washington	16,677.0000	27,533,727	1,725,243	9,867,528	17,666,199	1,059.32	164,625	704	17,666,903
Wicomico	10,829.5000	17,879,505	1,086,666	6,215,189	11,664,316	1,077.09	68,321	-	11,664,316
Worcester	4,884.5000	8,031,290	1,370,037	7,835,925	291,870	60.00	2,405	13,790	305,660

*Includes the following 1985 wealth figures: net taxable income, real property assessed for state purposes, public utility property assessed for state purposes and 50% of personal property assessed for county purposes. Public utility shares and one-half semi-annual are excluded.

TABLE
105

Average Salaries of Instructional Positions: Maryland Public Schools: October, 1986

Local Unit	Average Instructional Salary	School Administrators			Instructional Positions					
		Average	Principals	Vice-Principals	Average	Teacher	Therapist	Guidance	Librarians	Psychologists
State Average	$29,895	$44,462	$47,162	$41,149	$29,120	$28,893	$27,661	$33,702	$30,967	$35,292
Allegany	26,401	35,630	36,971	32,680	25,961	25,961	22,646	27,591	24,560	28,817
Anne Arundel	29,907	48,742	52,069	44,266	28,925	28,570	26,957	36,515	30,126	38,108
Baltimore City	27,202	41,077	45,143	37,000	26,397	26,332	20,272	29,941	27,533	23,683
Baltimore	32,923	46,005	48,079	44,462	32,041	31,762	29,459	36,301	33,362	41,634
Calvert	29,174	42,572	47,475	37,996	28,356	28,097	26,532	33,160	30,510	33,464
Caroline	23,795	36,107	38,019	31,902	23,111	23,028	20,741	25,684	25,473	26,590
Carroll	27,159	39,850	42,108	37,335	26,509	26,407	23,785	29,510	28,111	29,706
Cecil	25,574	42,098	43,858	38,719	24,702	24,575	23,237	27,896	24,975	36,571
Charles	26,720	37,526	40,494	33,851	26,205	25,887	25,970	32,990	28,259	29,505
Dorchester	25,753	36,979	38,446	34,165	25,100	24,981	24,033	26,730	26,594	28,380
Frederick	26,931	40,852	43,129	38,575	26,149	25,975	23,308	29,748	29,123	35,936
Garrett	23,476	35,322	36,212	31,929	22,712	22,090	25,406	27,081	24,840	31,428
Harford	27,661	39,710	42,895	37,186	26,977	26,852	24,120	31,145	27,415	29,161
Howard	29,285	46,938	51,349	42,085	28,426	28,178	27,657	33,626	30,264	33,304
Kent	24,877	36,768	39,997	31,117	24,043	24,224	23,361	28,374	23,911	30,888
Montgomery	34,626	53,608	56,740	49,517	33,774	33,508	30,961	37,111	36,595	48,090
Prince George's	31,613	47,234	48,910	43,274	30,948	30,785	29,750	34,444	32,702	37,689
Queen Anne's	29,596	45,388	47,654	37,024	28,865	28,816	27,367	32,665	24,339	29,559
St. Mary's	24,895	34,510	35,936	31,963	24,374	24,217	21,719	28,263	26,790	36,422
Somerset	22,114	29,043	29,775	27,285	21,574	21,493	21,469	27,878	19,775	20,500
Talbot	26,017	37,207	39,170	33,935	25,293	25,143	22,870	31,339	25,484	34,688
Washington	27,139	39,314	40,790	36,128	26,476	26,443	23,519	29,362	25,482	33,324
Wicomico	25,829	37,573	41,057	33,373	25,165	25,085	23,235	27,944	24,786	32,282
Worcester	29,063	42,428	44,054	39,409	28,336	28,188	27,326	30,815	29,420	30,691

TABLE
106

Average Annual Salary per Teacher and Principal: Prek.-12: Maryland Public Schools: 1976-77 - 1986-87

Local Unit	1976-77	1977-78	1978-79	1979-80	1981-82	1982-83	1983-84	1984-85	1985-86	1986-87
Total State	$15,227	$16,088	$16,941	$18,215	$21,536	$23,702	$24,692	$26,180	$27,806	$29,895
Allegany	14,225	14,610	15,998	16,964	19,537	21,103	20,886	22,764	24,648	26,401
Anne Arundel	15,331	16,553	17,189	18,423	22,752	24,936	24,676	26,631	28,260	29,907
Baltimore City	14,771	15,040	14,344	16,116	18,147	19,441	21,650	23,411	25,395	27,202
Baltimore	16,348	17,403	19,160	19,622	22,916	26,875	27,079	28,262	30,720	32,923
Calvert	14,176	15,193	16,017	17,412	21,210	23,142	24,235	25,652	27,747	29,174
Caroline	11,777	11,870	12,227	14,779	17,260	17,543	17,777	18,857	20,816	23,795
Carroll	12,616	13,061	13,712	15,754	19,456	19,815	21,426	24,039	25,180	27,159
Cecil	12,692	13,702	13,828	15,467	17,216	19,939	20,508	21,306	23,355	25,574
Charles	13,952	14,653	14,793	16,324	19,718	18,958	22,131	24,033	25,845	26,720
Dorchester	13,615	14,048	16,451	17,473	19,809	20,892	19,794	21,891	23,860	25,753
Frederick	12,484	14,133	15,230	16,328	19,649	21,759	22,673	24,007	25,459	26,931
Garrett	11,374	11,819	13,375	13,701	16,330	18,327	18,596	20,311	21,323	23,476
Harford	13,578	14,080	15,529	16,906	20,069	22,497	24,040	24,950	26,076	27,661
Howard	14,464	15,402	16,800	16,563	20,971	23,824	23,978	25,371	27,095	29,285
Kent	12,619	11,899	13,341	14,439	21,893	22,380	19,967	20,790	23,145	24,877
Montgomery	17,905	18,806	20,351	22,704	26,343	29,070	30,349	31,757	33,286	34,626
Prince George's	15,931	17,445	18,883	19,707	24,301	25,949	26,456	27,834	28,525	31,613
Queen Anne's	13,108	13,805	14,537	15,116	19,560	20,330	18,622	22,914	25,373	29,596
St. Mary's	12,701	13,636	14,301	15,599	17,832	19,920	21,260	22,999	23,887	24,895
Somerset	11,114	11,397	13,327	13,849	15,949	18,564	17,717	18,382	20,485	22,114
Talbot	11,613	11,059	12,066	14,511	18,286	22,006	20,951	23,221	23,797	26,017
Washington	13,126	14,071	15,043	16,472	19,208	20,530	21,866	23,554	24,933	27,139
Wicomico	12,547	13,314	14,493	15,382	18,396	19,633	20,948	22,718	23,627	25,829
Worcester	13,232	14,824	16,600	16,868	19,591	21,715	21,608	23,261	24,494	29,063

NOTE: Average salaries were not calculated for the 1980-81 school year.

TABLE
107

Assessed Valuation Per Pupil Belonging and Per Capita: State of Maryland: 1986-87

al Unit	Assessed Valuation for Local Purposes (Thousands)	Number of Pupils Belonging*	Assessed Valuation per Pupil	Population 7/1/86	Assessed Valuation per Capita
al State	$65,476,199	646,858.10	$101,222	4,463,200	$14,670
egany	844,115	11,076.50	76,208	74,800	11,285
a Arundel	6,195,629	61,471.85	100,788	406,000	15,261
timore City	5,966,897	105,587.75	56,511	757,500	7,877
timore	9,493,629	77,119.75	123,102	671,600	14,136
vert	1,323,798	8,171.65	161,999	43,100	30,715
oline	222,310	4,319.90	51,461	24,200	9,186
roll	1,395,289	18,706.25	74,589	111,100	12,559
l	700,518	11,500.45	60,912	67,100	10,440
les	1,371,295	16,303.60	84,110	88,700	15,460
chester	367,322	4,746.50	77,388	29,900	12,285
erick	1,735,853	23,479.95	73,929	131,600	13,190
rett	369,524	5,027.20	73,505	26,600	13,892
ord	1,843,641	27,127.15	67,963	155,900	11,826
ard	3,012,410	24,881.35	121,071	149,100	20,204
t	232,656	2,245.75	103,598	17,000	13,686
gomery	15,798,757	90,813.45	173,969	662,000	23,865
ice George's	9,097,522	99,146.05	91,759	683,000	13,320
en Anne's	459,838	4,606.95	99,814	29,500	15,588
Mary's	777,122	11,026.00	70,481	67,300	11,547
erset	188,076	3,270.70	57,503	19,300	9,745
ot	612,069	3,583.45	170,804	27,400	22,338
ington	1,202,048	16,608.55	72,375	114,700	10,480
mico	851,204	11,094.70	76,722	69,500	12,247
ester	1,414,677	4,942.65	286,218	36,300	38,972

ergarten are expressed in full-time equivalents.
es: Forty-third Report of the State Department of Assessments & Taxation
     "Maryland Population Report Estimates for July 1, 1985 and Projections to 1990",
     Maryland Department of Health and Mental Hygiene

TABLE
108

Historical Value of Maryland Public School Property* per Pupil Belonging+ : 1986 - 87

TOTAL STATE	$3,636,121,061	$ 5,621	$3,014,386,409	$ 621,734,651
ALLEGANY	1,638,298	147	1,421,250	217,048
ANNE ARUNDEL	373,418,758	6,074	300,578,092	72,840,666
BALTIMORE CITY	652,650,025	6,181	509,022,635	143,627,390
BALTIMORE	406,879,554	5,275	372,019,267	34,860,287
CALVERT	496,850	50	413,464	83,386
CAROLINE	18,808,935	4,354	17,662,601	1,146,334
CARROLL	113,343,218	6,059	101,631,075	11,712,143
CECIL	51,766,290	4,501	43,374,000	8,392,290
CHARLES	110,623,953	5,785	90,629,803	19,994,150
DORCHESTER	62,467,490	13,160	62,467,490	N/A
FREDERICK	138,515,454	5,899	105,484,210	33,031,244
GARRETT	44,057,907	8,765	40,913,280	3,154,627
HARFORD	141,223,591	5,205	128,122,403	13,101,188
HOWARD	159,631,647	6,415	122,034,541	37,597,106
KENT	20,161,399	8,977	14,969,843	5,191,555
MONTGOMERY	588,337,929	6,478	473,075,213	115,262,716
PRINCE GEORGE'S	455,956,318	4,598	372,450,815	83,505,503
QUEEN ANNE'S	N/A	N/A	N/A	N/A
ST. MARY'S	57,694,498	5,232	47,117,829	10,576,669
SOMERSET	18,101,600	5,634	18,101,600	N/A
TALBOT	21,212,953	5,919	16,696,620	4,516,333
WASHINGTON	86,891,383	5,231	86,891,383	N/A
WICOMICO	69,970,210	6,305	52,100,730	17,869,480
WORCESTER	42,262,800	8,550	37,208,264	5,054,536

* Excludes construction in progress.

+ Half-time kindergarten pupils are expressed in full-time equivalents in arriving at per pupil costs.

Includes furniture and equipment.

TABLE

109

Food Service Revenue: Maryland Public Schools: 1986-87

	Local Revenue			Federal Revenue			
Local Unit	Sales	Other Receipts	State Revenue	School Lunch	School Breakfast	Summer Food/ Special Milk Programs	Value of U.S.D.A. Commodities
Total State	$58,942,950	$1,945,102	$5,889,076	$33,582,251	$4,306,965	$145,852	$13,759,412
Allegany	1,028,019	36,354	203,512	950,936	223,895	0	305,188
Anne Arundel	5,756,621	296,311	263,797	1,585,530	253,155	0	892,458
Baltimore City	3,900,453	0	2,204,323	12,967,756	1,139,720	0	2,363,538
Baltimore	8,862,372	3,994	358,192	2,297,106	0	0	1,292,676
Calvert	650,764	47,474	38,967	253,626	32,998	0	153,459
Caroline	462,104	0	58,177	286,384	74,807	0	123,934
Carroll	2,038,600	66,732	37,864	428,993	24,527	4,266	408,441
Cecil	1,033,601	0	80,177	450,638	72,115	0	240,171
Charles	1,691,625	487	97,728	593,883	96,709	0	412,453
Dorchester	447,760	0	70,137	351,185	93,285	9,716	96,256
Frederick	2,721,032	0	119,531	804,788	82,088	8,058	674,610
Garrett	476,462	3,430	85,432	429,994	70,195	0	169,926
Harford	2,731,864	0	166,159	855,748	172,874	9,731	517,245
Howard	2,656,666	568,130	47,925	417,502	16,542	0	445,101
Kent	247,456	0	23,181	122,378	22,585	0	72,459
Montgomery	9,494,441	813,817	484,015	2,584,750	538,508	95,001	1,773,809
Prince George's	9,316,392	0	996,866	5,169,241	954,063	3,513	2,300,232
Queen Anne's	359,115	0	35,934	183,905	46,197	3,985	95,167
St. Mary's	1,036,260	0	105,061	548,503	69,353	0	239,482
Somerset	235,020	0	68,775	348,523	93,746	8,165	95,006
Talbot	376,805	0	17,065	166,876	17,218	0	104,901
Washington	1,809,223	72,504	175,742	925,966	84,853	0	560,803
Wicomico	1,065,534	35,869	90,045	531,519	66,077	0	283,074
Worcester	544,761	0	60,471	326,521	61,455	3,417	139,023

NOTE: Nonprofit private schools and state institutions are excluded.

TABLE
110

Meals Served in Food Service Programs: Maryland Public Schools: 1986-87

Local Unit	School Lunch			School Breakfast			Other Meals
	Paid	Free	Reduced	Paid	Free	Reduced	
Total State	33,138,794	18,698,361	3,888,710	802,293	4,566,511	591,896	2,816,999
Allegany	719,821	514,937	167,141	43,320	220,893	44,553	124,005
Anne Arundel	3,219,386	687,879	246,004	72,221	269,792	51,358	103,933
Baltimore City	1,077,476	8,820,329	700,970	10,459	1,272,384	37,398	429,997
Baltimore	4,431,584	1,005,472	375,482	0	0	0	355,038
Calvert	496,946	122,525	24,085	12,196	34,639	4,089	19,466
Caroline	267,293	156,596	41,307	8,357	76,520	11,514	13,350
Carroll	1,445,019	135,369	60,435	7,578	29,126	4,932	29,451
Cecil	575,507	236,767	57,594	11,408	76,278	7,559	26,979
Charles	1,099,906	284,864	67,963	22,653	103,744	10,793	60,177
Dorchester	220,937	201,529	41,992	10,102	96,427	14,256	31,068
Frederick	2,048,089	309,162	125,259	46,579	86,064	11,996	102,014
Garrett	227,712	250,656	63,615	7,405	74,007	8,249	65,458
Harford	1,588,924	364,348	162,823	64,058	174,126	36,583	61,125
Howard	1,566,385	124,411	47,429	6,698	18,627	4,497	134,312
Kent	130,782	66,354	16,195	3,643	22,331	4,404	8,238
Montgomery	4,255,125	1,237,843	371,002	232,194	578,872	93,430	546,359
Prince George's	6,631,971	2,551,540	889,788	173,256	977,879	188,379	371,679
Queen Anne's	231,651	96,260	24,459	11,224	46,990	8,391	20,956
St. Mary's	604,841	275,715	100,817	6,857	73,771	6,454	62,803
Somerset	164,153	209,529	36,716	22,628	95,650	11,785	33,213
Talbot	329,277	81,622	14,107	6,228	18,488	2,030	0
Washington	982,251	470,896	167,758	10,574	85,330	15,702	124,542
Wicomico	569,933	302,261	50,119	4,979	69,246	8,011	25,526
Worcester	253,825	191,497	35,650	7,676	65,327	5,533	67,310

TABLE

111

Maryland Public Libraries: Personnel: 1986-87

Local Unit	Total Staff	Professional Librarians	Library Associates	Support Staff	Minimum Salaries Professional Librarians
Total State	2,658.1	673.3	428.5	1,556.3	$19,193
Allegany	24.3	1.0	0.0	23.3	17,176
Anne Arundel	221.0	45.0	39.0	137.0	22,650
Baltimore City	554.0	142.0	64.0	348.0	21,252
Baltimore	519.5	93.7	92.0	333.8	23,733
Calvert	22.8	2.3	12.0	8.5	21,131
Caroline	18.8	2.0	8.0	8.8	17,280
Carroll	69.9	13.9	14.9	41.1	21,840
Cecil	21.5	5.0	1.5	15.0	17,401
Charles	25.3	2.3	20.0	3.0	22,500
Dorchester	12.3	4.0	2.0	6.3	15,253
Frederick	41.7	8.0	14.7	19.0	21,006
Garrett	10.4	1.9	1.0	7.5	11,361
Harford	98.4	20.3	16.4	61.7	19,240
Howard	128.0	18.0	40.0	70.0	20,070
Kent	8.3	2.0	3.0	3.3	15,920
Montgomery	373.2	180.5	2.5	190.2	22,854
Prince George's	349.0	103.0	49.0	197.0	22,195
Queen Anne's	11.1	3.0	2.0	6.1	22,650
St. Mary's	24.9	3.3	13.9	7.7	19,877
Somerset	7.8	1.0	6.8	0.0	N/A
Talbot	16.3	4.0	1.0	11.3	10,800
Washington	51.0	10.5	7.3	33.2	17,410
Wicomico	32.6	5.6	6.0	21.0	18,650
Worcester	16.0	1.0	11.5	3.5	N/A

TABLE
112

Maryland Public Libraries: Financial Statistics: 1986-87

Local Unit	Grand Total	Federal LSCA I	Total (State, Local and Other)	State Aid	Local Appropriations	Other	Estimated Population	Amount Per Capita
Total State	$80,907,135	$497,525	$80,409,610	$12,177,876	$60,865,862	$7,365,872	4,350,700	$18.49
Allegany	622,571	0	$622,571	316,531	269,571	36,469	76,100	8.18
Anne Arundel	7,396,060	46,873	$7,349,187	935,559	5,970,280	443,348	393,700	18.67
Baltimore City	10,267,953	40,200	$10,227,753	3,195,362	5,613,172	1,419,219	747,000	13.69
Baltimore	17,121,205	102,376	$17,018,829	1,767,805	14,445,024	806,000	682,400	24.94
Calvert	548,897	459	$548,438	59,399	459,039	30,000	39,100	14.03
Caroline	478,865	4,858	$474,007	93,500	372,814	7,693	24,400	19.43
Carroll	2,009,757	17,175	$1,992,582	287,103	1,566,487	138,992	105,200	18.94
Cecil	552,815	3,215	$549,600	235,775	281,330	32,495	65,700	8.37
Charles	762,138	1,442	$760,696	235,702	495,328	29,666	85,200	8.93
Dorchester	345,541	22,306	$323,235	106,903	198,050	18,282	29,600	10.92
Frederick	1,027,749	0	$1,027,749	346,111	608,387	73,251	126,400	8.13
Garrett	222,181	20,355	$201,826	93,101	79,800	28,925	26,600	7.59
Harford	2,852,547	3,926	$2,848,621	466,990	2,149,272	232,359	150,800	18.89
Howard	3,632,261	16,000	$3,616,261	180,700	3,147,320	288,241	139,000	26.01
Kent	199,303	1,023	$198,280	45,840	126,500	25,940	16,400	12.09
Montgomery	16,038,100	86,792	$15,951,308	813,540	12,872,648	2,265,120	625,800	25.48
Prince George's	12,962,132	81,914	$12,880,218	1,958,107	9,867,749	1,054,362	674,200	19.11
Queen Anne's	311,388	1,911	$309,477	63,897	201,930	43,650	27,600	11.22
St. Mary's	632,622	698	$631,924	229,436	387,302	15,186	65,500	9.65
Somerset	125,682	0	$125,682	72,499	53,183	0	17,800	7.06
Talbot	331,443	0	$331,443	34,970	207,646	88,827	26,900	12.32
Washington	1,241,948	27,136	$1,214,812	374,726	639,376	200,710	107,500	11.30
Wicomico	818,320	18,866	$799,454	221,810	500,507	77,137	65,100	12.28
Worcester	405,657	0	$405,657	42,510	353,147	10,000	32,700	12.40

TABLE
112

Maryland Public Libraries: Financial Statistics: 1986-87

		Operating Expenditures			
Local Unit	Total	Salaries	Materials	Equipment	Other Operating
Total State	$83,302,276	$56,188,105	$14,214,376	$2,569,061	$10,330,734
Allegany	594,353	404,856	87,263	7,057	95,177
Anne Arundel	7,354,524	5,130,834	1,322,753	43,607	857,330
Baltimore City	13,734,838	9,255,741	2,155,194	306,947	2,016,956
Baltimore	16,664,678	10,769,336	3,221,368	424,987	2,248,987
Calvert	541,530	327,684	100,805	5,196	107,845
Caroline	487,519	310,479	83,031	7,457	86,552
Carroll	1,974,586	1,254,620	361,162	11,303	347,501
Cecil	571,664	338,008	124,842	24,523	84,291
Charles	765,363	447,780	143,891	5,766	167,926
Dorchester	367,614	250,022	52,956	8,314	56,322
Frederick	1,012,556	685,438	259,020	0	68,098
Garrett	224,938	123,199	28,232	4,950	68,557
Harford	2,766,020	1,812,572	508,751	1,540	443,157
Howard	3,622,261	2,481,551	778,131	76,539	286,040
Kent	200,467	117,515	32,447	4,772	45,733
Montgomery	16,038,100	11,266,629	2,247,022	1,355,974	1,168,475
Prince George's	12,660,485	8,775,893	2,115,586	247,700	1,521,306
Queen Anne's	257,602	162,741	44,708	840	49,313
St. Mary's	615,420	399,420	76,537	5,150	134,313
Somerset	124,982	84,607	22,400	1,500	16,475
Talbot	337,355	215,188	43,681	6,247	72,239
Washington	1,238,469	853,781	197,518	3,193	183,977
Wicomico	747,269	492,772	113,178	5,499	135,820
Worcester	399,683	227,439	93,900	10,000	68,344

TABLE
113

Maryland Public Libraries: Collection: 1986-87

| | Books | | | Non-Books | | |
Local Unit	Total Catalogued Books	Total Uncatalogued Books	No Titles	Periodical Titles	Films	All Others
Total State	10,221,776	1,608,436	2,205,099	17,117	12,734	760,251
Allegany	164,447	8,415	60,520	169	43	13,097
Anne Arundel	1,710,321	0	92,843	406	0	119,307
Baltimore City	1,963,646	54,387	486,902	3,604	5,259	13,840
Baltimore	1,247,869	270,220	150,802	459	307	150,781
Calvert	64,224	20,495	46,940	280	38	18,739
Caroline	48,741	13,984	37,391	217	0	9,696
Carroll	223,451	40,730	99,767	362	0	13,285
Cecil	108,561	31,867	0	149	5	8,113
Charles	111,972	12,000	59,841	153	58	4,488
Dorchester	62,265	12,881	52,664	229	0	2,703
Frederick	195,610	11,000	80,946	236	291	9,078
Garrett	66,592	7,557	51,034	160	162	20,021
Harford	565,714	100,323	134,439	6,071	97	29,517
Howard	400,481	91,198	97,289	731	0	42,765
Kent	40,274	8,075	40,274	101	0	15,047
Montgomery	1,383,682	350,000	180,000	1,117	1,424	106,075
Prince George's	1,130,282	500,492	140,411	844	3,410	114,395
Queen Anne's	65,954	6,500	0	154	2	5,384
St. Mary's	101,471	18,000	59,551	162	0	21,749
Somerset	42,146	4,500	0	0	0	2,765
Talbot	92,789	2,500	82,275	133	4	4,981
Washington	215,504	14,500	80,054	633	0	5,032
Wicomico	131,213	7,723	120,437	568	1,619	22,796
Worcester	84,567	21,089	50,719	179	15	6,597

TABLE
114

Maryland Public Libraries: Circulation: 1986-87

Local Unit	Circulation				Registered Borrowers	Circulation Per Capita	Circulation Per Registered Borrowers
	Books	Audiovisuals	Other	Total			
Total State	33,071,708	2,679,395	1,340,170	37,682,430	2,487,139	8.7	15.2
Allegany	555,276	15,347	16,725	587,348	25,025	7.4	23.5
Anne Arundel	3,486,110	437,514	26,502	3,950,126	196,850	10.0	20.1
Baltimore City	1,459,644	60,072	0	1,519,716	286,649	2.0	5.3
Baltimore	8,947,988	946,067	48,154	9,942,209	658,673	14.6	15.1
Calvert	276,685	8,883	17,183	302,751	40,443	7.7	7.5
Caroline	136,915	66,121	9,117	212,153	8,950	8.7	23.7
Carroll	1,137,413	140,123	62,711	1,340,247	58,447	12.7	22.9
Cecil	277,562	31,892	3,532	312,986	43,183	4.8	7.2
Charles	303,683	8,272	15,138	327,093	58,137	3.8	5.6
Dorchester	147,028	6,088	0	153,116	24,343	5.2	6.3
Frederick	N/A	N/A	N/A	591,157	47,411	4.7	12.5
Garrett	177,678	12,114	25,092	214,884	11,499	8.1	18.7
Harford	1,608,697	284,244	91,289	1,984,230	49,736	13.2	39.9
Howard	1,725,452	227,827	25,924	1,979,203	127,110	14.2	15.6
Kent	82,289	7,039	35,544	124,872	13,489	7.6	9.3
Montgomery	6,758,935	158,383	887,112	7,804,430	328,059	12.5	23.8
Prince George's	3,964,680	92,131	0	4,056,811	328,315	6.0	12.4
Queen Anne's	107,211	43,661	9,618	160,490	8,881	5.8	18.1
St. Mary's	275,157	31,749	21,192	328,098	50,761	5.0	6.5
Somerset	51,915	4,103	5,529	61,547	6,000	3.5	10.3
Talbot	169,456	8,998	5,621	184,075	14,023	6.8	13.1
Washington	795,656	37,566	10,162	843,384	72,925	7.8	11.6
Wicomico	400,831	36,055	9,565	446,451	23,694	6.9	18.8
Worcester	225,447	15,146	14,460	255,053	4,536	7.8	56.2

CPSIA information can be obtained
at www.ICGtesting.com
Printed in the USA
BVHW06*1110091018
529683BV00020B/141/P